Pennsylvanian Voices
of the Great War

Pennsylvanian Voices of the Great War

Letters, Stories and Oral Histories of World War I

edited by J. Stuart Richards

McFarland & Company, Inc., Publishers
Jefferson, North Carolina, and London

Library of Congress Cataloguing-in-Publication Data

Pennsylvanian voices of the Great War : letters, stories and oral
   histories of World War I / edited by J. Stuart Richards.
        p.   cm.
     Includes bibliographical references and index.

     ISBN-13: 978-0-7864-1358-4
     (softcover : 50# alkaline paper) ∞

     1. Soldiers — Pennsylvania — Correspondence.   2. Soldiers —
Pennsylvania.   3. World War, 1914–1918 — Personal narratives,
American.   4. World War, 1914–1918 — Campaigns — Western
Front.   5. Oral history.   I. Richards, J. Stuart, 1949–
D640.A2P46   2002
940.4'81748 — dc21   2002004205

British Library cataloguing data are available

Manufactured in the United States of America

On the cover (top left and bottom right) Three Pennsylvania officers pose
with captured German officers and enlisted men; *(top right)* German
prisoners captured by the 28th Division near Saint-Mihiel, France;
(bottom left) Pennsylvania soldiers who served in the 3rd Infantry Division

McFarland & Company, Inc., Publishers
   Box 611, Jefferson, North Carolina 28640
      www.mcfarlandpub.com

To the Soldiers
of Pennsylvania

Contents

A Soldier

The bars upon your shoulder,
Or the uniform you wear
Does not say that you're a soldier
In this great world wide affair.

A man's a man in battle,
And the uniform so bright
Isn't worth an empty cartridge
If he don't stand up and fight.

It's the stuff inside the buttons
That counts when over there,
And you don't rate as a soldier
If you don't fight on the square.

The mud soaked, blood stained dough-
*   boy*
Fighting in the jaws of hell
Is the cleanest type of soldier
And fighting man as well.

Once I saw a soldier dying,
Yes he's worthy of that "name,"
Just an ordinary private,
My God, but he was game.

And as the bugle sounded,
And the troopers passed from view,
He shook me by the hand and said:
"Goodbye, Old Pal and true.

"Tell my sweetheart that I loved her,
"God bless my little Jane;
"Tell mother I died smiling—
"That I didn't feel any pain."

Gee! I envied him his rating
Though he died and did not flinch
His heart was inside bleeding—
That's a soldier every inch.

I knew another soldier,
Though she never fired a gun,
She never saw the trenches
And she never killed a Hun.

She is the Mother of that soldier
I saw dying over there
She's a sort of super-soldier,
For she gave more than her share.

She has given to her country,
Her love, her pride, and joy;
She's the finest type of soldier
For she gave her only boy.

—Corporal Herman F. Lehr
U.S. Air Service, A.E.F.

Introduction

April 6, 1918, marked the entry of the United States into World War I. The initial cause of our declaration of war was the repeated outrages of the German submarine force. According to some historians, Germany's actions with the use of submarine warfare against the United States were among the greatest military and diplomatic blunders ever committed by a nation.

Had Germany adopted a more conciliatory attitude toward the United States, it is very possible that America would have stayed neutral, and Germany might have gained a victory on the western front.

When the United States entered the war it put at the disposal of the Allied armies almost unlimited resources of money, food, equipment and manpower.

On May 18, 1917, President Woodrow Wilson passed the Selective Service Act. It authorized the president to raise, by use of the "Draft," one million men between the ages of 21 and 30. By the end of that year over 500,000 drafted men were in military uniform. The draft swelled the ranks of the National Army to over 287,000 men and the National Guard was now mustered into active military service.

The training of such a large army was the logistical problem that faced the military. In total, 32 places were chosen for the setting up of training camps. As many as 16 camps were set up in the southern states because of the more favorable weather conditions, while another 16 cantonments were built for housing and training of the drafted men.

On the 25th of April, 1918, the first regular divisions of the United

States Army, after months of training in relatively quiet areas, entered the active combat sector on the Picardy front, and remained actively engaged until the signing of the armistice.

Over 2,086,000 American soldiers saw service in France, and of this number 1,390,000 saw active combat in the front line trenches. Two out of every three soldiers who were sent to France took part in combat. The total number of men in the American armed forces including Army, Navy, Marine Corps, etc. included about 4,800,000.

The United States sent 42 divisions to France, along with several hundred thousand service and supply troops. Of the 42 divisions sent to France, 29 of these saw active combat while the others were used in a reserve roll or had just arrived during the last months of the war. Of the 29 divisions that saw combat duty, seven were regular Army divisions, eleven were made up of National Guard troops from the various states, and the other eleven were made up of National Army troops.

An American division consisted of over 28,000 officers and men, as compared to a British division which had about 15,000 officers and men or a French division at 12,000 officers and men.

For 200 days American combat divisions were engaged in 13 major operations, 12 of which were on the western front and one on the Italian front; 11 were joint operations with the French and British armies. Only two operations involved solely American divisions.

In the second week of October, 1918, all 29 American divisions were actively engaged. They held 23 percent of the Allied front, which equated to 101 miles of territory. From the middle of August 1918, till the armistice, American divisions held a front larger than that the British had held. During this time period American divisions advanced over enemy held territory an average distance of 17 miles for each division, or a total of 485 miles against heavy enemy resistance.

The first major engagement that American troops were involved in took place at Cambrai in 1917. Some engineering and medical units were involved but sustained no major casualties.

The Germans opened the 1918 campaign on March 21st, on a fifty-mile front on the old battlefield of the Somme. This was the first of five major offensives in which the German high command hoped to break the Allied line and bring the war to a quick end. Each offensive operation was timed to take advantage of the light of the moon. After 17 days of intense fighting the Germans were within 12 miles of the important railroad depot at Amiems. In this offensive over 2,200 American troops were engaged. The Allies halted this offensive temporarily when the Germans struck again to the north.

On May 27, 1918, the Germans attacked along the French front at

Chemin des Dames north of Aisne. On May 31st the Germans entered the Marne Valley, in a direct line for Paris. At this point the 2nd U.S. Division along with portions of the 3rd and Pennsylvania's 28th Division were sent in to block the advance. Blocking the German advance at Château-Thierry these American divisions stopped the most deadly of all the German advances.

The German offensives had placed Paris in jeopardy. The German high command still tried to deliver another blow by attacking along a fourth front of 22 miles between Montdider and Noyon. The French army held firmly against this attack and halted it after a German advance of only six miles. During this advance the American 1st Division held the extreme left. During this fight the Americans showed the Allied forces their fierce fighting qualities by capturing and holding the town of Cantigny on May 28, 1918.

Following a few weeks of quiet, the Germans reorganized their forces and prepared for the fifth offensive. On July 15, 1918, the Germans attacked on both sides of Rheims; to the east they gained nothing, on the west they crossed the Marne and made a small gain. Facing the Germans in this offensive were 85,000 American soldiers, and the German offensive was halted. On July 18th, the turning point of the war began. The tides of war had changed and now Marshal Foch, the Allied commander, began the great Allied offensive and began to drive back the German armies beyond the French borders. The 1st, 2nd, 3rd, 4th, 26th, 28th, 32nd and 42nd American divisions along with some French troops began the operation. In this operation American troops would be engaged in six major operations. In four of the six operations American troops were in support of the Allied divisions and under command of French generals.

On August 10th the American First Army was organized under the command of General John Pershing. Throughout the month of August the American divisions pushed the German armies back along the whole front.

From September 12th to September 15th, the first totally American operation began at St.-Mihiel. This operation was under the command of American officers. After four hours of artillery bombardment the attack began at 5 a.m. Troops of the 1st and 26th divisions met at Vigneulles and cut the Germans off in less than 24 hours. An interesting comparison with the operations at St.-Mihiel and the battle of Gettysburg fought July 2–4, 1863, is noted. Close to 550,000 Americans were engaged in combat at St.-Mihiel, while the Union Army at Gettysberg had 100,000 men engaged. At St.-Mihiel a record was set for a four hour concentrated artillery barrage of more than 1,000,000 rounds fired. While at Gettysburg in a three day period the Union artillery only fired 33,000 rounds.

On September 13th arrangements were made to move all the units that were not engaged in the St.-Mihiel fight. The first to move toward the Meuse Argonne front were reserve units of the artillery. To insure secrecy all the major movements were made at night. There were only three possible routes available; the roads were jammed to capacity.

By the night of September 25th the 1st Army stood ready for the attack. The battle order was as follows: the 3rd Corps, with the 33rd, 80th, and 4th divisions in line and the 3rd Division in reserve; the 5th Corps, with the 79th, 37th, and 91st divisions in line and the 32nd Division in reserve; the 1st Corps, with the 35th, 28th and 77th divisions in line and the 92nd Division in reserve; in Army reserve were the 1st, 29th and 82nd divisions in rear of the 3rd, 5th, and 1st Corps. Due to the fact that artillery organizations had not arrived with the troop movements of May, June, and July, their own artillery did not serve many of the divisions.

The Meuse Argonne offensive was divided into two phases: September 26th through October 31st, and the second phase ending on November 11th, 1918.

Six hours before the attack commenced the artillery opened up. At exactly 5:30 a.m. September 26th, the artillery changed to a rolling barrage and the infantry began to advance. Moving slowly forward the infantry met heavy resistance at Montfaucon. The initial movement caught the Germans with only 5 divisions in line of battle. At 11:00 a.m. on September 27th the U.S. 79th Division captured Montfaucon. Steadily advancing through the Argonne the enemy tried to reorganize and put six new divisions against the Americans on September 29th.

By the evening of the 29th some of the American divisions had suffered heavy casualties. By nightfall the American First Army line extended from Bois de la Côte Lemont-Natillious, southwest across the Argonne.

On October 4th the attack was renewed with only small advances being made. The fighting was desperate on both sides. On the night of October 8th the 28th Division was relieved by the 82nd Division. For the rest of October the general plan called for the consolidating of positions and relieving of certain troops. The last days of October were devoted to the preparation for the large scale attack to be launched on November 1st.

Up to November 1st the American gains included the southern half of the Argonne, 18,600 prisoners, 370 cannons, over a 1,000 machine guns. The enemy's morale had been reduced so low that his will to resist had reached nearly to the breaking point, while that of the American soldier swelled, so that they could carry on through almost any task assigned them. During this time other American divisions were working with the British and French armies. At this time Americans troops were requested by all the Allied commanders, as simply the presence of an American division assured almost certain victory.

Beginning on the 1st of November the American 1st Army started its attack. The attack was preceded by two hours of intense artillery bombardment. The enemy was overwhelmed and broke before the advancing infantry units.

By the evening of November 3rd, the German line was pierced to a distance of nearly 20 kilometers. The final objective of this campaign was now within reach of the American Army. November 8th saw the American Army on a hilltop overlooking the city of Sedan. Here the American advance was halted as Marshal Foch turned the American elements eastward so as to allow the French the honor of taking Sedan, the place were French troops were defeated in the Franco-Prussian war of 1870.

November 8th saw a German delegation discussing the terms of an armistice. November 9th the Kaiser abdicated, and fled to the Netherlands in exile. The terms of the armistice called for the Germans to withdraw from all occupied territory, move their armies to the east bank of the Rhine, and relinquish certain amounts of military equipment that would stop them from continuing the war.

Up to 1918, the Meuse Argonne offensive was the greatest battle ever fought by American troops. In 47 days of battle with over 1,200,000 Americans engaged, 34 miles of German line were penetrated. Approximately 150 villages and towns were liberated. The cost in American casualties was high with over 120,000 men killed, wounded or missing.

World War I ended on the eleventh hour of the eleventh day of the eleventh month, 1918.

Dedicated to the American Fighting Man

General Orders   France
No. 203   November 12, 1918

The enemy has capitulated. It is fitting that I address
Myself in thanks directly to the officers and soldiers of the American
Expeditionary Forces who by their heroic efforts have made
Possible this glorious result. Our Armies, hurriedly raised and
Hastily trained, met a veteran enemy, and by courage, discipline
And skill always defeated him. Without complaint you have
Endured incessant toil, privation and danger. You have seen
Many of your comrades make the supreme sacrifice that freedom
May live. I thank you for the patience and courage with which
You have endured. I congratulate you upon the splendid fruits
Of victory which your heroism and the blood of our gallant dead
Are now presenting to our nation. Your deeds will live forever
On the most glorious pages of American History.

> John J. Pershing
> General, Commander in Chief
> American Expeditionary Forces

The American Boy Is Fearless As He Faces the Hun

Mr. Wilbur M. Wilson in the uniform of the Y.M.C.A. drove his truck into the front lines and furnished the soldiers with coffee, smokes and sweets to men who had nothing to eat for days except their iron rations. Mr. Wilson spent time with the 28th Division on their push from Château-Thierry to Fismes and had this to say about the Pennsylvania boys.

"With my own eyes" said Mr. Wilson, "I have seen American boys steal out from the trenches to a frog pond in no man's land, calmly remove their uniforms and dive into the cool waters with German snipers not a hundred yards away in their trenches. The American boy appears to be absolutely unafraid. The greater the number of casualties in his own unit, the greater is his resolve to make the Germans pay the price. His morale increases noticeably every time a comrade falls with German bullets in his body."

1

1917: Lafayette, Nous Voici

April 6, 1917—United States enters war; fleet sails for Europe.

May 18, 1917—Selective Service Act in force.

June 5, 1917—10,000,000 Americans register for the Army.

June 26, 1917—First U.S. division lands in France.

August 28, 1917—United States rejects Pope's peace note.

I Had the Funniest Experience You Could Imagine

> October 21, 1917
> Lieut. Stanley Davis
> U.S. Air Service
> A.E.F.
> Paris, France

Dearest Mother:

You probably noticed in my other letters that I was constantly complaining about the bad weather and not being able to get aloft. Well, that is all over now and never again will I complain about the good weather. But this morning is damp and densely foggy and we can not work, so we all slept till ten o'clock. In fact my two roommates are still sleeping but I got up on purpose to write you a little word before lunch.

I have finished all my brevet tasks and now just finishing up with my time. It was very exciting all the way through and I have never gone through anything like it in my life. Some six or seven hundred miles in an airplane is no easy matter and especially as one does it all in different kinds of weather and times.

I had the funniest experience, which you could ever imagine on one of my triangles. A "Triangle" is one of the voyages which is necessary for the brevet, and simply means that you start at one point, say this field and then go to another town some 20 miles away, and then to another place some 80 miles away from the second and in a different direction, so that when you take your map of the district and draw lines connecting the three points, the result is a triangle. All the work is by map of course because none of us know the country. But when you get up to 3000 or so and have the map in a holder case in front of you, the entire earth looks almost identical with the map. It is almost too difficult to imagine until you have had the experience of looking down on actual living map and passing rapidly along roads, over towns, rivers, forests etc. etc.

Well, I did the one triangle successfully in the morning of a beautiful day. As the tests are official, one sets out with all sorts of papers that must be signed and officially stamped at different regular stations or landing points. Well, I started out on my second triangle late in the afternoon with directions to go to the first aid station and have my stop recorded etc. reset my barograph and then proceeded to the second stop and rest there all night in the hotel. Everything was all fine except that they had a little difficulty getting my motor running properly and it delayed me to such an extent that when I finally left for my night's stopping point, it was about 4:30 P.M. That left about an hour ordinarily before it started to get dark, and we allowed about that time for me to make that second leg of the triangle provided I went in a straight line.

Everything was wonderful. In the cool of the evening, at sunset, with the motor buzzing along at 1150 turns per minute and up to 2500 feet, following a course directly over a long straight road, bordered by trees on one side and white concrete telephone poles on the other. I won't take time to tell you my feelings, in fact I could not do it, for one feels so different being lulled to sleep by the buzz buzz of the motor, and with the cold air on your cheeks and face, suddenly I am awake however for it began to get dark, so soon and I could hardly see my friendly guide road below me. So I came down to 2000 feet and then in the darkness grew to 1500 and finally to 1000 and there I stuck as it was not safe to travel under 300 or 400 meters over strange country because you surely would be out of luck if your engine went bad and you had to pick a landing field with only several feet to glide in.

I was then as low as was safe and my hour was about up I thought I must be near my destination, and I began to look around and just about that time it started to rain buckets full and got dark as pitch, and the wind blew a regular gale, at least that's how it seemed to me. Then I couldn't find the road with the telephone poles, and I pretty nearly passed out in my predicament. Heavens only knows it is bad enough making landings in fine weather and when you know your fields. The wind and everything favorable to you. But here I was, at night or nightfall, in a strange place, with rain besides and absolutely compelled to come to earth or crash into something in the dark or fall down. I don't know how under the sun I did it but I got down, in a farm, and my wheels and skids came shooting along over a field, which loomed up under me, filled with little piles of hay, drying. I just managed to pass in between two apple trees, and came to a dead stop, with a jolt as my wheels struck the furrows of a plowed field at right angles. To say that I was happy at being down to earth again would indeed put it mildly. I was petrified and paralyzed and just sat in my seat, still strapped in, and sweated, and thanked the Lord he brought me down, for I knew I never did it myself. When I finally got myself together again, and the straps undid, and my gas and oil and one thing after another tended to, I was greeted by a flock of hurrying peasant men, (old men) women and children, all hurrying across the fields, slopping along in the rain in their wooden shoes, and wildly chattering and waving their arms, and as they came at me with a million words a minute in French and I stood there like a post with all my flying mitts, helmet, goggles etc. still on, they probably thought I was a dummy or a person from a strange planet. After they had all gathered around and looked the machine over and talked and waved the entire outfit finally I pulled off my head gear they congregated around me and waited and watched every single thing I did until I finally got myself out of my helmet and then you should have heard them-oh-oh-oh Anglais, Anglais. I heard the words and then more and more chatter and then an abrupt silence as an old man took center of the stage and looked into my face. Well the rest of the story you can fill in for yourself, mother, as I finally conveyed the information to them, that I was an American Volunteer, flying for France, "Pour la Patrie" and that I had lost my way and all I wanted was a place to couche (sleep) and something to eat. Then I felt the need for a little protection for the night for the plane and I got the entire assembly to help push the machine over the plowed field and against a little woods which offered as a sort of wind break for the wings. Then I warned them about touching the airplane and gathering up my things, the old man and I started out in the dark. I didn't know where we were going, he couldn't understand me and I certainly couldn't understand him. But in a little time we struck a road and about twenty minutes later came into a little village all dark and gloomy and drizzly with rain, and it was so late by this time that I was quite willing to try my French on anyone and when the old man mentioned the word "Maire" which means Mayor the town boss, I knew I was safe and sound.

I was only about six miles from my proper place and the mayor telephoned the next morning and a mechanic came out in a motor cycle and fixed a broken wire and we pushed the plane out of the mud and on to some dryer ground and I had a little runway off into the wind. It was a little dangerous getting off, due to trees and the short strip of the length of the ground, and the wind was still pretty high, as it had been raining most of the day. But the natives were all there fifty or more of them, and we had quite a time getting the dogs and kids away from the front of the machine and out of the road from the whirling propeller as we started the engine. But again providence was with me, and I got of and waved good bye to my friends and in ten minutes more was safely at my point and with some other boys who had arrived there and were stopping over night at the hotel. Snook my room mate happened to be one of the four and you will guess that we had a happy evening as we sat around the fire, over coffee and cigarettes and I told them of my luck, and then I heard what they would have done had they been in my place. It is always quite easy to tell a fellow what he has done wrong, but it is a different matter when you are in the air and things are coming thick and fast.

Yes I am through my tests now but still have a little time to kill to make up the required 25 hours and 50 landings, but the rest is simple and will only take a day under good weather. So I am ready for a three-day pass to Paris, and a good bed in a big hotel, and a little rest and a few letters to you and then down to another school for final perfection work on fast planes. No one can tell what will happen there after that but I will write to you and tell you everything promptly.

You're loving son,
Richard Stanley Davis

It was said during World War I that becoming a pilot required a young body, high spirit, quick wit, personal initiative and unshakable nerve. Thus the best and brightest of America's sons are the ones who take to the air with its perils and joyous ardor. The required 25 hours and 50 landings, along with the various cross country flights still would not qualify a pilot for the rigors of aerial combat, especially against the hardened German Aviation Service, as Lieutenant Davis would soon experience.

October 23, 1917—C battery, 6th Artillery fires first shot. Americans enter trenches.

October 25, 1917—Americans take first German prisoner.

October 27, 1917—The first American army replaces French soldiers on the battle front.

November 2, 1917—First Americans killed. Corp. Gresham, Pvts. Enright and Hay.

November 14, 1917—The third series of American soldiers have been successfully carried across the ocean and are located on French battlefields.

November 17, 1917—All electric signs in cities in the U.S. will be extinguished nightly at 11 o'clock to conserve power.

November 20, 1917—Germans have learned the whereabouts of American forces on the French battlefront, and shell them fiercely, trying to break their morale.

November 30, 1917—The 42nd "Rainbow Division," composed of National Guardsmen of several states, are now at various encampments in France.

December 7, 1917—United States declares war on Austria-Hungary.

December 8, 1917—The first U.S. destroyer is lost when the *Jacob Jones* is sunk in an attack while on patrol in foreign waters.

Take Your Fun Where You Find It

> December 20, 1917
> Miss Jennie Lennox
> Red Cross Nurse
> Base Hospital, Camp Pike
> Little Rock Ark

I am still at Camp Pike, and shall never forget my experience in this place. When we three nurses first arrived here on Sept. 24th we were the only ladies for miles around, and all we see is men, men, and they surely are being drilled hard from five a.m. until dark. We are wearing khaki dresses, as it is impossible to wear any others, on account of the dust. We also have ripped off all trimmings from our hats and are wearing plain shapes, but we do not get any chance to get off the reservation. The only amusement we had for quite a while was a ride in automobile truck which belongs to the National Guards, which they used to haul large machine guns. The epidemics are increasing daily and we have many cases of the different contagious diseases, and are working very hard but with all our hard work we are very happy for the reason that we are trying to do our bit.

I am working for Major Campbell on the rejection board. If a man gets into the army and is drilled and is found to be very nervous or unable to stand the hard work, he is sent before a board for rejection. There are about six Majors on this board, one a heart specialist, the other lungs and stomach, etc. So Major Campbell is nerves and I help him, it is very interesting but hard on one's own nerves.

There are a number of soldiers from France, who have been fighting. They are teaching the soldiers to operate machine guns. If behind the firing line is any worse, I do not know how the soldiers can stand it, as I did not go to sleep until three in the morning.

We have General Pershing's sister in law with us, she was a nurse when she married his brother. Her husband is not living and she is here trying to do her bit too.

I just wish you could see the room we are living in at present, two of us in one, and its about the size of good sized dog box. We got two bunks, and a chair, when both of us want to get in we are compelled to put the chair out, and we both could not think of getting up at the same time.

We went to see Al. Field's minstrels last week. They were not very good but we had a very pleasant time, as there were eight of us. We had dinner at the Hotel Marion and then went out to the theatre. We quote Kipling these days, "Take you fun where you find it." Even if we do have to go 12 miles for it, and suffer tiredness the next day.

We are hoping to get to France soon. The soldiers leave here as soon as the next quota of drafted men arrive, they are all anxious to go to France. The following is a rhyme written by one of the soldiers; it is very true.

> *Me and my two thin blankets.*
>
> *I'm here with my two thin blankets,*
> *As thin as a slice of ham,*
> *A German spy, I think, was the guy,*
> *Who made them for Uncle Sam.*
>
> *How do I sleep, don't kid me,*
> *My bed tick's filled with straw,*
> *And lumps and bumps, and big fat humps.*
> *That punch me till I'm raw.*
>
> *Me and my two thin blankets,*
> *As thin as the last thin dime,*
> *As thin I guess as a chorus girl's dress*
> *Well I have one heck of a time*
>
> *I pull them up from the bottom,*
> *My nightie's my B.V.D's*

A couple of yanks to cover my shanks
And then my tootsies freeze

Me and my two thin blankets
Bundled up under my chin,
Yes, a German spy I think was the guy
And gosh but he made them thin.

Jennie

Arthur Guy Empey was an American who served in the British Army during the war and wrote two excellent books entitled, Over the Top, *and* First Call. *From* First Call *the following excerpt is taken concerning nurses. "You will love them, you can't help doing so. They are noble men and women sacrificing all for your comfort and welfare. And people wonder how soldiers can be so cheerful. The great mystery is how any soldier can be grouchy after coming in touch with these heroes and heroines. The most romantic appeal to a girl is that of the Red Cross. The picture is touching, the white uniform bending over a bleeding soldier on the field of battle, impervious to fear and danger, soothing his brow as he whispers his last farewell message. But that is not the whole picture. The right to wear this uniform is the greatest honor to which a woman can aspire in this war. It is as glorious as the uniform of the soldier. He sacrifices himself for his country, she sacrifices herself for the soldier."*

December 31, 1917—204,965 U.S. troops in France.

2

The Early Months of 1918

January 5, 1918—President announces "14 Peace Points."

February 2, 1918—Yanks take over Toul sector.

How the Holidays Were Spent in France

> February 4, 1918
> Pvt. Harry C. Williams
> 19th Regt. Engineers (RY)
> Somewhere in France.

This has been a long Christmas for me as all during the month of January in nearly every mail there has been a Christmas greeting from some one of my friends and today I had the pleasure of reading a letter written to me on Christmas day. However I know Uncle Sam has quite a big problem in delivering letters here in France so we are all thankful to receive them no matter how old they are for it really is our chief pleasure to get news from back home in the good old USA the country we are all going to appreciate far more when we return than when we left. It has been my pleasure—yes a real pleasure even if we traveled two days and nights in one of the old style 3rd Class French railway coaches, to see many mountains, hills and valleys of old France, but it is rather hard to surpass some of our own Pennsylvania scenery. I regret very much the fact that I have not seen more of "America first." In one of the places I have been the snow capped peaks of the Alps could be seen far away in the distance.

At Christmas time some of us here had three days leave so I choose to go to Paris for that time. It was a trip that I had looked forward to, so I took the first opportunity to go. A few months previous, we had passed within a few miles of it but did not stop, so this time it was quite a treat to go entirely on my own time. A few of my comrades had been there before, so those of us who had not, had very good guides and with the help of a good guide book we had an easy time finding our way through the maze of Parisiene [*sic*] streets. Three days was hardly enough to see all of Paris but we made the best of it and saw all the places of interest we could. All I can say is that it is one beautiful city, regardless of its many historical interests and probably more beautiful in spring and summer.

Taking pleasure trips around France does not sound like the real business of a soldier to the folks at home but it is well to take advantage of them when the opportunity affords itself and it is quite a relief to be away from all things military for awhile.

Since being here my work has been very similar to the work in the States as this regiment is a specially organized one for railway work. So far we have been located well back of the lines and have not seen any of the big things going on to the north of us but know that we are all anxious to move forward and share the dangers along with the fighting forces. Our former location was in a large city in France of which I wrote you before but I was transferred to this small town which is typical of many towns in France. Very old and also quite a history connected with it.

Our barracks are located on the outskirts and as I look out of the window there is nothing to remind me that I am somewhere in France. It might just as well be somewhere in Penna. Our barracks are typical of what most of the men are using here and I believe many in the States now. Quarters are rather close inside as at the present time we are using what are called double deck bunks or in other words upper and lower bunks. Coming over in the boat one of my friends said he could lie in his bunk and touch seven men. I am not far behind that record for I can touch six. Can't say that I care to live that way for the rest of my life but we all soon learn to accustom ourselves to what ever condition we have to put up with so very little complaining is heard.

The U.S. has solved the food question here pretty well there is quite enough to live on, not always as much and the kind we would like to have nevertheless enough. What does it matter if the meat is tough, the rice without sugar, the bacon without eggs, and the lots and lots of other things we all had at one time, for none are losing weight on that account so here again the complainers are few and far between.

The Y.M.C.A. have a representative here too, in fact wherever I have been. In the town a house is set aside for the men to read, write and play and everything quite up to date and attractive. Religious services are held there and also here in the barracks, which keep the men close to things they were taught in their particular churches.

The Y.M.C.A. man is a very busy man and of the ones I have come in contact with have always found them willing to help whenever they had the opportunity. I was glad to hear that the people of the U.S. and especially of my hometown subscribed so liberally for it really means much to the men in service here.

The winter here seems to be over as the past few weeks have been much like spring but did get quite cold before that but as Uncle Sam is a good provider there was no suffering of the men on that account.

Sincerely.
Harry C. Williams

February 5, 1918—U.S. Troopship *Tuscania* torpedoed.

February 25, 1918—A great send off given to National Army men from all over the country.

February 26, 1918—American army furiously bombarded by Germans.

March 1, 1918—Major General Peyton March, Chief of Staff of the U.S. Army after 9 months abroad, states American Army is well trained in modern warfare.

March 2, 1918—German shock troops are beaten back with heavy losses but the American forces lose many in killed and wounded at Toul.

March 10, 1918—Secretary of War Newton Baker visits the front.

March 14, 1918—The 42nd "Rainbow Division" with many Pennsylvania soldiers, repulses a big German raid on the front.

It Is Really Surprising How Many American Women Are Over Here

March 20, 1918
Miss Elsie Mackey
Red Cross Nurse
A.E.F.
Paris, France

Letters are coming through better. Well this surely is a wonderful city, I like it better each day we stay here. I hate to think of Monday when we

German prisoners captured by the 28th Division near St.-Mihiel, France, 1918.

will have to leave and go back to work; although in one day one can see a great deal and the stores you see so many pretty things and feel as if you would like to buy everything.

We are seven in our party and we are staying at the Y.M.C.A. which before the war was a hotel. It is very pretty place and the food very good, plenty for all. It is really surprising how many American women are over here, doing so many different things. They surely are doing a lot of good. About 35 telephone girls are here at our hotel, who just came over who speak both French and English. They will be a great help to the Americans who try to phone and cannot understand French or speak it.

We have had wonderful weather up to yesterday. Was out this morning but thought I could spend the afternoon writing letters in place of being out in the rain. We have been on the go ever since we came and we feel pretty tired. We did see several places they said belonged to the Germans.

How we all wish the war would soon be over. One of the girls met here two brothers here in Paris she was very fortunate. Don't you think so?

The French people cannot understand the Americans. They say when there is an alarm everyone should go to the cellars, but the Americans go up to the roof to see what they can, of course that is like our people never want to miss anything. Our boys will surely come in for their share over here.

We are surrounded by water and expect to have a very nice time in the summer. We have about 260 patients at the present time, but only our Navy men. The other Army hospitals have more than we so many of the men are ill when they arrive on the boats from the states before they do any fighting. Remember me to every one with lots of love.

Elsie.

March 18, 1918—American soldiers now occupy a four and a half mile front in France.

March 21, 1918—Pennsylvania decides to care for its wounded soldiers.

March 23, 1918—Paris is being bombarded by a German long-range gun from 62 miles away.

March 24, 1918—Germans reach the Somme; American engineers stop a gap in the lines.

Tell Them I Am on a Trip

> March 25, 1918
> Corp. Anthony Dicello
> Co. E. 28th Regt.
> 1st. Division.
> Somewhere in France
> A.E.F.

Just a few lines to let you know that I am well and hope to hear the same from you all. Well. Frank, I was wounded on the 16th of March and had to stay in bed until this morning. But I am getting along fine again. I expect to be on duty in about a month. I was hit on the left leg with shrapnel but the injury is very slight. Do not tell my father and mother that I have been wounded and am in the hospital. Tell them I am off on a trip. Being in the hospital is just like being at home. We sure do get treated fine.

Anthony Dicello

On May 29, 1918, Corporal Anthony Dicello was killed in action at Cantigny, France. During the spring offensive of the German Army, the village of Cantigny was being held by the German 18th Army. During the month of May the Germans were attacking with heavy artillery and gas against the 1st U.S. Division. On May 28th the 1st Division was ordered to take Cantigny; the 28th Infantry regiment led the way, at 6:45 a.m. Advancing in three lines, their objective was reached at 7:30 a.m. Numerous counterattacks were sent against the American positions along with a heavy artillery bombardment. On the 29th, the day Corporal Dicello was killed, the Germans launched an attack early in the morning which was quickly broken up by artillery. At 5:45 in the evening the Germans launched a second attack. Elements of the 28th Regiment pulled back but the remainder of the regiment held firm. It is presumed that during this attack Corporal Anthony Dicello was killed. According to a friend who was with him at the time Dicello and two comrades, fighting to the last, went down with dead Germans lying all around them. A comrade stated that "Dicello was imbued with the thought that it was up to him personally to do his utmost to defeat the German hordes, and he went into his last fight a terror to the enemy." Cantigny was the first battle of the A.E.F.

March 28, 1918—General Pershing offers the American Army to General Foch to take part in the great battles.

March 30, 1918—Germans mass for another big drive.

April 6, 1918—Premier Lloyd George announces "That Germany would soon have the surprise of its life from America."

April 10, 1918—The American engineers, in an improvised army, save the day at Amiens. Four hundred twenty-seven Americans are killed and wounded in action. The number of fatalities is very small.

April 17, 1918 — First U.S. Division in battle line at Montdidier.

April 20, 1918 — 26th Division beats off German attack at Seicherprey.

The Sacrifices Abroad

April 21, 1918
Lieut. W. Ellsworth Gregory
Co. C. 30th Regiment
3rd Division
A.E.F.
Somewhere in France.

I guess you are all wondering where I am May. Well many miles away and settled at last and ready for some hard work. The sooner we get into it the quicker it is going to be over and all admit that it is up to America to finish the job and what I have been able to hear, they think it will be over in two or three months. Well the sooner the better now that we have come this far. Have sure traveled some and will have loads to tell you when I come home. We don't get to hear any news here and I am anxious to get a few letters from home to know what is going on. Am in a quaint place— all old people and comfortably fixed. Have the greatest bed—four mattresses—two of them filled with feathers. It is about four feet deep and when you get in you sink down and out of sight. Sure is good and warm. Very clean people for which I am thankful as it means no "Bugs" which I hate worse than bullets. That was one thing I hated to think of getting in a dirty lousy place. So no worry on that part.

Have seen loads of places of interest and they will take hours to tell about when I get home. Of course now we do not mention any names of places or parts of the country. The whole of Europe is on a war ration and believe me if the American people had to get down to what they are doing over here, they would know there was a war on. Why the waste would be grabbed up quickly as of great value. So don't let anything go to waste and save all you can for eventually it will come over here. They say we will have some hungry days ahead of us. Well I know what it is to be hungry and not able to buy anything for the time being. The women of these countries are doing a noble heroic work and they are going to have a big hand in winning the war. They do everything and work at all trades and nothing is too low or hard to do. That is a Great Spirit to have.

Sweets are impossible to get although at some Red Cross stations en route, we got chocolate bars which were soon brought up. Candy will go good at any time. Was in some drug stores on the way and they are hard up for drugs. Out of loads of things. Guess they depended on us for a lot and now it's hard to get anything. Take good care of yourself and don't worry. Give my regards to all the folks and tell them I am in good health. When you write enclose an extra sheet of paper. It is scarce here.

Lt. W. E. Gregory

There never was a shortage of food in the A.E.F. Soldiers at times did go hungry, but it was only temporarily. The main cause of this problem was transportation difficulties during active periods of combat, when the advancing units outdistanced the mobile kitchens. The American Army in France always had enough food and clothing.

Written from a Dugout

April 23, 1918
Pvt. Earl Haas
1 Cl. San. Serv. 637 USA
Ambulance Service
Somewhere in France

Well mother another week has rolled by and incidentally it was as you know the last week of my 21st year. I was just thinking at this time last year not one of us thought of such a thing as me being in France for my next birthday.

The week past I spent at post but there was very little doing, however this week is more exciting I am in a dugout 30 yards underground with three French stretcher bearers or bearcardiers [brancardiers] as the French call them, we have a fire going and are quite comfortable and safe as it is practically impossible for a shell to reach us here. They come very near us though when we are out in the field but we learned to dodge them very well by this time. This is at one of our front posts. We have a car here all the time to take the wounded back. Each driver spends 40 hours at these posts. I have lots of fun with the Frenchmen on these occasions. They come in and jabber away at me. I let them go on and when they get through say " Oh oui Oui" which means yes, yes and really I don't know if they are telling me I am crazy or that they have a wife at home. I sometimes understand things as I have learned a little French since I am abroad. Well we are notified that our section has to move but we don't know where to. The weather is still fierce so much mud and rain I hope we will soon have a little sun.

April 30, 1918

Just a few lines to let you know we have left our sector and are on our way to another one or perhaps "en repose" as yet we do not know which. Tomorrow we are going to make one of the biggest trips the section has ever made. It is to be a fine drive if it is a nice day. The fields trees and hedges are getting green and when the sun shines the scenery is wonderful but the Frenchmen tell me there are many more beautiful places in France. I do hope I get a chance to see them. The other night two fellows and myself had supper at a house in town and certainly had an enjoyable evening mostly trying to speak French. Received the carton of cigarettes you sent and believe me the good old Camels tasted good, many thanks. In June I get a 7 day furlough and if all is well I expect to spend it in Paris.

Earl Haas.

A dugout was nothing more than a large hole dug in the ground. Some could hold up to thirty or more men. The British Tommy stated, "dugouts are supposed to be shell proof, until a shell hits one." Also it was stated about a dugout, "Rat and soldiers find it an excellent habitation in which to contract rheumatism."

April 30, 1918—Germans capture Ypres Hill and make a tremendous assault. American troops take prominent positions on Paris-Amiens sector, holding their own.

3

The German Spring Offensive Begins

May 1, 1918—The Allied troops regain ground lost to Germans near Ypres.

That Flag of Old Glory

May 2, 1918
Corp. Frank Cooch
Co. D 103rd Engineers
28th Division.
Camp Hancock, Ga.
USA

Today we were presented with a flag of the National Colors of the United States of America and it was wonderful. The presentation was made by General Price and you should have seen the boys look around and tremble, and we shouted that we were going to bring victory with that flag of Old Glory; for one look at that flag and one look at the point of our bayonets and the Germans will suffer. That flag which waved for years shall wave forever in this country of freedom, The United States of America.

That flag of red white and blue center of stars, makes us all feel deep in our hearts that we must make one dash and bring back victory for the Red, White and Blue.

Frank

Presenting of the colors to a regiment has always been one of the most memorable moments to a soldier from the Mexican War to the present. Private Frank Cooch was wounded in action on July 15, 1918.

Hear the Wartime Jazz Band

> May 5, 1918
> Pvt. Thomas Whalen
> Co. A
> 1st U.S. Engineers
> 1st Division
> A.E.F
> Somewhere in France.

Dear Brother:

I guess you think I forgot how to write, but over here one seldom gets time to change his mind. Well, Tom, we are having some time of it at present, that is we know there's a war on, for the Boche have decorated a tree with our underwear that was hanging out to dry but we get even with them by sending back 10 shells to their one and they're hitting the mark too.

Our boys are doing fine work over here and the Huns sure know we are in it for blood. Say Tom, did you ever hear tell of the cooties? Well, they are great company, I'll say.

Have the Penna. boys left yet, or are they still at camp in the state? Well, what they did on the boarder will be child's play towards what they will get over here. Say Tom, this war has not treated me bad at all, for I got fine appetite and am in fine health and my nerves are still normal though this be my fourth trip to the front, which I never mentioned in other letters.

Well, Tom, out of a year and a month in the service, I got nine months foreign service, one stripe of gold on my left arm, shaped like an inverted V, which means six months at the front. Not a bad record, eh?

Say Tom, you ought to be over here where we are for just one week and hear the wartime jazz band, which ranges from 75's up. They sure make some noise, which we are well used to.

The doughboys sure pull some great stunts over on the Huns. They thought we were green but they know different now. How is Jack getting along by this time? Is he still working in the shops? Well, that's the spirit these days, do everything you can on that side and we will tend to them over here. How's everything going at home? I told mother to keep the home fires burning, for I might want to drop in for a warm some day. Oh. Boy, for a rice pudding that mother used to make. Well, that is all gone for the present and now we eat good old army slum and corn, Willie and such, but it's the stuff that keeps you on your pins and that's what counts these days. Well, I guess I will close my letter hoping to hear from you soon.

Your brother,
Thomas

The French 75 is one of the large artillery pieces used during the war; it fired a 2.99 inch shell, and if pushed, the gun could fire close to thirty rounds per minute. The 75 was known as the French artilleryman's "sweetheart." Upon arrival in France the American army was looked upon with skepticism until they proved themselves. A French lieutenant described the American soldier thus: "The finest thing was the dash of the Americans. It was splendid to see those grand fellows, with their tunics thrown off and their shirtsleeves rolled up above their elbows, wading the rivers with the water up to their shoulders and throwing themselves on the Boche like bulldogs. Anyone who has seen such a sight knows what the American army is good for henceforth and to the end of the war."

The Field Where Men Die Fighting Like Men

May 12, 1918
Pvt. Thomas Whalan
Co A. 1st Engineers

Dear Mother:

On this day the 12th every soldier over here is supposed to write a letter to his mother on the event of Mothers Day, I sure take great pleasure in writing to you for I know you will be glad to hear from me again. Well mother, things are going very well and I am in fine health and spirits. I am not the kid that left home a year ago to join the army but a man who has seen men die like men for the cause we are all proud to fight for. I remember Jack telling me I would be scared to shoot a gun but I out guessed him for I hear a few these days, and its only men that can die and fight where we are, slackers will never get near enough. Well mother I am glad Jack and Tom are still at home for it would be pretty hard on you to be left alone. Well as far as I hear there must be only a few boys left at home well here's wishing we won't need them over here.

Mother by the time you receive this letter I will be over here ten months and it seems a long time since I saw the states. I would like to be at home just for a day to taste some of your good cooking and to see what the place looks like but still and all we are perfectly satisfied to live in our little hole in the ground and say it is fun to live the life of a chipmunk. If I stay in this hole much longer I will have grown a tail. You sure get some great big experiences here you go out at night and work until the flare of the star bombs which are thrown up to find out where you are at so they can take a pot shot at you, but so far we have been experts in camouflaging ourselves. You learn to be on the alert always and that's what makes the soldier.

The Huns are very fond of shooting gas at us but they got to learn some new tricks for the present for we are on to them old tricks of theirs. I suppose you heard of the big 75 mile gun the Huns have, well don't get alarmed for that don't amount to much over here.

Well mother I guess I will close hoping to hear from you soon and pray for me for I need all the prayers I can get.

Thomas

The big 75 mile gun that Whalen is referring to was known as the "Paris Gun," a 38 cm naval gun machined down to 21 cm with an inner tube which projected beyond the parent gun and was further extended by a six metre smooth bore tube. The resulting 130 foot barrel was heavily braced in order to counteract the droop due to the weight of the barrel and the vibration during the firing of the weapon. The Paris gun was the most famous of the large weapons used in the war. The Germans also used 28 cm railroad guns with the same effect.

May 17, 1918—Washington reports large casualty list of American soldiers on the French front.

I Have the Feeling That I Have Done All This Before

May 18, 1918
Ambulance Driver Abe Gittleman
S.S.V. 623 Par B.C.M.
Convois Auto.
Somewhere in France.

We were sighted but escaped. I don't know whether it is good etiquette to minimize perils or not. Some parts of our voyages were thrilling. As our stay in Paris was only a little over a week. Mr. Greenburg and I came out to meet our new section which we are attached to. The way we work here is in sections, this section covers two front posts, next to the front line; each man stays 24 hours there and carries his wounded back to different hospitals, which specialize, on their individual cases. The next 24 hours are

German prisoners captured by members of the 28th Division in the Meuse Argonne, 1918. The prisoners pose with some officers of the 28th.

spent on evacuating these hospitals. Then we are relieved. We must wash and repair our cars for when we are in need of them we usually need them badly.

"Fritz" has quite a habit of shelling women as well as churches and homes over here. They are having a violent bombardment here at present and it seems strange to sit calmly and write letters. The work is interesting.

We are well fed and usually sleep in our clothes, with gas mask in easy reach. We sleep in anything from a dugout to an old chateau. I have yet to find out whether I would rather be gassed or suffocated in a gas mask. Strange that it all seems so familiar and natural to me. I have the feeling that I have done all this before or I am fulfilling a promise.

One has to see the wonderful old country to appreciate it, we often witness some terrible sights. If you could only know of the almost shameless masses of humanity we sometimes carry and the wonderful spirit that these people keep up. It is not pleasant to go unwashed and sleep in dugouts and stables.

We have just got our fill of tobacco, which comes very often, 15 packs of smoking tobacco and a very good kind. Part of this letter is written while seated on a three hundred and ninety dollar F.O.B. Detroit which was never noted for comfort.

Here comes an enterprising aviator with some things he hates to carry back home with him. We will have to give him a lift. One thing I have not yet accomplished and that is to teach these people to talk French my way.

Abe Gittleman.

Gittleman refers to a three hundred and ninety dollar F.O.B. Detroit. It was actually a Model T Ford military ambulance, and in 1916 could be purchased for $360 FOB (free on board). The Model T ambulance was used by the various ambulance services during the war. It was a 4 cylinder, water-cooled 20 horsepower vehicle; it had a top speed close to 45 miles per hour. Its light weight made it well suited for the use on muddy and shell torn roads. The vehicle could carry three litters or four seated patients. This vehicle was the choice of the American Field Service and Red Cross ambulance drivers.

One of Them Hit in the Gun Pit
About a Foot Behind the Gun Trail

May 20, 1918
Pvt. Russel J. Kantner
Battery B, 7th Field Artillery
1st Division.
A.E.F.
Somewhere in France.

Dear Mother:

I haven't written to you for almost a month and am very sorry. I could not do so sooner but it was impossible to write as we were in for a rather severe shelling at our old position, most of it being gas shells. One of them hit in the gun pit about a foot behind the gun trail and the liquid spurted around on the gun crew, myself included. I was fortunate enough to get most of the liquid on my overcoat but that did not save me from going to the hospital. They are very quick about treating you.

I was not anxious to go to the hospital, but was ordered there by an officer and so had to go. I was there seven days and would be there yet I suppose if I hadn't taken French leave. I was perfectly well all the time so I couldn't bear to stay in there. I didn't get a chance to write while in there and when I did get back to the position again, found that all my things had been shipped to the base storage room. I didn't even have a tooth brush left. But such is the fortunes of war.

We are getting good army rations now but will be glad when our American commissary supplies us again. I just received two rings from my Belgian friend. He is in the trenches in the thickest of the fight. One of the rings is made of an aluminum tip from a German shell and has the Belgian and French emblem painted on. The other is of bronze and is made of a piece of church bell, which the Germans blew to bits in Famacshel, Belgium. I prize them very highly and will send them home as souvenirs.

Russel

When war was declared the United States had on hand close to 900 artillery pieces. The 3-inch field piece was the largest type available. Fifty of these weapons were in each division. Of the original 3-inch guns manufactured in the U.S. in 1916 some were changed to fire the standard French ammunition and became known as 75-MM guns, model 1916. The United States had in France 3,500 pieces of artillery, of which 500 were made in America. And were used on the firing line 2,250 pieces of which 100 were made in America. (The war with Germany, A statistical Summary.)

Private Russel Kantner received a citation for
"Gallantry in action and meritorious services."
General Orders No. 1 Jan. 1, 1920 Extract No. 7643.
The Division Commander cites the following officers and soldiers for gallantry in action and especially meritorious services.
PRIVATE RUSSEL J. KANTNER
Bty, B, 7th F.A.
Who was wounded in action near Ansauville, France, Feb, 28, 1918 and on the Meuse Argonne October 1918.
By Command of Major General Summeral

The manner in which he was wounded was as follows: Two of his comrades were sitting on a caisson as he passed by. About ten seconds after he passed by, a shell burst and his two comrades were blown to atoms. While Kantner was helping to bury the remains another enemy shell exploded nearby and he was wounded.

May 22, 1918—Americans give the Germans a dose of their own medicine, when they use poison gas in the Toul sector.

We Have Very Many Men Here Who Have Been Gassed

May 23, 1918
Pvt. John August Wachter
S.S.U.639
Convois Auto.
Ambulance Service.
Somewhere in France.

I am glad to hear you are all well, as this leaves us at present. I am eating a piece of Hershey's chocolate just now. I have saved it for almost three weeks and take it from me I am glad. I did as the water is very bum up here, and there are no civilians left around here. We are up here for six days now and four days out of the six we are working steadily. We have very many men here who have been gassed and they are terribly just now from the effects of it. I am tired looking at them, every time I see one I wish for the war to be over. The French got the Germans the other day and gave them a little surprise gaining their objective and capturing many prisoners. Many of them were under 20 years of age and you should have heard them curse the Kaiser. One of them who was injured asked one of our men if he was an English man, the fellow said he was American, the German didn't believe him until he was shown the name of the American Field Service painted on the car, then sneered and said that all Americans who went over here were captured and all the ships were sunk by subs. I talked to one who was injured he was only 25 years old. They are glad to be prisoners, they had nothing to eat and some of them while marching past here picked up pieces of bread which laid in the gutter. We have plenty of noise around here, as there are guns all around us. They are shooting just now and the Boche are landing some shells in. Last night I saw an air fight in which the German was dropped. I am just realizing that this is sunny France. It is very hot just now. Our mail just came I must see if there is any mail for me.

I received quite a few letters, 20 of them four from you and one from Alois were among them, dated April 4, 7, 13, 18 and Alois 4, I'm thankful for all of them. I was out to our port last night and got sick in the stomach from what I saw and smelt. We get smells of gas here at night and this morning quite a few of us fellows were sneezing our heads off. I do not get to mass just now, as I am busy and the church is quite a distance from here.

Last night I was down to see several fellows I know from near home on a bicycle, on my way back a shell burst about 50 yards away I heard the pieces passing over my head. No one was near it except me. No one was hurt.

Hoping to hear from you soon,
John.

You Would Go Through Hades If You Saw a Hun

May 26, 1918
Corp. Lewis J. Goodman
Co. I 28th Infantry Regt.
1st Division.
A.E.F.
Somewhere in France.

Dear Father:

Just a few lines to let you know that I am well and hope these few lines will find you the same. My leg is pretty good and I can walk around now, but I cannot go back to my old job for a few weeks yet. There is so much muscle missing that if I walk around too much in the day it is weak at night, and I am glad to get off it, but it sure is coming all right. It is all healed up and all you can see is a big nick where the muscle is missing and a scare on each side about ten inches long.

I was in the hospital from April 2nd to May 9th; then I was transferred to another one and on May 12th I was transferred again and here yet, and believe me, I will be glad to go back on duty. It is too quiet here, the same thing everyday. I would like to get back to where there is something doing. There seems to be something calling me all the time. Once a fellow goes up there and gets a taste of things he isn't satisfied until he gets back. You don't get feeling good until things get lively and then you would go through Hades if you saw a Hun on the other side.

Once a fellow sees a good pal of his fall he is ready to start something. I have had no mail since the latter part of March, but expect to get some any day. I wrote to the company and told them to send my mail to me, so I suppose I will have some bunch of letters when they come. I do not know anything about the other town boys, as I have not heard or seen any of them since I was hurt. Give everyone my best regards.

From Your Son.
Lewis J. Goodman

"Damn the German"

May 27, 1918
Lieut. Surgeon Alfred M.
Bergstein
Medical Corps
18th Infantry Regiment.
1st Division
A.E.F.
Somewhere in France.

Dear Folks:

I received a couple of letters today from some friends that was sent to Greenleaf, and forwarded to me. I expect I will have some from you before long if you have written. It certainly was good to receive it and I am waiting to hear how you all are.

Have seen a little more of this war since I last wrote you and "Damn the German" will be my motto from now on. I ran into a gas attack and got a good chance to test out my mask. They surely did fill the valley I was in with it but didn't get but a few casualties. That is the damnedest thing of the whole war. We don't mind the shell's bursting so much as we do the gas, as we get under the ground where we can't get hit. Am back beyond the gas zone again now and probably won't get into it again, and besides we are always watching for it and prepared.

It is a fine day, but I can't tell you the day of the week it is. Have lost all track of the weekdays as all are the same and the date is the only thing we need in our business. My watch is broken so I can't tell the time except by the sun.

The weather is fine and I feel ok Haven't any ink here, as all my things are way back. My trunk is at the American Express Co. in Paris in storage, as I couldn't bring it with me. All my other belongings are at the regiment headquarters somewhere.

Am waiting for one of the men to give me a haircut and shave. Have several days' growth on my face and I will feel better after I am fixed up. Was up near the German line, but I am back to the point I wrote last time from and we expect to stay here for some time. I have been all the way from the rear to the front now and saw all kinds of things. Will be able to tell you some things when I get back. It sure does seem much longer since I was home than actual time. This traveling around makes it seem a great deal longer. If you didn't get my last letter I want you to send me the paper and some magazines.

Won't draw my pay this month, as I didn't get a voucher. Can't spend anything here anyway, except at the Y.M.C.A. canteen and then we get some chocolate or small cakes.

Alfred.

Gas, being heavier than air, lies low on the ground, and when caught by the wind, spreads across the land like a fog bank. When the gas reached the trenches and dugouts it settled down in the low parts. Upon the first indication of a gas attack a gong, usually an empty shell, was beaten upon. Several types of gas were used in the war. Arsenic and phosphorous were easily detected by their smell, which resembled garlic. Others were chlorine, phosgene, chlorine bromine, sulfureted hydrogen and yperite or mustard gas.

May 28, 1918—In hand to hand fighting near Aisne, British and Americans are driven back, but finally regain 200 lost yards. American 1st Division takes Cantigny.

May 30, 1918—American hospitals are bombed by the Germans and nurses are killed in Picardy.

Won Glory for America

May 31, 1918
Sgt. John W. Smith
13 Ambulance Co.
1 Sn. Tn.
1st Division
A.E.F.
Somewhere in France.

I have had the pleasure lately to receive several letters from you all, but have been unable to write much. We have been kept on the jump, but have good results. You have, no doubt, been reading of what the Americans have been doing in the big affair. Well, that happens to be our bunch and we were right in it.

We have been having some mighty warm times, but so has old Fritz and he is working his hardest to do what he can before he has more Americans to contend with. We have taken quite a number of prisoners and also some new territory. We are having ideal weather for our entertainment, and we sure are making Fritz busy. I wish I could tell you of the sensations one has when travelling through a shell torn area, the big shells exploding all around you, etc. it will keep, however, for a long time. One doesn't readily forget these things. The good lord surely has been with me, for I have been enjoying the best of health, and so far have escaped unhurt. Joe Thorn was gassed about four or five days ago, but not seriously.

I saw him before he was taken to the hospital. He was gassed in the eyes, but it won't hurt him any. He was lucky to get his when he did, for the big affair came the next day and he might not have come out so lucky. I believe he was sent to the hospital where Mose is, so he ought to get good care. Tell Aunt Belle not to worry, for he will be around all right in a week. I sure was glad I was able to see him right after it happened. I was in the same gas attack, but fortunately I was able to get my mask on in time, and only got a bit of it. Give my love to Mother and the rest and tell them not to worry about me.

John

Sgt. John Smith was an ambulance driver in the United States Army, being a member of the 1st Sanitary Train, of the 1st Division.

4

June 1918:
The Defense of the Line

June 1, 1918—Germans cross the Marne; 46 miles from Paris; 654,875 U.S. troops in France.

June 2, 1918—7th U.S. Machine Gun Battalion, 3rd Division hold Château-Thierry bridge. U.S. Marines stop Prussian Guards Northwest of Château-Thierry.

Something Tells Me I Am Going to Have a Chance This Time

> June 2, 1918
> 2nd Lieutenant Charles H. Ulmer
> 6th Regiment
> U.S.M.C.
> A.E.F.
> Somewhere in France.

Dear Parents:

Beautiful June is here; what will it bring? I am going into line again, and never felt happier over anything in my life. So far, I have been miraculously untouched, and it is surprising how much steel can pass you and yet leave you untouched. Something tells me I am going to have a chance this time. France has lost or sent all the young men, and only the aged and infirm remain, and the helpless and grief stricken women and children. If you could only see! Always so willing and ready to do anything to help. Sometimes I am so tired and weary that I stumble, and have to laugh at myself, but I am so thankful and glad of the chance to stand between these and the terrible enemy. Our glorious brave boys of German descent are out to fight down the wrong principles instilled for generations into the people; we shall live forever in the result of this war. The high cost of war has gone up in lives as well as money, but the higher price, the more valuable the purchase.

Five days later Lieutenant Ulmer was wounded in action during the Marines' fight at Château-Thierry on June 7th. Lieutenant Ulmer and another lieutenant had volunteered to take an important German machine gun nest near the edge of Belleau Woods. While dodging from shell hole to shell hole an artillery shell burst in the trees overhead and showered them with shrapnel. Ulmer was helping to dress the lieutenant's wounds when another shell exploded above him and he was gravely wounded. He died the following day, June 9th, and was buried in a courtyard over looking the Marne River.

On October 28, 1918, Lieutenant Charles Ulmer was awarded the French Croix de Guerre:

Lieutenant Charles H. Ulmer 2nd Lieutenant
80th Company, 6th Regiment U.S.M.C. 2nd Division
French Croix de Guerre with Palm.
Order no. 10,965 "D"
October 28, 1918
"Rejoining his unit on the front, he immediately led his platoon
with bravery and initiative and displayed great qualities as a leader
until he was severely wounded."

June 3, 1918—German submarines are reported in New York Harbor. Fifteen vessels are reported sunk along the Atlantic coast.

June 4, 1918—Americans hold a 12 mile front on the Marne.

A Prisoner of War

June 5, 1918
Pvt. Carl L. Fey
Co. L 28th Infantry Regiment
1st Division
A.E.F.
Darmstadt, Germany

A machine gun placed in a fox hole of the 28th Division overlooking a French town, 1918.

Dear Mother:

I thought that I would write you a few lines to let you know I was wounded. I got shot in the right jaw and also got captured on the 27th of May. Mother, how is Eleanore and Si. Mother, all my money I guess will come to you now. When you answer this letter, just address it to the hospital, Mother, how is dad and yourself by this time and how is Gussie and her family. Do not worry, everything will come alright for me and you sometime. Try and send me a package with some smokes and candy; Captain Von Watter said you can. Tell them I send all my best regards. I guess this is all for this time.

Son,
Carl Fey
Prisoner of War
28th Infantry Prisoner of War.
Camp De Prisonere de Guerre.

It required almost two months for this letter to reach the Fey family. The mail from Germany was first sent to Switzerland, then to Holland, then to England and then to the United States; it arrived on August 9, 1918. Private Fey was listed as killed in action on May 27th and the following Sunday a memorial service was held for him in his hometown of Schuylkill Haven, Pennsylvania. It is infrequently that one returns to read his own obituary and all the nice things that have been said about him, but Private Fey experienced this strange happening.

Fey was captured on May 27, 1918, and held in a German hospital and prison camp. On February 21, 1919, Carl Fey told his story to a reporter from the Call newspaper in Schuylkill Haven, Pa.

Carl Fey enlisted on May 27, 1917 in the regular army, Co. L, 28th Infantry. He sailed on June 14, 1917 and arrived in France on June 26th. After being in camp for two months he went into the trenches with the first division near Toul. After fighting two weeks they were given a week's rest and were then ordered to the Somme sector on the western front. On February 26, 1918, he was wounded in the arm with a rifle bullet and had to remain at a hospital for a month. After the wound had healed he was fortunate to reach his former company on the Somme front. Here with the French and English troops the Germans drove them back and in turn the Allied armies pushed the Germans back. This continued for several months under all kinds of conditions and the most severe fighting.

On May 27, 1918, he was hit with a piece of shrapnel on the right cheek. The shrapnel actually "blew" out the greater portion of his jaw bone and Fey states that for several minutes he was busy spitting out his jawbone and teeth same as actors on the stage spit out artificial teeth. All of his teeth on the upper jaw with the exception of two were spit out. This happened on the Somme sector. For thirty six hours he lay in a shell hole in no man's land without a bit of water or attention, no first aid or no other soldiers near him. Although his company may have known his whereabouts they could not reach him as the Germans were pushing them back farther and farther and the shell fire was too great and too heavy.

On the evening of the second day a German first aid soldier picked him up. He was unconscious at this time. He was taken to a dressing station and there regained consciousness. As soon as he came to the Germans began to ply him with all sorts of questions, as to the size of the army, the location of the artillery, the machine gun nests, etc. etc. The Germans did not bother so much in asking him about the United States army as they felt sure it did not amount to much. His questioners failed to realize that by reason of his wound he had practically lost his speech. Carl, however stated that even if he could have spoken they would have gotten no information out of him along this line. He also added that the Germans well knew the size of the Allied army and the number of men in the trenches. That they knew as much as the allied commanders themselves did, about the strength.

He was kept at the dressing station about an hour where he received only the very slightest and most simple first aid. He was then taken to a hospital at Damastard [Darmstadt]. Here there were only a few patients. They were French, English and Russian, and some Germans. He was the only American. And in all the hospitals he was sent to and later when in German prison camp, it is interesting to note that he was the only American patient and prisoner. He was kept at this hospital one month. In this time he received little or no attention either from the surgeons or the nurses. The Germans did not even bandage up his wound nor did they do anything to prevent infection from setting in. They did not even wash it out. This he had to do himself with warm water. Not even an examination was made of his wound by the surgeons and while the nurses would have been at least kind enough to help him they had received instructions from the surgeons not to bother with him. However, he had three bandages in a kit and from these he managed to bandage his own wound. Attention was given to the wounded English and French, and to the Russians that were exceptionally, kind and attentive.

After being stripped of his uniform and clothing, every piece of clothing he had with him and every article on his person, he was given paper clothing. This quality of clothing was "poor dope" Mr. Fey stated, as would tear very easily. His shoes were taken from him and he was given a pair of wooden shoes, no underwear or socks.

He was kept at this hospital for a month and was offered as food, saw dust and hot water. Questioned about whether it really was sawdust, Mr. Fey stated that it certainly was as he was sufficiently alive to tell the difference between saw dust and anything else. But he did not eat it as he had been sufficiently wise to inform the Red Cross immediately upon his having reached the hospital, of his whereabouts. The Red Cross sent to him all kinds of good food such as corn, peas, corned beef, biscuits, salmon, tomatoes, sardines, etc. Most every day he received a package of food from the Red Cross. Asked about whether he was not afraid the Huns poisoned the food for him, he stated they could not do so as it was only canned food that was sent in and in every package was a warning from the Red Cross as to his being careful to examine every can and see whether it had been punctured in any way and soldered shut again.

He then was transferred to a hospital at Mainz on the Rhine. Here he stated the scenery was very beautiful but that he could not eat the scenery did not help his jaw any. He received no better treatment at this hospital. Absolutely no attention from nurses or surgeons. In addition to sawdust and hot water, here the bill of fare was increased by the addition of black hard bread and potato peelings. How ever the Red Cross kept in touch with him and continued to send him food. There were only Germans at this hospital, and only one American soldier, a Schuylkill Haven soldier, Carl Fey by name. Frequently the packages from the Red Cross would be robbed and the only thing he received then would be the package. He continued to be warned of using any of the cans that seemed to be tampered with.

Instructions or the warning was specific, telling him to throw the whole can away. No concern was manifested for his comfort or attention and the only treatment his wound received was that given it by himself by washing it with hot water and that he had to be mighty careful was not poisoned.

He cites an instance of the brutality of the Huns at the hospital when he stated that at the first hospital a French soldier lying near to his cot had his leg so badly shattered that the surgeons began to amputate it without giving him an anesthetic. The fellow during the operation cried out by reason of the great pain. This made the surgeons so cross that they immediately packed up their tools and left him bleeding on the cot. The fellow simply bled to death in a few hours time.

Mr. Fey was then sent to West Prussia to a prison camp located at a place that from pronunciation one would spell something like this, Cresch. It was located along a railroad and was a large camp. There were about 4,000 Russians, 1200 English and 2,000 French and one American Carl Fey. A portion of the small town and the outskirts had simply been boarded up with an eight foot fence. For sleeping quarters on barracks there were old dilapidated barns. Asked about whether it was not possible to escape he stated not as there were guards inside and outside. That they were Irish of the Irish brigade who had turned traitors in 1914.

Asked whether his wound did not give him great pain, he stated it did not. That he never had any pain. He received mail from home right along, also packages of cigarettes, candy, clothing, etc. that had been sent by his mother and relatives. That oft times the packages would be robbed. He remained at this place for three months.

He was then sent to Denmark, Holland and here is where this soldier boy put it over on the Huns. He learned one day that 250 non-commissioned officers who were prisoners, since 1914 were going to be sent away or released the next morning at 5 o'clock. Carl mingled with these fellows and when the morning came he stood inline with them and marched away to safety. Whether or not his absence was discovered after he left is not known as he did not bother about making any inquires or waste any time about this matter.

At the time the armistice was signed, Mr. Fey states there was little or no demonstration on the part of the people of this particular country, it was a neutral one. The Red Cross paraded the streets but that was about all there was to it. He was then shipped to Edinburgh, Scotland, to a hospital where he remained a month and a half.

Upon his arrival in New York City he was sent to a hospital. He wired his relatives and within a short time they were with him. It was then that he first learned he had been reported missing and later reported killed. It was also the first time he learned that funeral services had been held for him in his hometown. He expects to have bone and flesh fitted into his badly shattered jaw and check when he gets to Baltimore hospital.

Mr. Fey wears three service stripes for 18 months' overseas service. Also a gold star showing he was one of the first 100,000 men in France. He wears two wound stripes and the insignia of his regiment, being from Fort Snelling, Minn, namely a white star and half moon.

June 6, 1918 — U.S. Marines take part of Belleau Wood. American soldiers use Indian war whoops to great benefit, taking over a thousand prisoners.

The Americans Are Giving Old Jerry His Hands Full

> June 6, 1918
> Pvt. William O'Conner
> Co. H 112th Infantry Regt.
> 28th Division
> A.E.F.
> Somewhere in France.

Dear Mother:

We are in France at the present time and believe me it is one beautiful country. They don't have a lot of stuff for themselves, like the people in America have. We are quite a few miles from the front, but we can hear the big guns crack at night. If you were to look up in the air every time you hear an airplane your neck would be broken, because they are as common as birds flying in the air. Once in awhile a Jerry as they call the Germans over here, comes over us and drops a few bombs around and then he gets chased. It is a real fourth of July every time one comes over because the allies are always on the look out for him. It is a great site to see two of those airplanes in a fight. They keep climbing until one machine gets on top of the other. Then they start their machine guns a going and one must come down and that is wonderful to see. At present we are in camp with some British and I think they are fine people. We have not arrived at our American camps as it takes a long while to move the troops. The Americans are giving old Jerry his hands full and I think they will soon bring him to time, but it will take a little time to do it, but the Americans are sure to win. We did not get our American Y.M.C.A. fixed up yet and that is why I did not write, because we could not get any paper, but I will write often now. I received all the mail you sent to Camp Upton.

Tell all my friends I was asking about them and I send them my regards. I am in a large barn without the usual straw, therefore the ground floor and a few army blankets is my regular bed. At night I am not bothered much by the pigs, cows and chickens making noises about me as some of the fellows in other quarters are; the worst I have to contend with is a few rats and mice running over top of me now and then, but one soon gets used to that.

Paper and envelopes are scarce materials, therefore the different kinds. Time is also very scarce, although a feature over here is that it never becomes dark until about 10:30 P.M., so you see although it is sometimes late when we get in from training and other duties which it is necessary for us to learn before we hit the front lines, nevertheless we still have time before bedtime to write.

It is now June 6th, and as yet I have not received any mail since coming here, with the exception of a letter from a very nice girl I met while in England. I will enclose this letter and send it to you. It will give you an idea of what the English girls think of we American lads, as they call us. I also wish you would save it for me for some day when I get back home I may wish to read it over again.

Well brother, although I have not been in any battles yet. I will say at night, at times I can hear some awful hammering of the big guns at the front. At such times we look at each other and say I hope Tommie Atkins is giving the Boche "Hell."

Air raids at night also are frequent occurrences. About those I would like to tell you more but the censor will get after me if I do. Therefore "Nuff said."

Read the newspapers of the day, brother, and you'll learn more of the war than I can tell you. The little I see is all I know for we very seldom get a paper of any kind.

To get any luxury here is almost impossible; no candy, no Ice cream, no cake. The best we get now and then that makes us think we are back home once again is a pack of Piedmonts.

Yes brother, she's tough. But things look favorable for us and when we start we never stop until the old Kaiser Bill is canned and we will all fight hard to do that and get back again to good old America and all the luxuries she holds for us. Tell mother not to worry as I am in the best of health and as yet in no danger.

Love to all.

Jess.

One thing that was very important to the combat soldier was his need to write and receive mail. The Y.M.C.A. or Young Men's Christian Association helped supply the soldier with the various items he needed: writing paper, envelopes, reading material, etc. The fascinating thing about the Y.M.C.A. was they were located near the front line trenches. In all the big cities of France where the American men passed through, the Y.M.C.A. operated hostels where a soldier could get a bed for minimal cost. There were Y.M.C.A. dugouts right behind the front line trenches, where soldiers could get hot drinks, crackers, cigarettes and other comforts at all hours. In England a fleet of motor cars roamed the streets to pick up soldiers who were wandering about; these vehicles were operated by English women. The importance of this service can be estimated by the fact that at least 50,000 soldiers were on leave in London every week. Over half of these men slept in the Y.M.C.A. Members of the Y.M.C.A. followed the soldiers right up to the front lines, and the last contact a soldier had with the life he loved so well was a cup of tea given him before he went over the top. And if he came back wounded, before his wounds were dressed the Y.M.C.A. was waiting for him with tea and sweet chocolate. The well known symbol of the Y.M.C.A. is the "Red Triangle," or as one soldier called it, "The last evidence that anybody cares."

Tommie Atkins was a reference to the British soldier.

The Sooner Its Over the Better

June 10, 1918
Pvt. Robert Whitman
Co. D 103rd Engineers
28th Division
A.E.F.
Somewhere in France.

We had a very nice trip over and enjoyed it very much. We had a little bit of rough weather and very few of the fellows were sea sick. I did not even get a headache. We had a little excitement in the way of submarines but none of the ships were bothered. We got two of the subs and probably three. The boat on which I was fired two shots and the gunner claims he got one of them. No one seemed to worry about the boat for all they did was to run to the deck and watch the gun at work, telling the gunner to get them. It all passed very nicely. We have seen some very beautiful countries since landing and have done some moving around as we are now at our third camp since getting over.

At the first one we met a fellow from home who had been torpedoed but came out of it safely. His name is Frank Downs and he lives on the east side. I taught him to run the elevator at the P.&R.C. & I Co., but he is the only fellow I have met so far that I know. I have already heard and learned lots of things that I would like to tell you, but of course that is impossible but hope to be able to tell them, some day. We have already been under fire as we have been in three air raids, but no damage done very close to us, although in one place they raided a man, woman and their five children were killed when a bomb hit their house. They were to move the next day. I tell you there are hard lines and we did not realize how war seems and the people at home don't have the least idea about it, so you can imagine how we feel about such things but the sooner it is all over the better it will be for all and we will be happy to get away from it. We were given a wonderful reception in the first town we landed and we saw lots of American flags.

I saw an air raid the other afternoon in which one of our hospitals was burned and also saw a German plane meet its Waterloo and fall to the earth from the clouds through the marksmanship of one of the Allied aviators. You should have heard the fellows howl when they saw him go to the ground. We have had a few afternoons in the surf and the first afternoon that we were in we had a lot of fun. The fellows put their clothes on the beach near the water and were enjoying themselves very much when the tide came in wetting their clothes, and floating different articles of wearing apparel around. There was a grand rush for clothes everyone grabbing all he could and carried it to shore, some fellows lost watches and money, but that was about all.

For two or three days we were having an inspection of our barracks bags and I had fourteen big packs of tobacco but when I came to put them back I had seven. This afternoon I opened a new pack and went out of the tent. Jim Eisnehower was sleeping in it and when I came back it was gone but Jim had not seen or heard anyone in the tent, and he does not use it. I will be satisfied if I can break away from the habit. According to all the talk, it does not seem as though the war will last very much longer, and all are looking for it to be over before the fourth year and that is in August, but it sounds as though it won't last through the winter and we are all hoping it won't but of course there is no reason for building fake hopes. So we will wait for future developments. Only hope it comes out the way people are saying it will. If it does we may eat our Christmas dinner at home.

Robert.

The Ambulance I Brought to the Front Is Now Captured

June 10, 1918
George L. Whitmeyer
Sec. 502 Ambulance Corp.
A.E.F.
Somewhere in France.

Well, I wanted to get into action and at last it came and we ambulance men certainly have been on the go since we landed at the front. Hardly any sleep, and what sleep we do get is during the day, as we are at our busiest time when it is dark, and are going strong at night. I cannot tell everything that happens during the day, but this is some hot place, always dodging shrapnel and high explosive shells. We have been fired on by machine guns and some of the ambulances have been hit.

The ambulance I brought to the front is now in German hands, the assistant driver took it out while I was at breakfast and the last anyone saw of him he had a load of patients and was headed for the hospital, but took the wrong road and went into the Boche lines. The Marines had tried to stop him but he must have thought the Germans were firing at him and went faster. So, many toilet articles and half of my clothes are being worn and used by the Boche.

On Friday morning Charles Ulmer was seriously wounded and died on Saturday, June 8th. He was buried at 10:45 on Sunday June 9th, by a Y.M.C.A. worker, who when in the U.S.A., is a Methodist minister. I was at the grave and have it marked, also the name of the place and near what city. I'll try and get in touch with Joe Ulmer and I'll see whether it will be the last time or not. It certainly is hot at present.

The work we are doing now with the American Army is doing the work the French Award Croix de Guerre for in their army, and I don't doubt but what we would all have medals if we had gone through such hot work with the French.

George L. Whitmeyer

George Whitmeyer and many of the ambulance drivers attached to the French army during the war were members of local Ambulance Corps units, such as the "Bobby Jenkins Unit," the "Robert D. Heaton unit." All the units from eastern Pennsylvania formed into one main Ambulance Corps in early June of 1917. After training in Allentown, Pennsylvania, the units departed for France in December and arrived in early February 1918.

We Had to Stay Low from Flying Stray Bullets

June 12, 1918
George L. Whitmeyer
Sec. 502 Ambulance Corps
A.E.F.
Somewhere in France.

Yes go on, I know what you are about to say. I'm pretty long between letters, but then that cannot be helped even now I'm writing this, not knowing whether or not I can get it off, for we are not allowed to write letters send them front to front, too many spies around. However, we do send little cards saying I am well, some of which I already sent you, and guess you understood why I delayed my letters. If possible, I'll get this censored and carry it in my pocket until I can have it sent to the rear and mailed.

To begin with, we have been on the go continuously for three solid weeks, hardly any sleep and very much driving. At the start we were all kept busy during the big drive the Marines made, then after 72 hours some of us got some sleep, but only six hours a day. This kept up for a few days, and things began to go a little better and one of our men even went across the Fritz lines and with a load of wounded. He was lost and just turned into the wrong road. Our outposts saw him but could not run out and stop him without letting Fritz know their location.

We have many machines blown up while going after wounded through these shelled towns and woods, but none killed, only a few wounded. Then the last day Dr. Boone, of St. Clair, was here at the dressing station, where he had been stationed for a few weeks, and which was always under shell fire, the place was hit and four of our ambulance men had to be dug out from under the debris, not badly hurt, but giving us less ambulance drivers, and more duty for those able to work. I lost one machine there, mashed by a big shell, another went up in flames being hit by shrapnel, one half mile to the rear, and Sunday, June 23rd, I went into a town the Hun had just been driven from and had to wait for patients. I camouflaged the Ford under the branches of a tree, crawled to a dugout and from there it was not more than 100–150 yards to the front lines. The Fritz were about 300 to 400 yards further on, and snipers were firing at every moving object, which you know can be seen pretty plainly from a tree 500 yards away unless one gets down and crawls. About dusk the Marines made an attack and we could stick our heads out see them make a run toward the Hun, and such a racket by small arms. Fourth of July was nothing like it. They gained another strip of woods, and we had to keep low from flying stray bullets. Did not hear much then until midnight when somebody from Berlin sent Fritz another basket of shells and they immediately got ready to use them. They fired about five hundred shells into this little town and literally tore what remained to pieces. Our dugout was not hit, although shrapnel flew all over the top and only a direct hit could have hurt us, but my goodness, gas was thick as smoke and there we were pinned in that hole for two hours with gas masks on. One minute we'd be praying and the next cussing the Boche. Another crowd of men who had been to the rear for food were caught and got to another dugout (namely French wine cellars) and it was hit, wounding five, one dying a few minutes after being given aid. I then sneaked, mostly crawled, like a snake, to my car, and poor Henry was no more. The body that remained was like a sieve, and the wheel and engine were all on the ground. Old Fritz had made a direct hit. So they sent for more cars and a truck for the remains of Henry Ford's little wonder, but by then it was day light and the firing was too heavy to get near the place. So they had to stay there with us, without food or water during the firing, and when it became dusk the ambulance and truck came out taking the men and part of the Ford to the rear. I then slept the rest of the night and am now waiting for a call to go out to some post in another Ford.

Oh! this is a great life. We live on a few hours sleep, lots of poor coffee, canned meat and hard tack, but, our section will soon be all used up and will have to be relieved till we strengthen up. We hope to be relieved soon and if practicable, get to Paris for the Fourth of July.

Now if you receive this little epistle you can consider yourself lucky, for until we leave this fighting zone no kind of mail is supposed to leave here, but when we get relieved for a rest I will send more news.

Good luck to all.
George Whitmeyer

The Doctor Boone whom Whitmeyer refers to his Lieutenant Joel T. Boone of St. Clair, Pennsylvania, a Navy doctor who was awarded the Congressional Medal of Honor for action with the United States Marine Corps. Boone's MOH reads: "For extraordinary heroism, conspicuous gallantry, and intrepidity while serving with the 6th Regiment, U.S. Marines, in actual conflict with the enemy. With absolute disregard for personal safety, ever conscious and mindful of the suffering of the fallen, Surg. Boone, leaving the shelter of a ravine, went forward onto the open field where there was no protection and despite the extreme enemy fire of all calibers, through a heavy mist of gas, applied dressings and first aid to wounded Marines. This occurred southeast of Vierzy, near the cemetery, and on the road south from that town. When the dressing and supplies had been exhausted, he went through a heavy barrage of large caliber shells, both high explosive and gas, to replenish these supplies, returning quickly with a side car load, and administered them in saving the lives of the wounded. A second trip, under the same conditions and for the same purpose, was made by Surg. Boone later that day."

Surgeon Boone was also awarded the Distinguished Service Cross for service June 9, 10, and 25, 1918, at Bois de Belleu, France. In this instance the regimental aid station in which he was working was hit by heavy shells and demolished on two successive days. Two men were killed and a number were wounded or badly hurt by falling timbers and stones. Surgeon Boone worked without cessation on wounded men, setting an inspiring example of heroism to the officers and men serving under him. On June 25, 1918, Surgeon Boone followed the attack of one battalion against enemy positions in the Bois de Belleu, establishing advanced dressing stations under continuous shelling.

Typical trench system that the soldiers from Pennsylvania fought to control. France 1918.

The Flashes of Our Guns Behind Us and the Rattle of Machine Guns

June 14, 1918
Pvt. Charles I. Saylor
Headquarters 117th Engineers
42nd Rainbow Division
A.E.F.
Somewhere in France.

Last night I think was the longest for me since being in France. I slept in the car as I had to go to the front at 2:30 a.m. and did not want to take a chance on over sleeping. One of our infantry regiments went over the top at dawn and the Colonel was going out to see the raid. We left HQ at 2:45 a.m. and arrived at — —, at 3:15 a.m. It was rather dark and in the low places misty. The best I could do under the circumstances was 20 miles an hour.

When we arrived at the town where I was to leave the car, the Col. said "Saylor, put her in close to the building and come along and see the fun." You can just bet I was tickled to death for the chance. There were four in the party, the Colonel, Lieut. Colonel, the Captain and myself. We started out across the fields and before we had gone very far we were all wet and muddy to the knees. We had to cross two lines of our own barb wire entanglements and a like number of our trenches, besides numerous shell holes filled with water and high wet grass and bushes. This was all done in the darkness.

The Colonel had been up there several days previous and picked out a good place to watch the "doings." The big guns were very active all night long and also our machine guns. The barrage fire stopped right on the minute of four, and all the big guns stopped firing (the calm before the storm). Then one of our machine guns would fire a few shots occasionally. We were standing then on a little hill about 100 yards behind our front line trenches. We had a good view from here.

At the stroke of four, a 12 inch about two kilometers away fired. Then there must have been over a hundred big guns took part in the barrage. I know of one eight inch gun in particular that fired 150 shots itself. Another battery that I know of used up 6,000 shells. This will give you an idea of the intensity of the fire. It was a sight that never will be forgotten. The flashes of our guns behind us, the rattle of machine guns on each side and the bursting shells and flaring sky rockets in front of us made a display of fire works that I will always remember.

We could see all our shells bursting in the German lines. When a big one would burst it would send up sparks in all directions for 50 yards. Every so many minutes we could see a row of red star rockets go up. This was the signal from our already advancing infantry to the artillery to advance or lengthen about an hour and a half, or as long as it took the infantry to go over the top, make their raid and come back. The Huns reply was very feeble. The first "Bertha" was let loose at 4:20 a.m. They didn't send any gas over.

I will be in bed very early to night and make up for last night. I am feeling fine and it seems as though the life at the front agrees with me. For I am not losing any weight.

Charles.

Charles Saylor was a member of the famed 42nd "Rainbow" Division (NYARNG) the first National Guard unit to be sent to fight in the trenches of France. The 42nd arrived in France in November of 1917 and entered the front lines in March of 1918 where it remained in continuous contact with the enemy for 174 days. The 42nd participated in six major campaigns and had one out of every sixteen casualties suffered by the American Army.

Our Eating Here Is Very Good Its Not Beans, Beans, Beans

June 14, 1918
Pvt. William G. Schappel
Quartermaster Corps.
A.E.F.
Tours, France.

Dear Father:

Gee it is a pleasure to be located again, so I can write to you often for when one travels around he cannot write very often. At present I am fine and feeling great and would be surely well pleased to know you all at home were feeling good.

The camp here is an ideal spot and we have shower baths and fine wooden barracks, and they are putting in the electric lights now.

Here we get up at 5:15 and have breakfast at 6:00, then at about 6:45 we fall in for work. I am working in the rubber department repairing gumboots. By the way, I was transferred to the Q.M. corps early this week although I am sorry to leave the boys I had been with all along. The fellows here treat me just like I was with them all the time and I can say now I believe I will like them very much.

Say, I wish you could see the life the most of the boys are leading over here, early to bed and early to rise is the motto and I am right in my little bed every night at 10 o'clock and our eating here is also very good it is not bean, beans, beans, but a change of menu every meal, and I say, I guess I don't do damage to the eats, I eat more than ever.

I have not been to town yet, but when I do I may be able to tell you something about it. I understand it is a very remarkable place.

Well I will have to close and want to say please tell Mae and Lavern and Kyle as soon as I get a chance I will write them all, and you both I will write twice a week.

Your most loving son.
William.

"Lets Go" I Will Never Forget Those Two Words

June 16, 1918
Pvt. Harry (Hap) L. Golden
S.S.U. 637
Convois D Autos, B.C.M.
Somewhere in France.

Dear Parents;

Received 3 letters two about 10 days ago and one this morning. The one I got this morning must have traveled all over France, because it was dated March 3. I had quite an experience since my last letter and never want to have another like it.

It is just one week ago today that the big drive started and I was close to the middle of it. I had gone to bed about 11:30 on the 8th and at 12:10 I was awakened by one of the fellows who said, "Lets Go." I will never forget those two words as I had hardly gotten on my socks when a shell burst next door, which broke all of our windows. I ran with my shoes under my arm to the cave where everyone else had been a couple of minutes before me. We at once put on our masks and found that the long expected attack had come. I did not feel very safe in our cave and wanted to go to the one under the headquarters building which I knew was better and, furthermore, there would be some officers there who could tell us what to do. The fellows persuaded me to stay were I was because it meant almost certain death to try to run to the other cave, which was about 200 feet away. Well, I stayed until 4 o'clock and then made up my mind I was going so another fellow and I started and left the other three they're [*sic*] who could not go. We ran and crouched close to the walls of the houses, which were being shot to pieces very fast. It was raining shells I never thought that the Boche had so many guns. Well, my partner and I got there safely and remained there until 7:30. We had our masks on for the gas almost eight hours and I was nearly smothered. The Medicine Chief told us to leave and not take time for anything. So I lost everything of my own, all my clothes and toilet articles and my car. The Lieut. Bought seven new outfits for the ones we lost. I think that was fine. We worked for five solid days and nights and were given a Division citation for our work. This includes all the section and in it are Charles Dougherty, Earl Haas and Guy Eisenhuth and my self from the former Pottsville section 19. We may now paint the Croix De Guerre on all our cars. And believe me we are some proud boys being able to wear this war cross on them.

I am well and hope everyone is the same. Give my regards to all and my love to the family.

HAP.

The men of the United States of America Ambulance Corps were not under the control of the American Expeditionary Forces. They were directly under the control of the French Army. Their designation included S.S.U—, U.S.A.A.C. Convois Automobiles, Par B.C.M. Paris, France. B.C.M. is an abbreviation for Base Censor Militaire, and S.S.U. is Service Sanitary Unit.

Harry "Hap" Golden was awarded the Croix de Guerre for bravery. The citation reads:

FRENCH CROIX de GUERRE
With Bronze Star
General Headquarters French Armies of the East:
"A very courageous driver he displayed the greatest qualities of endurance
and spirit during the entire very severe period from October 20th to
November 10th 1918. He had been wounded by shell fragments previously
in the attacks in the month of August at Ecovillon."

Our Machines Are Being Smashed Every Day

June 16, 1918
George L. Whitmeyer
Sec. 502 Ambulance Corp.
A.E.F.
Somewhere in France.

Dear Mother:

Well another week has passed, but it has been one very hard week. We are kept on the go all the time, getting very little sleep. In fact, we get no sleep in the night time, it's always the day time that we are off, then we get six hours sleep and go back to duty. Our best time to get the wounded is when its [*sic*] dark and we can go closer to the firing line. We hope soon to be relieved and get back away from the fighting for a good rest and we certainly need one. Half our men are out of business, being sick, wounded, and badly gassed also our machines are being smashed every day. We don't have half enough, so we are compelled to take a rest, if we soon don't get new cars.

So far I have been lucky and have not been hurt, although I went up real close and was hit by a flying piece of shell; it did not hurt me, only took a piece of my coat. So there is no need to worry about me, as I am very much alive at the present.

Our little Fords are doing great work. They get in and out of most any kind of a hole and our tires are easy changed, so after all its not so bad.

There is no need of our being worried about being hurt for [if] we are hit we won't know anything about it and unless our name is written on a Boche shell we are o.k.

Now mother dear long before this letter reaches you, I will be back away from the danger line and having a good rest, so now cheer up and don't worry about me. I am O.K. and in the very best of health.

Lovingly your son,
George

Whitmeyer's unit the 502nd Ambulance Corps was under the direct control of the American Expeditionary Forces, in France.

Tell Mother if I Get Killed She Will Get $10,000 and Be Rich

June 16, 1918
Private Francesco Janarella
Co. H, 110th Infantry Regt.
28th Division
A.E.F.
Somewhere in France.

My dear Cousin:

I received your welcome letter and was certainly glad to hear from you. I am certainly in the best of health. I am a little tired but every body feels that way very often where I am. I was very glad to get to see you before I came across. I was late getting back to camp but nearly all of us were late coming back. Most of us got lost in Jersey City.

I arrived safe a couple of months ago and I am still safe. I am going to kill my share of Germans so don't worry. I won't stop until I get a couple dozen. Don't worry about me because I am glad I am here. I wrote to mother about 15 days ago. I tried to send some money home but I couldn't because there is no post office around. When we get paid we try to spend our money quick so if we go to the trenches we can say we had a good time before we went.

Tell mother not to worry because if I get killed she will get $10,000 and she will be rich. Give my regards to all.

Francesco.

You might tell Francesco's mother that he is one of my best boys, Yeager, Lieut. Censor.

Francesco, although wounded in action, did survive the war.

Off for the Front

June 19, 1918
Lieut. Stanley Davis
U.S. Aviation Corps.
77th Aero Squadron,
French aviation Corps.
Somewhere in France.

Yesterday Saturday I got so that I thought I'd go crazy if I didn't get somewhere. So I took my plane about 4:30 P.M. as it seemed to be clearing up and flew for one hour and 40 minutes, and I had fog and clouds and rain but landed carefully in one of the fields they have for the defense of Paris, a large aviation field. Then I came into the city in an American truck and last night alone went to hear "Thais" at the Grand Opera House which is wonderful. Then I slept the sleep of a tired man and the day Mothers Day dawned with your son in between clean white and fluffy sheets, elder down quilts and a hot bath being drawn in the tub. Then I hopped out at 10:30 and tried to get my uniform which I gave them to have cleaned during the night. Well, I had a fit! The garoon told me it would take six days as they sent it to the cleaners. Think of it, Mother but then I got an English speaking man and finally got my uniform. Think of it six days in bed without a uniform, because it is my only one, as I flew up here without even a toothbrush.

Then the following Sunday we were en route between two places and spent another Sunday in church in Paris. There was a fine sermon by a minister from Pittsburgh, pretty near home, how about it. Well after that we had lunch with some girls from Bryn Mawr who are over here in Relief Work or something and then we all went to the movies and what do you think we saw? Bessie Barriscale and a dandy Triangle picture, once more my thoughts went flashing home. And just as we were going in the cinema we heard a distant boom! And knew the long-range gun was again in action and another shell had landed. The long-range gun really does shoot there as the paper say and sometimes does some damage to innocent people and kids, but it is really quite rare.

While there we met a chap, a friend of Walt Snooks, my pal, and he had just come into Paris on 24 hours leave, due to bad weather. He is in a French bombing escadrille and told us of a recent trip he took into Germany, along with about 20 other bombing planes. They knocked the deuce out of things around large munitions works etc. Just imagine that and he has the Croix-de-Guerre for faithful service and being always on his toes I guess. He told us a lot of other stories, too, but I guess I better not write them because of their military value.

The other day the orderly came to my quarters and told me HQ wanted me on the telephone. Well, a general was going to visit the camp today and they suggested that we have some formation flying for his pleasure. I got busy and this A.M. we had our show for the general, a formation of 15 planes and we circled round and round just as it is done at the front as some of these chaps will soon be doing and as I hope to do, too, when they think I can be spared, I guess. It was really pretty and I got quite excited at times, going chasing up and down along both sides and weaving one after another to close up and get together and then dropping down in front to take the lead and steady things up. It sounds like drilling men doesn't it, or forming boats or something. I guess you can hardly imagine chasing airplanes into a formation but it all seems sort of common place to me now and not at all unusual although I will admit that eight months ago I would strain my neck and eyes for an hour trying to find a plane in the sky. And in those days an airplane was an airplane to me. I never thought of the different types and makes and varieties in each make. Why, I swear there are almost as many different kinds as there are automobiles and one gets to name them as readily when they pass high overhead, Nieuport, Spad, Farmer Caudron, etc. Innumerable to say nothing of the German planes of which I know little and of which I have got to learn or meet the fate of the gods. For each type has its weak points and points of attack and one must be well versed.

June 19, 1918

It is a rainy morning and so there is no chance to fly until this afternoon at any rate. I just stopped here to think a minute whether I had better write what I first intended writing or not and as I glance back over the first part of these letters I find I am becoming worse and worse in my penmanship. I wonder if you can really read my writing at all. This mixture of letters reminds me of my flying. I never try to fly in a straight line but always zig zag up and down, around and over and over. One great long S S S S in the sky. That's for safety only I can't understand why my letters should be this same way. Now I'm going to write one good line, there just to show you. I can do it.

Well, mother I have some good news to tell you this trip, you can guess it, of course, but I am going to tell you anyway for they are such sweet words to me. And I have waited so long to receive the orders containing these precious words. "I am on my way to the front." Yep honest to John and here is how it is. The man at the head of Aviation decided that if some of the men who had been acting as training officers were given a chance to go to the front and then made good and were recalled at the end of a few months they would make all the better instructors and the students would, of course, respect them 100% more for advise [*sic*] gained through experience. And so three of us are here with some other Americans about a score or more, all great chaps, most of whom passed through the field in the course of their training.

We are all happy and I will write to you real often as soon as we start moving again. There are some airplanes, now I wish I dared describe one. Maybe next time I write you will be able to hear the big guns in my letter who knows. We heard them last night way, way off and soon I guess the shells will be whistling as they did a year ago, over my head at the front.

You're loving son.
Stanley

His Last Letter

June 20, 1918
Pvt. John Miller
Co. D 103rd Engineers
28th Division.
A.E.F.
Somewhere in France.

My Dear Parents;

Just a few lines to let you know I am in the best of health and enjoying the life "over here" immensely. The weather is fine. We had very little rain since we arrived. Although the nights are a little cool but in the day it is quite warm.

The boys are now training very hard. In the evening we amuse ourselves with boxing matches and playing cards. I am getting to be a good player.

I was at church last Sunday. It was held in a field. The Chaplain held a communion service. There were quite a few of the fellows from our company who took it. We then had the rest of the day to do what we wished.

I will now tell you about the first air raid which I saw. It was about midnight when I was awakened by the boys in the tent who told me to listen. I did and I heard shots being fired. I went outside, and saw several search lights scouting all over the sky. At least one searchlight found the objective, a German plane. At that instant the whole bunch of lights were centered on him. Then they began to fire, and the plane was forced to retreat towards its home. This was the first air raid I ever saw.

I am having an awful time trying to understand what the French people are saying to us, so I got a book and am carrying it around with me where ever I go in case I get stuck, out will come the book and I am saved.

I hope everyone at home is well, I hope your throat is alright as it is summer now, and all colds should be gone. Hoping to hear from you, I am.

Your Loving Son,
John

Editor's note: Private John Miller was killed on July 15, 1918, on the opening day of the German offensive. On this day Company D, 103rd Engineers, 28th Division would hold the record for the most casualties suffered by one community in the whole United States. That community was Pottsville, Pennsylvania.

Pvt. Walter Spearing a Marine
Beneath the Green of Belleau Woods

June 20, 1918
Written by his friend, to Spearing's mother.
Pvt. Sol Segal
23rd Co. 6th Marines
U.S.M.C.
At the Front, France.

Dear Mrs. Spearing:

There is grief in my heart and in the hearts of all my comrades for the great sorrow that this war has brought to you and to us. We all unite to express our heartfelt sympathy and condolence to the mother and family of one who has fallen in a cause as imperishable as will be the names of those who have fallen to defend it. Should there be anything my comrades and I can do to mitigate your grief and to allay your sorrow—some little keepsake of Walt as a Marine perhaps, but name it dear lady and it shall traverse the ocean to you.

Because you do not know me please do not think it presumptuous for me to write. You are Walter's mother, I was his inseparable friend and comrade, that makes us two kindred souls in common grief for our nearest and dearest. Then too this letter fulfills a duty that I am bound by oath and will to perform.

Many months ago, Walt and I promised each other, that should the God of Battles call to one, the other would console the sorrowing mother. Now Walt has gone west to home and to you forever, but his figure, his

Pennsylvania Marines fought in this wooded area of France during the great battle for Belleau Wood.

voice, his wonderful personality will always be living truths to me. I myself, should the great call come will go gladly, confident of a reunion and with the faith in the eternal truth of that cause for which I die.

"Beneath the green in Belleau Woods forever connected with the Honor of the Marines," lies Walt with two comrades dead on the field of Honor. Above their graves, the stately pines sway in their grandeur, an imperishable monument. But greatest of all epitaphs is that engraved within the hearts of his comrades. "A man, than whom there was no peer in kindliness, in understanding, in comradeship, beyond compare." We alone know what could have been, had circumstances so willed it. What ever befall, whatever sorrow fills us, one thing I swear to you, here hard by that lonely grave, the very paper that I write upon taken in a captured German dugout. I swear that Walt is well avenged, that he has not died in vain, for his spirit leads us on to ultimate victory. You are proud I know, for you are the mother of a martyr, a martyr in a holy cause, Freedom and Liberty.

Dear Lady, the very thought that you are in grief tears my heart. Do not sorrow, death after all is not so terrible, and here, why here, it is glorious. Mother, in the name of the 23rd company, in the name of the Marines I salute you and all my comrades salute you.

Devotedly
Sol Segal

Walter Spearing, a University of Pennsylvania man, was one of the first Marines to ship over to France and received the wound which caused his death in the fight at Belleau Woods. Sol Segal, a 20-year-old comrade of Spearing's, wrote this letter on captured paper while sitting beside Spearing's grave.

I Started on One End of the Line and Mowed Them Down

June 20, 1918
Pvt. Herbert K. Lennox
Co. G. 141st Infantry Regt.
36th Division.
A.E.F.
Somewhere in France

Dear Parents:

Just a few lines to let you know that I am getting along fine. I am up and around again but still at the Hospital. I received my clothes this morning and feel kind of natural once more.

I have not received any mail for some time back, but I wrote a letter to Bob Hughes and told him to forward my mail to this hospital as yet I have not received any. The last letter I received from you was in the front line and it sure made me feel good to get a letter while I was there.

I saw Franklin Miller when I was going back to the hospital, and he was in good health and getting along fine. He sure was surprised to see them carrying me out wounded, but I was a lucky boy to get away with it as lightly as I did, without being cut to pieces.

I was out on an outpost in front of the front line trenches, or what was supposed to be trenches, when the Huns put a barrage on our line and started after us. The first thing we knew they were throwing grenades on us, which forced us to go back, but I had only gone about 25 yards, when I was hit in the back and knocked down; so I got up and picked up an automatic rifle, and there was a big line of "square heads" about 20 feet in front of me, so I started on one end of their line and began mowing them down, when I was hit by another grenade and knocked down. I laid there a few seconds and "bang" another fell under my leg. I felt sure my foot was shot off, but luck was my way and the foot was still there.

So I had to lay where I was until they drove the Germans back, and then they carried me out and now I am just as good as ever.

Hoping this letter finds you all in the best of health, as I am the same, I remain.

Your loving son,
Herbert.

*Private Lennox was awarded the French Croix de Guerre on May 16, 1919,
for the action he wrote about. The award reads as follows:*

*French Croix de Guerre with gilt star.
Under order No. 17465 "D" dated May 16, 1919.
General Headquarters French Armies of the East.
"Although severely wounded and incapable of falling back before
the assaulting wave, he allowed the enemy to pass over him by feigning death
and dispersed them by firing at them from the rear."*

June 22, 1918—The U.S. has sent over 900,000 soldiers across the ocean.

June 25, 1918—American troops beat off German attack at Torcy.

I Thought I Would Go Blind

> June 25, 1918
> Pvt. Frank A. Moyer
> Co. D 151st Machine gun Btn.
> 42nd "Rainbow Division"
> A.E.F.
> Somewhere in France.

Sir:

Just a few lines to let you know I am better again. I was gassed last Tuesday evening, June 18 and it sure did knock me out. It was called mustard gas. Believe me, it sure did smell like horse radish and very strong. I got it in my eyes. I thought I would go blind but now I can see again.

This is the third time I have been in the hospital. Once before I was hit on the forehead with a small piece of shrapnel, on May 6, and the second time I had trench sore feet and 48 boils. I got out in the French hospital and this is my third time I got gas in my eyes.

How is everybody in old Pa. How is Mayor Mortimer. Tell him I send him my best regards. I am doing my bit over here. You can hear over head the big shells bursting. Our Captain, J. M. Leightner of Lancaster was sent home but some of the boys say he was made a Major in the same 157th M.G. battalion. I don't know where he is.

We have lots of big shells. We call them the 120 big header shells. We have been in the front line trenches a long time and just got relieved. The 77th Regt. just relieved us. We are in the 42nd Rainbow Division. The 77th are drafted men.

I only met one fellow from my town. He is in the 168th D. Co. Inf. His name is Lewis Flatto. He lives on Minersville St. He was drafted on Dec. 5,

1917 to the Iowa battalion. I received the Republican regular I am glad to get the news from my old home town. I was made a mule skinner and help to dish up soup out to the boys at the posts. I am going to try to get into the field bakery.

Last month I made eight raison pies, five apple pies and 287 sweet biscuits. The boys said they liked them very much.

The French girls can't understand the American language and we can hardly understand French. I picked up the French language pretty good since I am over here.

Well I guess I gave you all the news so I will bring my letter to a close. Love and regards to you and to my parents on West Sanderson St.

Frank Moyer.

Each infantry division contained one machine gun battalion, commanded by a major and containing four machine gun companies. Each company had 178 officers and men and utilized 16 guns. Within the company were three platoons. Each platoon of four guns had two sections and each section contained two gun squads, with one gun and 10 men led by a corporal. The squad had one cart pulled by a mule which was used to pull the gun as close to the enemy as possible.

The machine guns were used for both indirect and direct fire. Machine guns were high priority targets both by artillery and infantry, and in turn manning a machine gun was a very dangerous occupation.

Took a Bath in a Pond Filled with Old Dead Germans

June 26, 1918
Pvt. Jack Kaiser
Intelligence Section,
80th Division, HQ.
A.E.F.
Somewhere in France.

Dear Mother and all:

Since my last letter I have had quite some experience and no doubt you will be surprised to learn that I have just returned from the front line trenches.

During the itinerary of this trip from our division, we passed through a great portion of the front. The destruction done by the Germans will take years and years of hard labor to replace and a good number of places it will never be done. One town we passed through "Jerry" threw 300 high explosive shells into it in one hour and completely destroyed same. All towns within ten miles of the present front have been evacuated by most of the inhabitants, only a few remaining. Another city we passed the cathedral was bombarded seven times and all that remains is a portion of the wall. It seems the Germans shoot very true at churches although none are ever used by the allies for observation purposes. It is quite hard to describe all that I have seen in travelling through this country, so I will endeavor to tell of life in the trenches.

Four of the boys, in the same section that I am attached to left our division at 4 A.M. one morning and after being on the road for 48 hours, we arrived at a point 9 miles from the front. After waiting for another twelve hours we were taken to within 3 miles in a truck from which place we hiked to Battalion HQ which is about 1–2 miles from the front line. We arrived at 3 o'clock in the afternoon attached to a Scotch Division. The Yankee doctor who is in that division then took us for a bath in an old pond which he said was no doubt filled with dead Germans, but nevertheless we enjoyed it very much as we were some dirty. After tea, we had our first official trip through the lines with the First Lieutenant returning about 9 p.m. to our dugout, which by the way was built by the Germans. It was built in a railway embankment and was about 40 feet undercover. This dugout would accommodate about 200 men. This is the place were "cootie" makes his home and after he becomes acquainted stays with you for some time, at least they have been with me ever since. In dry weather the trenches are not so bad but it is not so nice when it rains. Then a fellow is covered with mud. I have been within 20 yards of the German trenches and one evening we crossed a railroad 50 yards from three German machine guns. We had no sooner reached the other side of the road into high grass when Old "Fritz" started to shoot away but we kept nice and low and were out of harm's way.

This is all the paper I have at the present so I suppose I shall have to close. Trusting you will receive these few lines and hoping you all keep well, as I am feeling fine.

Your loving son,
J. Allen

5

July 1918:
The Allied Offensive

July 1, 1918—Americans capture Vaux, on the Marne front.

The Wounded Beg for Water from
My Radiator Even Boiling Hot

> July 2, 1918
> George L. Whitmeyer
> Sec. 502 Ambulance Corp
> A.E.F.
> Somewhere in France.

Wow, but it is hot—both weather and shells coming over, the Hun must have their dates mixed and are trying to celebrate the 4th of July but we will set them right at midnight tonight when we start our third drive.

It will be on the celebration of the 4th and a barrage will be kept up for 72 hours then they are going to show old Kaiser Bill how to celebrate the fourth. Just now we are not firing much, just living up to the old adage, always calm before a storm, and if the Boche knew what we have in store for him they would all be rushing from the front before midnight tonight.

They started a terrific barrage Monday July 1st and got a few of our boys, killing two of our ambulance drivers making our section daily report read somewhat like this: killed in action 3; captured 1; sick and wounded 27; available for duty, 14, 2 sergeants, 12 drivers, and with this drive coming off we will be some busy. We have 12 machines at different posts and I have been on duty since 5:30 p.m. July 1st with no sign of relief. Guess I am due to be active till after the drive and then I'll be busy till our wounded are hauled away.

You folks at home cannot imagine how much excitement we go through. Just imagine what a stir the Eddystone explosion caused last year when only 130 people were killed then picture the boys going over the top and many more killed, 130 being killed or wounded, and yet no end of the war, then you can judge how we feel and what we are going through.

During the day no fires are lighted on account of the smoke, and in the night a guarded fire in a dugout to warm coffee and only the people in the rear can get that. While the boys at the actual front line live on hard tack, canned meat and water. They get one canteen of water each night and the party of 8 or 12 men going after the water lose 5 men on each trip.

When I go crossing through a wood at night and up to the boys for wounded they rob my extra tank of water and beg water from the radiator even boiling hot.

There are very few army men doing the fighting at this front. It's a Marine division, the 5th and 6th Marines who are doing all this good work but are paying dearly for it, and they not having any ambulances we are called on to do the work. Some large ambulances which came here to help out are too big to do the work but the little old Fords sneak up close to the lines, taking rations up and bringing prisoners back, always on the go and for good work both General Pershing and Colonel Jones our Ambulance Chief has commended us for our excellent duty.

We have another verse now for " Pack up your troubles" it goes.

> *Pack up your wounded in your old Ford Car*
> *And drive, drive, drive.*
>
> *Although the shells are bursting near and far*
> *You'll get there alive.*
>
> *Now's the time for hurrying*
> *Speed up and you'll arrive, so*
> *Just give a yell and go like hell,*
> *And drive, drive, drive.*

George.

From a Multitude of Iron Mouths
There Belched Forth a Rain of Fire

July 2, 1918
Sergeant John T. Duffy
Co. D 103rd Engineers
28th Division.
A.E.F.
Somewhere in France.

Dear Father:

We arrived at this point in France and this is really the first opportunity that I have had of late to write to you.

The 103rd is the first of our boys selected to see real service and we are the first of the 28th Division up in the fighting zone and everything indicates real active work ahead.

Just a hurried thought of my first sight and impression of America's challenge to the Boche and I need hardly say that what I saw will remain fixed in my memory. We assembled in the dead hours of the night and as the columns were ready to move there was a quiet and feeling hard to describe. And as we moved off and up the mountain to the point where work was to begin, we felt a new experience. Far across the ravine the boche sent his challenge and from a multitude of iron mouths there belched forth a rain of fire that sent the Hun to cover, but the firing continued until dawn. I watched the morning break, streaks of purple shoot out from the horizon and slowly the great sky seemed to soften. The birds in the trees sang their lays and I marveled to think that in this country where nature has been so kind to the people that autocracy was to meet his master democracy and that the sons and sires of this old world, who left it many years ago to take up new homes in the land of the free, should march back and on the same mountain sides crush the foe which drove their ancestors across the sea. The reign of militarism is dying and the men who founded a country on principles that represented privilege for the few, whose despotism and tyranny would make slaves of us all is over and I feel that before long we will celebrate a Fourth of July of the peoples of the world.

Our American troops have been very successful and last night they gave the boche a push that was wonderful and took many prisoners.

Our work is chiefly construction and of course we must take many risks and while dangerous, don't take any stock in the hair brea[d]th Harry tales which usually are circulated so freely and while danger lurks everywhere. We use every precaution and with the help of God we will be spared to do the duty in this great cause.

All of our boys are enjoying good health and if any of their families inquire say to them that there is no cause for worriment and we hope to get through the contest without much trouble.

Sincerely, Your Son,
John.

Sgt. Duffy and Company D arrived at Romeny on June 28th and stayed there until July 8th. Here they were engaged in trench building and guarding the bridge that crossed over the Marne River. Here company D suffered its first casualties, having one man killed and five wounded.

A Dugout Is a Hole in the Ground

July 2, 1918
Pvt. Alfred Bowe
Co. D 28th Infantry Regt.
1st Infantry Division.
A.E.F.
Somewhere in France.

Dear Mother:

Everything is o.k. here as this letter leaves us. I am writing this letter in the trenches. It isn't as bad here as you would imagine. The only thing you have to do is to keep as far down in the ground as possible. I am up at night and sleep in the day but this morning I am not a bit sleepy so I thought I would write to you. I will not get a chance to mail it until we get out but it may not be long.

Well mother I saw the Republican where there are 100,000 troops marching to the front. Well I was one of them and we were hiking for a month. We are having fine weather here. It was almost too warm to hike but I really would not have it otherwise.

I am pretty far from the place where I had my picture taken and I don't think I will get back to get it.

Dad, do you remember the night you saw me crawl out of that culbert [*sic*]? That was a good drill for me as that is the way I must go in and out of my dugout at the present. A dugout is a hole in the ground. The deeper it is the safer but this one is not very good as it was just built, also it has no bunks in, my pal and I lay on the ground, all we have to do is to make up our bed, to pick up the sharpest stones where the heaviest part of our bodies lie and everything is o.k. I broke my watch the other day and

A common sight in 1918—American soldiers marching into battle. American soldiers would fight in France for 200 days.

needed one so bad that I tried to fix it but did not make a success of it. I received a letter from Joe Beir the other day that he wrote in February. He did not have the number of my regiment on the address so it took much longer to come.

Alfred Bowe.

July 4, 1918—Americans celebrate the fourth by taking Hamel.

I Went Swimming in the Famous River
Once Red with Blood

July 5, 1918
Lieutenant Thomas Beddall
1st Gas regiment.
Warfare Service.
Attached 30th U.S. Engineers
A.E.F.
Somewhere in France.

Dear Father and Mother:

I have just written to Marsie and told her most of the news. We arrived here at our new station after two days of travel in motor trucks through a very fertile country, about a 200 mile trip. This is the most beautiful part of France I have seen yet. One of the Captains of our command live[s] in the room occupied by Von Gluck during his brief stay in these parts. It was about this country that the story about the hilltop was written that you enjoyed so much, "Hill top on the Marne."

Yesterday, the fourth we spent very quietly. I went swimming in the famous river, once red with blood, and enjoyed myself immensely.

Stories from eyewitnesses of recent fighting, in which the Yanks covered themselves with glory, are very interesting. In the cleaning up of Huns from the cellars of houses, after the assaulting troops had gone to the other side of the village, a yank of Polish birth found himself in a cellar with ten Boches and a battle royal started. Being greatly outnumbered it looked badly for Mr. Yank. At the rear of his little group of Huns he heard two of them converse in the Polish tongue. Instantly he recognized it and shouted something to them in that tongue. They immediately attacked the remaining Boche from behind and in a few minutes the Yank came out of the cellar with the two Polish compatriots and eight other prisoners.

As I told Marsie recently. I am to receive the Croix de Guerre in appreciation of what we did for the French Government in a recent attack.

Thomas

Lieut. Beddal received the Croix de Guerre:

First Lieutenant Thomas H. Beddall
1st Gas regiment, Chemical Warfare Service.
French Croix de Guerre with gilt star.
Order no. 11,399 "D"
November 8, 1918
"An officer of great valor who displayed veritable qualities of leadership and bravery during the course of special operations executed by his company."

July 12, 1918—Eleven U.S. Divisions on the battle front.

The Other Night We Were Playing Hide and Seek with Fritz's Shells

July 12, 1918
Pvt. Carl Feger
Co. C 103rd Engineers
28th Division
A.E.F.
Somewhere in France.

Dear Dad:

Well I had luck enough to get hold of a couple of envelopes and some paper, so I will try and make up for the time I missed. I have received about five letters from you since I came over here, and I am going to answer them now.

The other night we were playing hide and seek with Fritz's shells at supper time, and we were having some good time until he sent a bunch of gas shells over and then we had to leave our baked beans and fried potatoes get cold. We had a good wind so it did not last long, but believe me, it is a darn sight worse than shrapnel. That night we pulled out, and from that time on we spent sixty one hours in the trenches, and maybe the stuff didn't fly around.

This is some place up here. Today I washed for the first time for several days. It rained two nights and it sure is fine lying in the mud. I was on my knees or my back all the time, outside of when we could go for our meals, which were few and far between.

I can't tell you just where we are for the censor would not pass it. But I can say if you read the newspapers you can tell just where we are. We are on the most active front, that is the French and American front.

We had a rest for two days and will go out again very soon. The hardest thing to get over here is candy or sweets of any kind and writing paper and envelopes.

It takes just about one month to get a letter. The last one I got was dated June 12th. I do not see why you didn't hear from me before. We cannot smoke or have any lights at all, and in the day time we have to keep under cover all the time, for it would only be a matter of a short while until we would have a whole lot of Hun artillery on us. Of all the boys over here I have not met any one yet that I knew.

Your Son,
Carl.

From June 30th till July 13th Company C was engaged in the construction of reserve trenches and wire entanglements about two kilometers north of their billets at Charly, France. Also during this time period they were detailed as a reserve infantry company.

Crank Up Little Henry and Chase
to the Dressing Stations

July 14, 1918
George Whitmeyer
Section 502
Ambulance Corp.
A.E.F.
Somewhere in France.

Viva [*sic*] la France, July 14, 1918. At last things have quieted down and we get plenty of time for cleaning up, even to getting a bath, and that is going some at the front. We have moved our quarters to a Chateau, a real large house with plenty of room to throw our clothing about, and at a house further up front in the evacuated district which our boys have just captured, there were two pianos, so we salvaged one and brought it to our new quarters, so now we have a large writing room and music all the time. The windows have been camouflaged and every night there is big doings in the room, a piano, fife, violin and bugle, with our lieutenant and his traps, it makes some jazz band, and the French soldiers in the vicinity congregate in the yard and have a high old time.

Our duties are quite easy at present but we are always ready to crank up little Henry and chase to the dressing stations in case of an attack. We have twenty machines, ten on duty all the time, and our duties run for 24 hours on and twenty four off giving us plenty of time to repair the machine when off duty and to clean up. That also gives us one night's full sleep every 48 hours besides the sleep we get while on our posts in the daytime, but at night when we move closer to the lines we don't dare sleep, as it is an advance dressing station and the least little attack and gain by the Hun would mean our capture, so we stay always on the alert with the machine ready to evacuate on a minute notice.

Some days on post we don't have more than two trips, other days it is nothing but go, go, with just enough rest to fill up with gas and back to the lines. But there are no nights when we have much rest, for that is the time the men up close must be taken in, and then the time flies so quick we just pray for the dark hours to creep by so we get all the men safely through the danger zone.

Our food up here is not so very good, we cannot have fires going, for any sort of fire means smoke and draws the Boche's fire, then in the night it makes a light, and no matter how careful might be a light is not exactly covered, so it means canned meats, hard tack and bread three to five days old. In the rear where the kitchens are, we always stop and bum a meal when we happen to get that far back with patients, which is seldom, for the big trucks generally take such trips, for they are obsolete away up front where we work, so are used from the field hospital a few miles back, to base hospitals.

In the night these kitchens send hot coffee, stew, beans and other such things up to their respective companies, but these ration wagons are generally caught coming up close, and every so often one is knocked off the road and the men seriously wounded or killed, then these men whom the rations were meant for are due to wait 24 hours longer for their hot coffee and the warm food, and even though they do get it each man only gets enough to fill up for one meal, and must go on all day with out hot food, no water except what he gets during the night in his canteen, and it is suicidal to venture from their small trenches during the day for up here it is open warfare, and we have nothing but quick trenches thrown up, in these the men keep under cover, not out of danger, but quick enough to keep them from flying pieces of shrapnel and small arms ammunition fire and it takes a direct hit to get them, so you see they are cramped up in small holes or trenches all day. It don't get dark until after nine and daylight at 3:30, so to them darkness is a God send and daylight means to sit in a cramped position and sleep as much as possible, for at night all must be on the job.

I understand our boys from old Schuylkill are camping about ten miles away from the field hospital, making it about 12 miles from the actual front, and ready to come here in case the big attack starts here at this point. It may happen any day now, but the Boche will think all hell broke loose if they do start on this point. They have Bull Dogs to fight here, the kind who bite and hold on till the last, and plenty of them, and the Boche kind of knows that too for he met the Marines and knows what kind of bull breed they are. This division here now is the Yankee division from New England States, so the Yankee bull dogs will meet them first if they ever decide to break through.

This place the Chateau Thierry district is on a direct line to Paris, and when we came here it was never thought that the Boche was kept from going right into Paris, but the Marines stepped in and took a few towns the Boches strong point, the Belleau Woods, and have stopped them at every turn they make. Suppose the next division will be the 28th Division who goes to the front, then I will go to see the engineers, Co. C and D also the others who have been sent over from Pennsylvania. Will then have plenty to write about, and much news for the folks at home.

George Whitmeyer.

July 15, 1918—The Germans launch a major offensive on the Marne toward Epernay and 200,000 Americans are before them.

July 17, 1918—General Pershing sends news to Washington that the big German push on the Marne was stopped by American troops. This will be the high tide for the German Army.

The 155 mm Shell Fell Right in Front of Them

> July 17, 1918
> Private Kenneth T. Lavelle
> S.S.U. 560 Convois Auto.
> Ambulance Corp.
> Somewhere in France.

Dear Mother and Dad:

Yesterday at 1 p.m. a shell fell in the midst of our camp killing two and wounding five. Among these were John W. Crane killed and Walter J. Lecher wounded. "Harp" was killed practically instantly. Lecher is comparatively lucky as he was never in any danger of losing his life. He suffered terribly, of course for a while as his right hand was badly mangled and his left arm in the upper part was pierced by shell fragments. He was the same old game boy though and walked unaided to the ambulance holding his hand. Luckily for several of those wounded, the hospital was only a mile away so that they got their wounds attended to within several minutes.

Harp, Lecher and many others were seated together talking, waiting for the call to mess. The call came and most of the fellows hurried away. Unfortunately Harp and Lecher stayed with several others. About fifteen seconds after the dinner call, the 155 mm fell right in front of them about two yards away. It's a wonder they weren't all killed.

For God's sake use all the discretion in your power in breaking the news to the Cranes and Lechers, if they have not already heard of it. That's all for that I guess, excepting that Harp's grave is well taken care of by both the Italians, with whom we were working at the time, and by our boys. Needless to say we will continue to do so as long as it is possible.

Reassure Lecher's family as to the certainty of his recovery and his personal courage. I suppose you still believe I am wounded or some such thing, so I can but assure you that at the time when that shell fell I was up the road about a kilometer with an axle that turned without moving the car, and the mechanics had just left camp to help me in when the thing broke right where they had been. No I am very much alive and glad of it.

> Son.
> Kenneth.

John W. Crane was 22 years of age and was educated in local Pottsville schools and later at Villanova College. At both places he was a tremendous baseball player and football player. He was the fourth man to enlist in the C. A. Snyder Ambulance Unit where he enlisted in May 1917. He was assigned to section 643. He later was assigned to Unit 506 and sent to France.

Hell Had Certainly Broken Loose

July 17, 1918
Pvt. Charles Saylor
HQ. Co. 117th Engineers
42nd "Rainbow" Division.
A.E.F.
Somewhere in France.

Dear Folks:

I suppose by this time you are anxious to know why I haven't written for such a long time. The reason is very simple, our division has been sent to help stop the Germans on their next drive, which started at 12:00 o'clock on Sunday night.

Just at 12 o'clock on Sunday night I was awakened out of a sound sleep by a gas signal. I never in all my life heard such a terrific bombardment, as was going on at the time. The expected German drive had commenced. We expected it to start the night before, but for some reason or other, it didn't materialize. It didn't come as a surprise for the time and the place had been figured and worked out almost to the minute.

In less time than it takes to tell we were all packed up and every man at his post ready to move up at a moments notice. I put my things in the car and stood by, waiting to hear from the Colonel.

Shells were dropping all around, the sky was full of planes and the din and road was terrible. Hell had certainly broken loose, and right where we were too. Sherman knew what he was talking about.

At 12:20 a.m. a mounted dispatch rider came down and told me to report at the office at once. I will never forget the night of the 14th. It was a terrible night for driving. The flashes of hundreds of big guns all around made it even more difficult.

At 2:20 a.m. on the 15th, we moved our regimental HQ office in a dug out. This dug out was 45 feet deep and about 2150 feet long. We slept down there for two nights. Even at that depth we could hear a dull rumble every time a big shell landed near; the candle flame would flicker and the bunks would shake. It reminded one of a coal mine in Penna. That same night I had the unpleasant experience of having a Hun plane swoop down on me as I was driving along the road and pumping his machine gun on me as hard as he could pump. It was a bright moonlight night, a straight road and no traffic. I was rolling along between 35 and 40 and the first intimation I had of his presence was a stream of machine gun bullets striking the road along the side of the car. I stopped the car short for I knew that was something that he couldn't do. He had to keep on going. By the time he turned, I was gone.

Our division played a big part in stopping the Huns from gaining their objective in this drive. We were there only four days and then we made another big jump. We have been unable to keep up with our infantry, and last but not least the Post Office was lost altogether. They were just re established two days ago.

Editors note: Saylor's letter was in two parts and was finished on August 20th.

For the last month I have been driving on an average of 18 and 20 hours a day and of the worst kind too. Many a day I drive into camp in time for breakfast after driving all night. Sometimes I am so dead tired that I don't even eat breakfast, I'll just throw a blanket on the ground and "flop." My beds (when I sleep) vary very much. Sometimes I lay in the woods in the grain fields, in the car and not a few times I have slept under the dirt bank along the roads. This last time when we were under shell fire.

The drive the Germans made on the night of the 14th was as near as I can learn, the fiercest attack they ever made during the whole war. Our division also helped to give them the worst licking and set back they ever received. From 12 o'clock on Sunday night until 10 o'clock Monday morning, more shells were fired than any two days fighting at Verdun. This all happened in our sector too.

The things that happened between the 14th of July and the present time I shall never forget as long as I live. Certain things have been so impressed on my mind that it would be impossible to ever forget them.

There are so many things, but perhaps, in the eyes of the censor, I have already overstepped the mark. Just leaving on a four hundred mile trip.

"DART"

July 18, 1918—French General Foch strikes back at the Germans and gains over four miles.

The Propeller Stopped Dead and My Heart Did Too

> July 18, 1918
> Lieut. Stanley Davis
> Attached to
> 77th Aero Squadron,
> French Air Service.
> French Army.
> Somewhere in France.

Another month has rolled around since I left the old Etats Unis and when they ask me how long I have been over here, I say in an off hand sort of way… "Oh only seventeen months." But it is some time, some long, long time, and I'm heartily fed up on the whole business.

But I must not tell you my troubles, when I am really very happy and full of pep, and feeling that I'm doing something—yes—yesterday I felt that I earned all the salary the government ever paid me.

I'm still in the French Army, and our group has been moved bodily from one section of the line to another, the very worst in the entire outfit, I guess. I have been having considerable trouble with my motor in different planes, and while they were installing a new motor in my plane, I flew a different plane down to the new location, and then they sent me back to the first place via Paris for my original plane, and so I had two days and nights in Paris again. Saturday morning at 6:30 I left our old aerodrome in my plane and the new motor went dead and I managed to creep along until I saw a large aviation field and I landed there. It was right outside of Paris and saw the wonderful fete of July 14th the French National holiday, never have I seen such troops in parade, they were from everywhere, and our boys would do your heart good.

I got back to this place Sunday evening in my plane and yesterday morning at 4:00 a.m. we were awaken[ed] by an alert, the Boche had pulled a grand attack at daybreak, and it was no fun, another chap and myself got off, he is an ace, 24 Boche to his credit, and did a patrol at 500 meters, due to the deep low hanging clouds, never have I been so scared in my life. Everything was in an uproar and the great guns burst right under your plane, you'd think a powder mill blew up or something—and the vivid flashes of red and all the time, one rush up and down, and I was completely lost and you could see the Huns crossing the river on specially built bridges, and all the Spads were going up and down, diving at them and shooting at them as they tried to cross, and the earth would go leaping up in big clouds of dirt and dust and water as the big shells landed up and down around the advancing troops.

We flew up and down along the river, it was the old line of the night before, and by George, when we got back to our aerodrome, we found we were at least five kilometers inside the Hun lines, they had advanced so quickly, golly it was some excitement.

In the afternoon we were off again, a big formation of seven this time as the clouds were very high 3,000 meters, and never have I seen such a sight as below and above. We got in several mixups and I am not sure whether I got a Hun or not. I never waited to see, because as I pulled both triggers with all my might shooting between two big crosses one on each wing, I saw four other crosses and two other planes moving around, and well, it was a thriller, and I was one happy boy. When the leader, I found him after the scrap, pointed down and dived and we were comfortably heading north for home, and I was all smiles and riding close to him, sort of snuggling under his left wing, because my wing was up a little after the thing was over. Just about that time I felt a lot of hot oil on my legs, the crank case had sprung a leak and my motor stuck fast, the propeller stopped dead and my heart did too. But I managed to hit a good field somehow, and a second later the leader of the group number 3, shot down over me and waved and a second later another one came whizzing down and loomed up again, and I knew they would soon come and get me. I read and smoked and thought it all over, and then the auto came. They had to leave my plane there under the trees and we got home in time for supper at 8:15.

Our next patrol got moved up with the famous Hun outfit, Richt[h]ofen's Circus. I had two Huns on my tail before I knew I was alive, there were three others above me and my guns stuck. I dove almost 8,000 feet vertically and managed to cross the Marne into safety when I landed, lost, at a strange aerodrome. We found the plane pretty badly shot up, to say nothing of a number of holes through the wings and fuselage. One bullet cut half through my control rod that works the ailerons on the wings, one cut half through a hollow steel rod that works the elevation of the tail, it stuck there. And about six others in a group severed the main spar of my lower right hand wing. I guess I earned that two days rest in Paris, while mechanics practically rebuilt my plane. I didn't sleep much the first night after the scrap, every time I'd doze off I'd hear the bullets whiz pass my head and ears. And that long dive, I'd still be going, if the Huns hadn't started shooting from low, I came that close to the ground and it brought me to my senses with a rush.

Now we are waiting, the French and Americans are going, perhaps it is on now, for the cannonading is terrific, to push the Huns back again onto the river. We are waiting orders any moment to come and do our part, perhaps keep the Hun planes off, perhaps dive on the Huns as they try to re-cross the river. Think of it, mother, having to drive the devils into a river, but don't be scared, it is only a day or two days work, perhaps after this is over, we will be around for a week, but by George, we have earned it.

It is getting fine out of doors, I wonder how soon we are going off, I get nervous waiting.

Your Loving Son,
Stanley

Lieutenant Davis's aerial victory was confirmed and on October 30, 1918, he was awarded the Croix de Guerre for this action.

French Croix de Guerre with Palm.
Under order No. 11,054 "D"
October 30, 1918.
General Headquarters, French Armies of the North and Northeast,
with the following citation:
"A very spirited pursuit pilot who volunteered for all the perilous missions.
On July 17, 1918, he shot down an enemy airplane. (First victory)"

A Piece of Shell Hit Three Inches from My Head

July 18, 1918
Pvt. Allen D Knarr
Co. C, 112th Infantry Regiment.
28th Division.
A.E.F.
Somewhere in France.

Dear Sister:

Just a few lines to let you know I am among the living. The boys went through quite an experience since my last letter I wrote you. I will try my best about telling you a little about it, without giving details, subject to the censor and useful to the enemy. It was the beginning of the German offensive, which began about 12:15 a.m. Nearly everyone with the exception of myself, my platoon commander, sergeant and a few others, being in camp. All the rest were out in the trenches. I was sleeping very soundly in my pup tent when I was awakened by the sentinel who told me to put on my shoes and get the H— out of there. I heard the shells bursting all around me. Well, I didn't lose any time in getting out and hunting a dug out.

The dugout was only one of the two or three which happened to be located there. I wasn't there but a few minutes when my platoon commander came over and asked me if I was alright. I told him I was and he said he probably would be with me in a short time. Well, he certainly had

Soldiers creeping along the trench lines. The men are typical of what the Pennsylvania soldiers would have looked like in the field.

a lot of nerve he ran a half kilometer to the trenches, through thick shell fire, shells that were composed of high explosives and various gases and it was luck that pulled him through O.K. When he returned, he had with him a team of machine gunners, which he brought back to the dugout.

During his absence a shell burst about 20 feet from the dug out, which threw mud and stone all over me. The dug out was the only thing that saved me. After the firing quieted down a trifle, I returned to my tent. I wasn't there but a short time until another shell burst but a short distance from me. A piece of shrapnel came through my tent and I thought that it went on through, but I found out different when it hit three inches from my head. I don't know whether you call that lucky or not. But I'll make that my conviction without any doubt. There were several casualties from our company, killed and wounded.

The Americans, according to the reports brought in, are doing some wonderful fighting, which of course, is all American blood. It is up to us to bring this great war to a close. Which I imagine won't take very long to accomplish. I was thinking won't it be great to have Christmas peace.

Sincerely
Allen D. Knarr.

July 19, 1918—1st U.S. Division takes Bersy-le-Sec; 2nd U.S. Division takes Tigny; U.S.S. *San Diego* sunk off New York.

July 20, 1918—26th U. S. Division takes Epieds; 3rd U.S. Division takes Jaulgonne.

We Stayed at Our Guns Till the Water Came Up to Our Knees

July 20, 1918
Seaman Norman Robertson
U.S.S. San Diego

Dear Mother and Father:

Just a few lines to let you know that I am safe in Port, and am well and O.K. We were on our way from Portsmouth, N.H. to New York. We were torpedoed about 11 o'clock in the morning about ten miles off Fire Island. I was on the main deck when it happened. I ran up on the boat deck and cut down two life rafts and got a life preserver on and then ran down and relieved a man at the gun which was my station. We fired six shots at what we thought might be a submarine. We stayed at our gun till the water came up to our knees and we were ordered to leave the ship to save our lives.

When the ship was hit it put the generator out of commission and we could not hoist out any of the life boats or send a wireless for help. So when I left the ship every life raft was full. There was an oar floating by and I got that. After floating about a half an hour with an oar and my life preserver I got hold of a piece of wreck with six other shipmates and after floating around in the water for three hours we were picked up by a ship called the Bussum and two other ships. I tell you I was pretty nearly all in when we were picked up. We got to New York about midnight and are stationed on an army transport for a few days. They gave us all a suit of pajamas, sweaters, a comfort kit and a blanket and best of all something to eat as soon as we came aboard. I got a suit of white and a pair of shoes and a cap yesterday and was left go on liberty. I went off to Flossie's and stayed until after supper. She told me Melvin was up here so I am going to find him sometime this week if he is still here. As soon as I get clothes and money which I expect to get in a few days. I will tell you all about it when I get home. Don't answer for I don't know what address and don't worry for I am o.k.

Your loving son
Norman.

Where Do We Go from Here Boys

July 20, 1918
QM 3rd Cl. Joseph Mussina
U.S.S. Maui
Atlantic Ocean

Dear Parents:

We sure have been a busy bunch around here all last night and today. You of course know about the San Diego being sunk. Well, last night at 7:00 p.m. we received word that the survivors would be sent to us, to be taken care of. All hands were called and no one was allowed to turn in. At 11:00 p.m. they started to come aboard. Well we worked all night getting them fed and bunked up comfortable. Some happy bunch they were dressed in all ways imaginable and singing " Where do we go from here boys." At Point of Woods where they landed they were treated loyally. Many were naked, others in underclothes and some in whites. Very few had shoes. The people and Red Cross there gave them clothing and many offered money but few would take it. When they came on board here most of them were dressed in pajamas and wool socks, some sight. On coming across the gangway each one was given a Red Cross comfort kit and a blanket. They were pretty tired but many of them told us the story. Not until the order was given. And that was when she was lying on her side and nearly under. The gun crews stayed at their stations until knee deep in water. The majority think they sunk one of the submarines. Our captain and theirs are at work at the present time checking up the crew. They say between fifteen and thirty men were lost. The actual number is not positively known, but is about twenty four. Work was continued all day today. A navy barge came alongside and each man was given a suit of whites, underwear, socks, shoes a white hat, and given shore liberty at once to last until 9:00 p.m. on Monday. Many of them live in New York. On Monday a court of inquiry will be held to settle things officially and the men will probably receive last months pay over again, $100 to cover the cost of new clothes, bag, and hammock and then be given thirty days leave with pay. None of them are sick the main trouble is a bad case of sunburn. Frantz used to be on the San Diego and knew all the signal bunch so we took them on the bride and fixed them up to go ashore. The cake arrived and we had a feast of that, you should have heard them rave over it, and they all send their best, wishes, praises etc. They sure were grateful for it. I wish I could tell all the tales they tell. It must have been a wonderful sight. Makes me wish I could have gone through it. They cannot get through praising the Red Cross for their kindness. You can imagine what our ship is with all that bunch coming unexpectedly.

Guess I'll quit now and call my relief. It is possible that I may get home next Saturday and Sunday. I hardly think so but you never can tell. Received your letter today with the cake. You can bet I eat my share but I had to share up with my shipwrecked shipmates too, who wouldn't. Will close now and turn in I need the rest. Write right away.

Joseph.

Editor's note: The U.S.S. San Diego *was a 503-foot 13,600-ton armored cruiser that was commissioned on August 1, 1907. Her armament consisted of 18 three-inch guns, 14 six-inch guns mounted in side turrets, four eight-inch guns and two 18-inch torpedo tubes. On July 8, 1918, the San Diego left Portsmouth, N.H., en route to New York. She rounded Nantucket light and was heading in a westerly direction. On July 19, while zig zagging as per war instructions, at 11:23 a.m. an explosion tore a huge hole amidships. Two more explosions tore through her hull created by the exploding of the boilers and ignition of the powder magazine. The ship immediately started to list to port. The crews manning the guns fired at anything that looked like a submarine. Captain Christy tried to steam toward Fire Island but never made it. The order to abandon ship was given. Captain Christy was the last man to leave the ship and was cheered by the men in the water. The official casualty report listed 30 to 40 men but the finalized death toll after checking all muster rolls was only six seamen. It was later determined that a mine not a torpedo laid by the U-156 sank the vessel. The U-156 was sunk by an American mine on its homeward journey. The* San Diego *was the only major warship lost by the United States in World War I.*

July 21, 1918—American forces capture over 21,000 Germans.

It Was Plain Hell on Earth

July 21, 1918
Sergt. Harry Lankert
Co. C 103rd Engineers
28th Division.
A.E.F.
Somewhere in France.

Dear Brother:

This is my first letter to you, Earl, and I dare say that you came very near not hearing from me. Listen to this little story about the first real battle I was in.

The Germans started a drive on the night of the 14th. It was a French holiday and it seems to me the Germans took the French a bit off their guard. But the Dutch didn't figure the Yanks right. He started a drive on a fifty mile front with about 480,000 troops. His main drive was in the sector which we are working in. There were only three companies of infantry and three companies of engineers at this one certain point. Our company was one of them. We hiked about two miles to meet him and we stopped on top of a high hill about two in the morning. The Captain ordered us to scatter and hunt protection behind trees, in holes and anywhere. Well, we were not there ten minutes before the show started with the big act on first. We were shelled from two in the morning until three in the afternoon. It sure rained iron and steel enough to built a railroad and enough for engines to run the road. It was plain hell on earth. The Germans took a bunch of French Artillery and turned it on us. I cannot begin to explain it to you. I certainly was lucky. We had no dugouts to creep into. So the only thing we had to do was to lie flat on the ground. The shells came so close to me without hitting me that they would burn my hands face and neck. I don't mean burnt hard, but just as hot as a piece of steel would feel if it passed under ones nose. I heard one fellow yell, Help. Help I'm shot in the jaw, so I started to crawl towards him on my stomach. Well, every time I would put my hand down I would put it on a piece of shrapnel and every time I would burn my hand. I imagined I was shot. I crawled about 20 yards and called to him, but could not get an answer.

By this time they were getting slight flesh wounds all around me and our platoon was pretty busy getting the wounded to the dressing station. But here is the best thing of all. Not one of our fellows was killed. I cannot understand how on earth any one thing could have lived within a square mile of our location.

Well, after we had dare wink an eye without being shot at, which was about three in the afternoon, our platoon (50 men) started through the woods looking for dead and wounded. The woods were full of German snipers in French and American uniforms; we did not know who were our friends or enemies. We got a few Hun prisoners and I made them carry our wounded back. A fellow from another company shot a German Sergeant out of a tree. He had a machine gun also a camera with five films. He told me and a great many more that if the Germans failed in this drive the war would be over in six weeks. He told us how little they got to eat and that the papers in Germany state that there are scarcely a thousand Americans in France, that the submarines are sinking them as fast as they come over. Can you imagine that!

Well, that night it started to rain very hard. Three of us were in a hole trying to sleep, we were might tired and hungry. The rain came through our poor roof and we put on our slickers (raincoats) and sat on our steel helmets from 10:30 P.M. until 5 A.M. without even a place to lean our backs against. The thunderstorm, along with the hot sun afterwards certainly did everything but help the dead bodies smell good. The fellows not being accustomed to the stench put their gas masks on. We finally got reinforcements and started the Germans back. When we came back the hills were full of artillery and now the Germans are so far away and still retreating that the artillery can hardly keep up to them. Everyone thinks the war will soon end now because the Huns are quitting cold. I think our company figured in the battle that is going to end the war.

Send me a letter once in awhile; I did not get any from home yet. Also a few clippings from the newspapers, things that would interest me. Good bye, and good luck.

Yours in good health,
Brother Harry

On July 13th Company C marched to Charly, leaving there at 1:30 a.m. on motor trucks and arrived at Conde-en-Brie at 5:30 a.m. On the 14th they moved to the forest south of a public road between the village of Grand Fontaine and La Fourche farm. On the 17th the 1st, 2nd and 3rd platoons left the forest and marched to the forward slope of St. Agan. Simultaneously with the arrival of platoons on the forward slope of the forest, the Germans opened up with a heavy artillery barrage, before the men were put into position. It was very dark and little shelter could be found. In all, 20 men from the company were wounded.

July 22, 1918—The 28th Division from Pennsylvania are fighting desperately and the Germans are being forced back miles every day. This is the Germans' first big retreat.

The Devilish Business of the Hun

July 22, 1918
Pvt. Edward Duby
Co. C 103rd Engineers
28th Division.
A.E.F.
Somewhere in France.

My Dear Sister:

We are doing regular engineering war now and are hiking all over France. We were at the front a couple of times. I'll say its nothing like home in a dug out but it won't be long till old Liberty Bell will ring all over the U.S.A.

It certainly is a fierce sight to go into a village that was recently occupied by the Germans. They tear the homes inside and out to find valuables.

I am writing in one of these homes now. I have a bed and a soft one but the floor is full of old clothing that the Germans pulled out of the closets, lots of expensive goods, silks and satins all over the floor. Across the street is the foundation of a small house that was torn down by shell fire. The people in France certainly do feel and realize what a war is and its up to the good old U.S.A. to finish the devilish business of the Huns.

Most of the Germans I've seen laying around have written on their belts the words "Lord go with us" but when they shoot a shell in a church and watch the church fall in a heap, it don't look very good. After the Americans and French drove the Germans back all the fellows went into the field to get souvenirs. I am going to get things a little later on as I have enough to carry around, helmets, bayonets, pistols, rifles, leather pouches.

Edward Duby

July 23, 1918—American troops capture Jaugonne.

I Would Say That No One Is Giving Too Much

July 23, 1918
Color Sergeant Foster Berger.
H.Q. Company
103rd Engineers
28th Division
A.E.F.
Somewhere in France.

Dear Mother:

I received a letter from Anna the other day which had been addressed to Camp Mills. We have not been receiving any mail for some time, but late this evening I received one from you dated June 27. This is the latest one I have. It sure makes [me] feel a little better to read a letter from [home] that is not so old.

Mother, about the Red Cross, Y.M.C.A., Liberty Loan and War Saving Stamps, which you say requires sacrifices. I would say that no one is giving to[o] much at any time, because they are speeding it in the right way over here and are doing wonderful work. They take tobacco, cigarettes and other articles right to the boys in the front line trenches where it is needed the most. Troops riding trains for long distances always get a handout at the Red Cross stations if they stop long enough. Sometimes only a cup of hot coffee, but that goes a long way and is greatly appreciated. Upon getting off the boat on this side the boys had a good breakfast and then started to unload the ship. They worked very hard and didn't get much of a dinner. We then boarded a train and after riding about two hours we struck one of the Red Cross stations and they gave us coffee and buns. I certainly must say that it was very good at the time.

Mother, you said I should make Old Glory wave, but the flag is not carried in this war, not until we go marching through the streets of Germany. I sure will take good care of it when we go through Germany, which I think will not take to long. We are giving them a very hard fight at the present time.

I am in the best of health at the present time. In fact I feel as though I could lick the best man the Germans have. Hoping to here from you soon.

I am your son,
Foster W. Berger
Color Sgt.

The rank of color sergeant was still an honor, but the time tested method of carrying the colors into battle and leading the regiment ended with the Spanish American War.

He Stood the Test of This Life Like a Man

July 23, 1918
1st. Lieut. Alfred M. Uhler
American Ambulance Service.
A.E.F.
Somewhere in France.

Mr. and Mrs. Crane,
Dear Friends:

Will you allow me what is perhaps an indiscretion in your deep sorrow, but which is prompted by my own sincere feeling?

In our life here, I came to know your son rather well and the same fine qualities that you loved evoked the fondness of friendship in me. You may feel sure that he stood the test of life like a man and that is no easy thing to do. He made the great sacrifice in an undertaking, which I hope will accomplish something substantial toward relieving youth from its fate of always paying the penalty.

He lies in a valley along the Marne where in other times than these, there must breathe the peace and graciousness of one of the loveliest parts of France.

I trust that you will accept this note as the sincere expression of one who shares in a way your great loss.

Alfred M. Uhler,
1st Lieut. A.A.S.

The terrible duty of writing to the family of a soldier killed in action always fell to his commanding officer. It was a job which needed much courage.

July 24, 1918—The 42nd "Rainbow" Division takes Forêt de Fere. The Germans' loss was said to be 180,000 men in ten days.

John Crane Killed in Action, Giving the Last Full Measure of Devotion

July 24, 1918
Corporal Homer Riegle
S.S.U. 650 Convois Autos
Par B.C.M.
Somewhere in France.

My dear Mr. Crane:

In this great hour of your suffering, I do not wish to add more to your burden, but I feel sympathy of myself and all the boys in the death of John. It was indeed, a great shock of me when I read the brief telegram "Killed in Action." I immediately got in touch with his section commander to ascertain more fully the details of his death. From my information it appears that during the day of July 16th the cars of quite a few members of the section were at the park at H—— Marne where the section is billeted; and awaiting a call to go to convoy to poste de secours, when a shell burst in the centre of the park killing two men and wounding severely three others among the former being John.

He was buried in the American cemetery at D—— (besides the bodies of so many of his American comrades who so valiantly fought and died with the spirit transcended to them by their forefathers). A beautiful little village near S—— and overlooking the historic Marne, a river made red by the blood of thousands of our brave allies, who with their never dying. "They shall not pass" held the vast hordes of Huns thrown across the river to gain the road to their goal, Paris.

The death of John touched me more than I can ever tell, and it is a loss felt keenly by everyone of the town boys. To us it is the loss of a personal friend, whom we had known for many years, one who shared every

Yanks in the front line trenches wearing gas masks. Many Pennsylvania soldiers suffered from the effects of German gas attacks.

joy and hardship and came through smiling. The ray of light coming to one, is the knowledge that he took such an enthusiastic part in the organization of the units from home, in the early days of the service, being one of the first to enlist, and with high hopes, and looking forward to the day we would leave for France and do the wonderful work called for by the men of Ambulance service, filled with that same glowing spirit which made him a favorite in the school room. In games out of school, in work and in the service, he soon became a favorite with the members of the section to which he was lately attached. It was that joyful out look on life his ever ready smile that cheered many of us in the training camp, when everything became monotonous and unimportant. And this spirit he carried with him to the battlefield of Europe.

Whenever work of any nature was to be accomplished, he was the first to volunteer; whether it be work around section quarters or a dangerous mission to the front line trenches to bring back blesses [blessés—wounded people]; and with that radiant smile emanating from him, he was sure to inspire others with that high courage and splendid, unselfish devotion of his nature.

The most beautiful sentence ever written was the one "Greater Love hath no man than this, that he lay down his life for a friend." Now where, and no truer example of this can be found than that set down by the men of the Ambulance Service and by the deeds of John. Called upon at all times to rush up to the front posts, to bring back the wounded; through the enemy barrage, into the path of the shrieking shrapnel and bursting shell, the ambulance men are ready at the first call and if need be, ready to live up to the very sentence and give their lives while trying to save their wounded comrades. The spirit emanating from the ambulance men and which became instilled in John is one of the highest examples of the type of patriotism with which all are imbued, the love of country and of all the ideals set dear that bind the two great republics for whom we are serving.

It is indeed a sad loss, but you can be comforted by the knowledge that your son proved faithful to the trust and when the last Great Honor Roll is written and the Ambulance men who sacrificed their all for the sake of the country of freedom and of Ideals, go down to history for their valiant deeds, the name of your loving son and our beloved friend John will be among the highest. Enfolded by the flag of his glorious country he died, giving the last full measure of devotion, he died a hero.

Very sincerely yours,
Homer Reigle.

Editor's note: John Crane received the French Croix de Guerre; following is the citation.

Crane John W. 7761
Private
Section No. 506, Ambulance Service.
(Posthumous award)

FRENCH CROIX de GUERRE WITH GILT STAR.
March 5, 1919
General Headquarters French Armies of the East.
"After having displayed an example of the greatest bravery during 5 weeks
of battle, he died for France on July 16th 1918."
Residence: Pottsville. Pa.

I Suppose the Kaiser Has Changed His Mind About the Sammies Now

July 24, 1918
Corp. Stephen Mitchel
Co. D 103rd Engineers
28th Division.
A.E.F.
Somewhere in France.

Dear Mother:

Just a few lines to let you know I am safe and o.k. No doubt you have read of the misfortune our company had; but don't worry about me as I escaped and have only been a little gassed. I am at a base hospital but will be back with the company before you receive this. The only reason I am telling you this is that you may know the truth. Am enjoying the fruits of the American Red Cross now. The hardest thing I have to do is stay in bed. There are a good many from our division in this ward and we are having a good time. Plenty to eat, white bread at time. It sure tastes good. Everything cooked like home. A good spring bed. Far enough from the front that we can't hear the firing. What more could a fellow want? I feel like a king. So don't worry about me no matter what you hear.

Am still here in the hospital but feeling fine. Yesterday the doctor examined the fellows in this ward. Nearly all are getting uniformed today. I would be getting one too only I was wandering around the other wards when the doctor was here.

We have good times here in the ward. With the exception of a few, we can all walk around. The other day they brought in an empty stretcher and told a big husky patient to get on it. This patient has been running around ever since we came here. After carrying him around and having him on a liquid diet for a day, they discovered they had the wrong man. It sure was a joke on the stretcher bearers as the man they carried was nearly as big as the two of them together.

Then last night, they came in and placed a tray full of instruments and bandages, beside a big Indian who is next to me. He was asleep when they came and on being awakened, you should have seen his face. It was another case of getting the wrong man. In the dark, the ward master read the name wrong. We are kidding the chief, as we call him all day.

The ward master just told me I would get a uniform tomorrow. I will be glad, for I can then take a look around the place. We are on the outskirts of a good size city and I sure would like to see it. Since we arrived here, we have been in the wilderness all the time. In travelling by train, we passed through some big places but we didn't stop-off.

The other day who should walk in the ward but Herbert Lennox from home. He was wounded but getting along nicely. I suppose the Kaiser has changed his opinion of the Sammies by this time.

I can't tell you much about this country for all I have seen is the back woods. We passed through some large places but didn't stop. I can mention though that the women in many of the country places wear hob nail shoes. How would you like to be one of them?

The French soldiers sure do like us, they give us anything they have except their canteens. The reason is it is always filled with wine. They have it issued to them daily. Have been living in vacated houses and stables. There is plenty of company at all times. At one place, one of the fellows coming in from work went to lie down and discovered a bed full of kittens where his bed had been. Another place, the rats had a marathon and occasionally would use our heads for a race track. One soon gets used to these things and after a hard shift or long hike you just " flop" down without examining your bed.

Can't begin to handle the language over here. I must do nearly all my talking with my hands.

Stephen.

I Was Overcome by Gas

July 24, 1918
Pvt. Joseph Kirkpatrick
Co. D. 103rd Engineers
28th Division.
A.E.F.
Somewhere in France

Dear Mother:

I am in a Base Hospital over here but I am not serious at all. On Sunday night, the fifteenth of July I was overcome by gas. It was one year ago that night since I enlisted in the service and I hope by the fifteenth of next year I will be home and all the rest of us also.

The Germans opened up on us at midnight and shot gas, shrapnel and high explosive shells at us from twelve that night till nine the next morning, but have been getting the same dose from us and lots more ever since from our boys. Our cook wagon had come up with our supper and we were just starting to eat when they started to shell us and our wagons and horses were blown to pieces. Most every one had their mouths full eating at the time and couldn't get their masks on and some of us got gas. We had two ambulances with us but both of them were blown off the road in pieces. An ambulance hit a tree where we were at and the driver was overcome by gas. I was all in and my mask was torn to pieces. I got started and we loaded it up with wounded and I drove to the first dressing station but could not hold out any longer. I didn't know anything else after that till I found myself in the hospital the next day and I am still in but expect to be back with my company soon again. Don't worry about me for I coming around fine and I hope this finds all of you in the best of health.

I am down in the southern part of France and the weather is fine down here. This is a summer resort and a fine place. It is the finest part of France. I am over a hundred miles from the front now but soon expect to be back there with the boys again. I guess you see in the papers about our boys and the great advancement they are making and are still driving and having great success in their work.

News is awful scarce and we get only one newspaper a day and read it so often to pass the time away that we know it by heart. I often wish I had a good book to read but I will be out soon and I won't have the time to read then. I am going to try and get transferred to an ambulance unit if I can when I get out of here.

Joseph.

There Is No One Like the Bosche

July 24, 1918
Sergeant John Duffy
Co. D 103rd Engineers
28th Division
A.E.F.
Somewhere in France.

My Dear Father:

Well you know by the time that we are located on one of the fighting fronts. I did not mention this before feeling that it might cause undue worry and that the news would be published as events transpired.

Recently we came into a town that the Germans were forced from and we saw the worst condition of havoc and destruction imaginable. They evidently thought they would locate in the town for some time because they had made their quarters in the houses from which the people had fled and what they did not or could not use, they destroyed. You may talk about barbarism but of all the men you could imagine, there is no one like the Boche. They smashed works of art, beautiful furniture and everything they thought was useful and they ransacked and plundered everywhere.

We went into a convent, which they used for their brawls and saw many articles strewn on the floor and they seemed to have taken a fiendish delight in destroying the precious gems venerated by all the good people for centuries. I saw vestments of the Bishop, the Chalice and many other things piled up as plunder to be taken away by these inhuman monsters. I will not mention about their other outrages excepting that it is enough to say that they are everything you have ever heard they were and nothing is exaggerated. We went to the Post Office and found piles of plunder wrapped up and addressed to their people back home, but they had to leave as we secured them and turned over everything to the proper officers.

We are delighted to say they are getting a good licking and I really believe that the turn of the tide is here and from now on the Hun will be on the defensive.

Every one at home should be a good American because anyone who is not heart and soul for the U.S.A. in this conflict is not fit to live among the people who love liberty. I am not giving you hearsay. The Huns drop bombs on hospitals, Churches, Ambulances containing wounded soldiers and any one who stands for those fiends should be promptly dealt with and all should realize that an open enemy is no worse than a hidden foe. Every time the Allies get him on the run, he went holler kamerad, but when he enters a town where there are women and children, he is the despot that is pictured.

The American troops fight wonderfully and they are a credit to the U.S.A. Our regiment has been very active and did very well and our company constructed a bridge over a river that brought up the troops on their advance.

The Red Cross is doing a great work and if only those at home could see some of the fruits of their labor over here. I'm sure they would feel that all of their work was worthwhile.

It is wonderful to see the way the boys behave themselves, for their conduct is very fine. There is no nonsense of any kind because they are engaged at a mans job and they are going about it at a way that is commendable. You may meet people who will try to make you believe that any boy over here is subject to so much temptation but all we see over here is work and do not have time for mischief. I believe that any boy that comes through this war will return home a finer man mentally and a bigger man morally and will be a credit for those who sent him.

> Give my best to all the friends,
> Sincerely,
> John

I Felt a Crack on the Right Leg

> July 24, 1918
> Pvt. Robert Whitman
> Co. D 103rd Engineers
> 28th Division
> Somewhere in France.

Dear Folks:

Another week has gone by and still no word from home. You cannot begin to imagine how anxious I am for word from you. Do not be alarmed at this report, but I am in a base hospital with a punctured right leg. I claim the honor of being the first boy from both companies to be wounded and sent to the base hospital, with (Doc) Frank Gore a close second. The company had gone to the lines on Sunday afternoon but my ankle has not strengthened quite enough to allow me to go, so that I was put on guard again in the evening. When on post at ten o'clock and everything went along very well until exactly 12 o'clock when the enemy started to bombard close to our billets. It was my duty to wake the fellows who were back in the town and tell them to get into the dugouts for safety. Many of them went into them but a few … went into the house close to the hills who did not go to the dugouts as the town had not been hit, but shells had dropped in back of it, or on the hills in front. It was only a few minutes from the time I started out until I had told them and made for a dugout myself, but on reaching one of the dugouts I met Doc Gore, who was the corporal of the guard, with his gas mask and then it was up to me to make the same rounds again and tell the boys there was gas. By this time, shells were dropping all around us and hitting squarely in the middle of the street, making it very difficult to proceed, but by sticking close to the buildings I escaped being hit.

I had only two places to make before I would go back to safety. The one I made but found they had all gone to the dugouts, at least, I could find no one or get any response. Just across the street was my last stop and that is where the Top Sgt. was and I knew he had not gone out. Tried to make it but it got too hot to be safe, so I went back to the dugouts and arrived there o.k. Was only there a few minutes when the bombardment stopped. I thought they were playing for the artillery which was close by and had given up the attack. I said to Doc, "I am going to try to get up and tell the Top Sarg. to put his mask on," as there was a slight chance that he could have already been gassed, so I started out and Doc came after me. I think he was going along with me. I had got to exactly the same spot where I turned back before, when a shell dropped at my feet on the right hand side. When I saw it, I tried to think but it exploded before I could even do that, but it seemed to be God's will that I was not to be killed as most of the shells flew away from me and against a stone wall. I felt a crack on the right leg and thought it was some of the stone from the wall. The shell threw out a dense black cloud. All I could hear was stone and shells falling in all directions around me. I wanted to keep on going but found that I had difficulty in doing so and shells started falling thickly again so I made for the officers dugout which was close by. I made it in a short time, but I was figuring that another might come along and finish the job. I made it though and called to the fellows inside that I had been hit. They sure did get on the job. To fix me up, but they had just started on me right when Doc came in. They fixed both of us up and as luck would have it, our ambulance was there and in a few minutes time, we were on our way to the hospital. It seemed as though the Huns had picked us out as they just followed us down the valley with their shells which broke within a hundred yards of us several times.

Finally, we reached our own infirmary and were dressed by one of our regimental doctors whom many of you know. From there we took another ride to the dressing station where we were transferred to another auto and finally landed in a field hospital where we were again dressed and prepared for the operating room. This was five thirty a.m. Monday morning. We were shot about twelve thirty a.m. A fine looking Major came in and questioned me as to what I knew was going on. Had heard news on the way that had not sounded encouraging and told him about it. He thanked me and started issuing orders and in no time nurses started to come from every where and every thing was made ready for a busy twenty four hours at least but it lasted for almost seventy two. At six o'clock a.m. the first truck filled up and from then on, all you could see was ambulances one after the other.

Just an American Woman Over Here

> July 25, 1918
> In reference to:
> Sergeant Sylvester Hoy
> Co. E
> 28th Division.
> Tours, France.

My Dear Mrs. Auman

I visited the American Hospital at Tours today and your brother asked me if I would write to you, which I very gladly do. I do not know if you have already been notified but he was injured on the 18th I think it was and brought here to base hospital on the 27th and will remain until well enough to be sent home. You will be glad to hear that he is doing well and the doctor reports everything favorable. His left leg is badly shattered by one of the devils machine guns, and it is strung up in a frame high in the air so it will knit together firm and in the right position. Of course there

Men from Pennsylvania's 28th Division, 103rd Engineers, built pontoon bridges like the photograph depicts in France and Germany during the Great War.

is a good deal of suffering but each day makes it a little easier and he told me the pain was better than the last few days. He is now out of it for good and some day you will have him back again. He has done his duty bravely and has not had to lose his life or any part of his body, he comes home with both his legs, eyes arms and all his fingers. We have seen some very dreadful wounds of course, one dear boy today has lost his right arm. It just wrings your heart to see all this suffering but we are proud. They are so fine and noble and have such splendid things and our men are the best in the world.

I am not a nurse, or Y.M.C.A. worker, just an American woman over here trying to do some little bit to help out wherever I can and if I can do something to help them over the hard places, I am rejoiced. I shall visit the Hospital again in a few days and again write you so you can be informed as to your brother's progress. He is a handsome boy, isn't he. I just admire him so and you must be so proud of him.

I helped to serve vanilla ice cream with chocolate sauce this afternoon. I don't know who provides it, the Y.M.C.A. I suppose and how they all love it. They get just the best of food and the best of care. You will be glad to know this. Civilians don't begin to have the good things to eat. White bread is an unheard of luxury. They all have sugar, chocolate and meat, all they want and everyone at home can be satisfied they are having the best. It will be some time before he can write himself as the doctors are very strict, but he will write as soon as he is able. I know, I am glad if I can relieve your anxiety, concerning him.

Unknown

Just Remember I Am Doing What I Want to Do

> July 26, 1918
> 1st Lt. Douglas B. Green
> Co. H 168th Infantry Regiment.
> 42nd "Rainbow" Division.
> A.E.F.
> Somewhere in France.

Sister:

I am as well as I have ever been in my life. Everyone I see tells me how well I look and I think I'll be able to stand most anything they put me up against. We have good men in our regiment and they will give a good account of themselves and help to make things easier for their officers and make us proud of their record after we come back.

There isn't anything that I would rather do than go over and fight the Germans. So, whatever you may think about it, just remember that I'm doing what I want to do and something that I wouldn't give up my chance of doing for all the rest of my natural life. When its all over you'll be glad to be able to say that I went over and did my duty. Everyone has to suffer some to win this war, and if my going is hard for you think that is the part you are taking in the greatest thing that [the] civilized world has ever done. Giving up something for the cause is a real privilege, it seems to me, and you certainly would not want me to be deprived of that privilege.

Douglas

Lt. Green was killed on August 1, 1918, while in action with his company.

July 27, 1918—The 3rd, 4th, 28th, 42nd U.S. Divisions on the heights of Ourqc.

You See Men Shot Down Killed and Torn Into Pieces

July 29, 1918
Major. G. O. Santee
Medical Reserve Corps.
A.E.F.
Somewhere in France.

My dear Friend Bright:

Stationary [*sic*] is very scarce, so I am pressing an old form, taken from the desk of a lawyers office, into service. We are using this office as our Medical Headquarters while stationed here. From all indications, the occupants left in great haste and we found things were left without any provision for a protracted stay. When we look for the reason we find, in 1914 the Germans, while on the way to Paris, occupied the town, and in anticipation of this and without much notice the better class of the inhabitants simply pulled out leaving everything behind.

I am quite well and enjoying things to the full. This surely is the life of course, there is always danger, but it is remarkable how soon you forget about it and find it to be the least of your troubles. You see men shot down, killed, wounded and torn into pieces, but after a while you get so that you feel you can take your medicine the same way if necessary and not think much of it. I have had several close calls since I am over here but these are just matters of course.

There is plenty of excitement all the time and instead of going out to look for it, we have it with us continually. Music all the time. We go to bed with it and what the band doesn't furnish, the airplanes, cannon, rifles and bombs do.

I hope you may find time to write a few lines once in a while. Mail is rather scarce and a fellow certainly enjoys hearing from his friends at home. Please remember me to everybody and convey my regards to them. Ask them to write. Things look very bright at present as we have the Huns on the run.

Sincerely,
G.O.O. Santee, M.R.C.

World War I was the bloodiest war ever fought up till 1918. Of every American soldier, sailor or airman who took part in the war with Germany, two were killed or died of disease during the hostilities. For every man killed in battle, six others were wounded. Records showed that 85 percent of the men sent into hospitals with wounds were eventually returned to duty. About half of the wounded were reported as slightly wounded and most of these wounds would not have been reported in previous wars. The final total of battle losses for the American Army was 50,000 killed and 206,000 wounded.

This Life of a Machine Gunner Is Great

> July 29, 1918
> Sergt. Lewis M. Krebs
> Co. B 4th Machine gun Batn.
> 2nd Division
> A.E.F.
> Somewhere in France.

I sure was glad to hear from you as a letter from home to us boys is like a dish of ice cream to you folks at home. I heard from Bus Bowe and he expects to go into the trenches. We hear a lot about fellows that are in the trenches, that you folks back home never read of.

Well kid, Bus will have his second service chevron when I receive my first one. This sure is a great place. The Boche make it pretty warm for us sometimes. The shrapnel shells burst all around us in the trenches.

This life as a machine gunner is great, we get more Fritz shells on us than the doughboys get. We can see all over no mans land in the day time. All there is out there is a mass of barbed wire entanglements, trenches, trees cut down and towns destroyed by shell fire. I sure will have a lot to tell you when I get back home, things I cannot write to you, thing that would open your eyes.

One time I was in a train wreck, but escaped uninjured, and I have lived in every kind of a dugout and billet that a soldier lives in. I have not been sick since I am in France. I was entitled to my first chevron in April.

While I am sitting here in this dugout thinking of old Port Carbon. I am in the best of health and hope you are the same. Say, Arden you should be over here with me. We have the finest little dugout in this line of trenches. We sit at our gun positions and see all over no mans land; that is a great place. We never see anything living move out there in the daytime, for if they did it would not be a very healthy place for them.

I suppose all the people back home are reading all the newspapers all about the war, and they believe all the "bull" in them. Why, when some of the boys get some of the Phila papers they just say it sure is a lot of "Bull" those newspaper guys are giving the people back home. Some of the things are true but many are not. You know we boys are in this little game of war and we know when some one is giving us real news or dope.

When the war is ended you will read all about it; not before. Why, I'll bet most of you fellows back home do not know what a shrapnel shell or hand grenade or even machine gun is. Well, I will tell you that they are three great things in this war.

It rains six days out of seven each week and the seventh is cloudy. The country is always muddy. We will soon look like ducks, as we already walk like them, but you should see us pull through, and we go at it just like we would go at a good meal in the good old time fashion. Talk about mud why we will soon be that used to it that we will put it on the meat we eat in place of mustard.

If you know any of the boys that are soon coming over here tell them to roll in the mud about four times a day, use it in their bread in place of butter, sleep in it, wash in it, take a four or six mile hike when it is muddy back home; if they do that for about six weeks they will be used to the mud before they leave home.

But with all the mud and rain, I would not give up this experience for anything else. Believe me, I have seen a great many things of great interest since I left the states and think I will see many more now before I get back home again.

I have been up to the trenches and it sure is one great life in them. Talk about working in the rains, it's nothing on the life over here. A fellow has all kind of friends in the dugouts, from rats down to lice of all kinds. I believe that some of them have a dozen legs. You told me about the brush fire on Salem Hill. Well, kid, we have plenty of Boche fire over here, and it takes more than water to get the best of it. Sometimes steel duty is a mere trifle when it comes in contact with the Boche fire.

There are good times and bad ones in the trenches, but it could be worse. I will send you my picture, when I have it taken. You cannot get things so easy. We have to pay one franc, or 20 cents for three small cards. I tell you, everything over here is not as pleasant as they publish in the states. The women are not plentiful as men. I have not seen a woman or girl in three months.

As I am writing everything is quiet outside, but it only takes a few minutes to start things lively. Let me tell you old boy that the American Artillery men sure hand out the shells to the Huns. Every now and then the enemy makes a little drive but they only hold the ground a short time, and they are losing men in great numbers. Most of the Germans are young fellows. I believe this year will end the great struggle for liberty. I could tell you many things personally but it would not pass on the paper at the present time. I suppose you are reading in the newspaper about the big drive that is going on. I guess we are all reported dead by this time. Brother Jacob is up on the front somewhere, not very far from where I am located, but as you know we cannot run around when ever we would like to. I will try to locate Jack and get a chance to see him.

> Your Pal,
> Sergt. Lewis M Krebs.

The front line trench was the one nearest to the enemy. A barbed wire entanglement was built about ten feet in front of the trench and slightly lower than the parapet, so that sentries could observe the enemy and be able to fire over top of the wire. This wire entanglement was miles long. It was so constructed that it was almost impossible to go through unless it had been blown open by artillery or cut by wire cutters. Within the trench were barricades supported with sandbags and wood called traverses. Traverses were used to prevent enfilading fire. A traversed trench prevented multiple casualties. If an artillery shell fell inside a long straightaway trench it could possibly kill many men on either side. But if a shell dropped in a traversed trench it would only injure those in the immediate area of impact. The front of a trench was called a parapet, and the rear the parados. The top of the trench usually had anywhere from two to four layers of sandbags. At the bottom of the front wall of a trench was a wooden platform called a fire step, and by standing on it a soldier could see over the top of the trench into no man's land. The average English trench, which the Americans used, was about eight feet deep. Dugouts were usually built into the rear wall of a trench, and would be protected by the traverse. Communication trenches connected to the front line trenches but were made in a zig zag method. In the rear of the front line trench ran the support trenches, used for the bringing of supplies and ammunition to the front line trenches. They also acted as a method of retreat for troops that lost their positions in the front line trenches. All communication, support, and fire trenches were named to help one find his way through the maze of confusing trenches.

July 29, 1918—U.S. 42nd Division takes Sergy. Reports from Germany state they misjudged the American soldiers' fighting ability.

July 30, 1918—U.S. 32nd Division takes Grimpettes Wood. Americans attempt to cross the Ourq River. German gunners are holding them where they dug in. At the order the Americans rushed the river, swam across, climbed up the bank and put the Germans to rout.

French General Mangin Pays Tribute to the 28th Division

> July 30, 1918
> General Order no. 318

Officers, Non Commissioned officers and soldiers of the 28th Division:

Shoulder to Shoulder with your French comrades you were thrown into the counter offensive battle which commenced on the 18th of July.

You rushed into the light as though to a fate. Your magnificent courage completely routed a surprised enemy and your indomitable tenacity checked the counter-attacks of his fresh divisions. You have shown yourselves worthy sons of our great country and you were admired by your brothers in arms.

91 guns, 7,200 prisoners, immense booty, 16 kilometers of country reconquered, this is your portion of the spoil of victory.

Furthermore, you have really felt your superiority over the barbarous enemy of the whole human race, against whom the children of Liberty are striving. To attack him is to vanquish him.

American comrades! I am grateful to you for the blood so generously spilled on the soil of my country. I am proud to have commanded you during such days and to have fought with you for the deliverance of the world.

Mangin

General Charles Mangin was known as the most aggressive French general on the Western Front. He was nicknamed the "Butcher" because of his total offensive tactics. Mangin was relieved of his command for the failed attack at Aisne, but in the summer of 1918 with the Germans in full retreat he was given command of the French Tenth Army.

July 31, 1918—In the town of Seringes, Americans trick the Germans by a fake retreat, and when the Germans arrive they are surrounded and captured by American troops in hiding.

A Whistling Sound Came Singing Through the Air and Bang!

July 31, 1918
Corporal Harold A. Brennan
Ambulance Co. 5
A.E.F.
Somewhere in France.

Dear Father:

At last we find ourselves actively engaged and this letter is being written in a dugout on the front where I am in charge of a little bunch of boys mostly from home. The shells are continually whistling and singing overhead. We are glad to get on a front where the boys are doing such good work. We worked hard for days and nights and when things got quiet we went back to the barn for some sleep. Well everyone was enjoying a fine rest when a whistling sound came singing through the air and Bang! Goes the roof of our sleeper. Everyone ran to the dugout and there we sat in our gas masks listening to 3 inch shells biting at our door trying to get in. Perhaps it may seem terrible to you but it is great after all. I saw a great bombing plane fly over us the other day and the sky was full of smoke from the anti aircraft guns but Fritz didn't seem to mind it. But all of a sudden from way up in the clouds came a rattle of machine gun fire and another Fritz came crashing down to the ground. It's a great experience. We are located in a village where even our own shells meant for the Hun pass over us. We have watched the shells burst from the entrance of our dugout. When we are out in the open and hear one come we drop flat on the ground. By doing so the shrapnel, which bursts and rises to a height of four or five feet passes over us. They make very peculiar noise—just a whining rattle or a whistling through the air. But then its not so dangerous after all.

Harold.

The normal dugout, which could hold one or two men, was usually dug out of the ground to a good safe depth and surrounded by sand bags or wood. Some of the larger dugouts were called "Elephant Dugouts"; they were supported by steel girders resembling the ribs of an elephant. Some of these dugouts could comfortably hold thirty to fifty men.

My Eyes Were Glued to the Front Looking for Germans

July 31, 1918
Pvt. William Montalto
Co. E 9th Infantry Regiment
2nd Division
A.E.F.
Somewhere in France.

Sis:

I have a surprise for you in the next few lines for I have gone over the top with the best of luck, and it sure was something real new and big for me. And the best of it was I got a letter from home half an hour before going over. I will try and give you an idea of it. About 8:30 a.m. of July 1st we were told to get out of our holes to get ready to go over. At that time I felt a little shaky. We were ordered to lie down on the side of a bank in a ravine. Shells were flying all around us and you could hardly hear your own voice while the air was thick with dust and powder. I was lying there about fifteen minutes and I forgot about everything but the town we were to take and the Boche we would meet at 6 p.m. Then we started to go over. I was in the first wave. Boche shells ceased to bother me no matter how close they were striking. My eyes were glued to the front looking for Germans. We kept going until we hit the town when a few machine guns opened on us. We put them out of commission in short order and went on. We never stopped until we reached our objective. Then we began to dig in and looking back into the town we could see Germans coming out of every cellar and cave with their hands high in the air. When we got through we had 500 of them and many machine guns. But it is much more to be there and see it than I could ever explain. Now we are on are [*sic*] way back to a rest camp. We are to get new clothes for these we now have on forty days with out a chance to take a bath, and the cooties refuse to let me sleep at night, and during the day all I do is read my shirt. I mean by looking for cooties. They are bothering me while I am writing. Hoping that you are all well in health and spirit and write often.

> I remain,
> William.

Going over the top was a catch phrase used by all the infantry soldiers in World War I. In general it meant going on the attack. On the Western Front going over the top usually was preceded by a massive artillery barrage, for the purpose of destroying any barbed wire or other type of defense the enemy had. It had to be smashed before the infantry could advance. For the defenders an intense bombardment meant an oncoming infantry attack. At a designated time the artillery stopped and the infantry moved out or went over the top under the protection of overhead fire. While advancing in a long wave many men were killed or wounded while crossing the area known as "no man's land," the area between the opposing trenches.

6

August 1918: The Allies Gain the Initiative

Pvt. Joseph Maleski's War

August 1, 1918
Pvt. Joseph Maleski
30th Infantry Regiment
3rd Division
A.E.F.
Somewhere in France.

Sir:

I had never been on such a big ship before. And I had never seen the ocean before. Of course I had seen Lake Erie, but this was different ten days steady steaming across the ocean. You know it's still wonderful to me. I don't know where they get all that water.

The first day our bunch was busy shaking down into quarters. We were a bit crowded, but we slept all right and we had good eats and smokes. What did we talk about? Well, mostly about two things whether we were going to be sea sick or were we going to be attacked by German subs. We didn't have thrill.

Of course we had life drills and learned how to put on appliances to keep us afloat. I guess some of us didn't think how serious things might get until our officers told us about what life boats or rafts we were to get into in case of an attack and how we were not to move until we were ordered.

We were April fooled on the trip after all. We saw land and we thought it was France. But when we got ashore found we were in England where everyone talked the same language we did and turned out to show us how welcome we were and how glad they were to see us. We were there three weeks, being billeted from town to town and always on the move toward the south of England and the channel ports. We were getting some final touches in our training. I remember one thing that ticked our fellows. In one training camp they had some Englishmen to show us how to throw out a skirmish line. Then our officers showed them how we do it. You know the old fashioned way, the first Americans had when they fought the Indians. Guess may be we weren't proud when the English said they couldn't teach us anything that we had it all over them when it came to that open fighting skirmish business.

Of course there were things that they showed us that came in handy, angles of the trench game, grenade throwing, etc.

Then one night we were moved to France in a quick trip on the train and across the channel in a swift boat. It was funny to be in country where you couldn't understand the lingo and read the signs, but we were kept to[o] busy to bother about that. They moved us along from one town to another and we had our share of hiking. It rained every day and when it didn't rain it poured. But we didn't care we were in France.

We felt sure we would get our chance at the enemy. They were coming down the line like a house afire, taking down and smashing armies. Of course we didn't hear the news. You folks back home get that quicker than we do. But via lip-to-lip telegraph we knew things looked bad for the French and the English and that General Pershing had offered all his army to General Foch. Gee, you ought to have seen how busy our bunch got. The officers didn't have to tell em to. Of their own accord they got out their rifles and oiled them and polished them. And you'd see a fellow slipping away to where he could put a little more edge on his bayonet. The Frenches call their long slender bayonets "Rosalie." We didn't call our[s] by any pet names, but we put an awful lot of trust in them, and we made up our minds there would be a heap of big doings when we got in touch with Fritz.

We didn't have any tour in quiet trenches like some of the fellows. So we didn't know what it was like to fight cooties and the Fritises [Fritzes] at the same time. We didn't even know what shell fire sounded like or looked like. Of course we heard about it and read about it, but that's not like the real thing. We were still coming along in France from one billet in a little town to another when the Germans reached the Marne. Then one day they loaded us up in trucks and hustled us along crowded roads, TO THE FRONT.

I don't see how those drivers got us through so fast. The roads were jammed both ways with all kinds of autos coming and going, and all on important business. Going forward there would be trucks loaded with men and shells or food and then maybe detachments going along on foot; tanks crawling along; horses or mules pulling guns up to the front; coming back would be empty trucks going for more supplies; ambulances taking wounded men back to the base hospitals and messengers hustling back to general headquarters on motorcycles.

But with this exception and until we got where the Germans had been, it was hard to believe there was a war. The little towns had their little town life and you would see old people out on the farms hard at work, or children tending to the cows. And sometimes, busy as they were, they would take time to pull wild flowers and give them to us as we passed.

We were dumped out of the trucks just about three miles from the French third line trenches. That is where for the first time we heard the roar of the big shells, the whine of shrapnel and the put put of the machine guns. Two big shells dropped near us the day before we went into action. After the dust and smoke had cleared away our crowd went over to have a look at the holes they made, but the sight didn't worry us any. I didn't see any fellows who looked scared.

I knew I felt good. This is what I had enlisted for. This is what I came for. I was going to get a crack at the Germans. I have been a good shot for years. When a boy I roamed the hills and hunted fox and rabbits and squirrels and duck. And we had been told time and time again by our officers not to do like the Germans, shoot from the hip. We were told to keep cool and fix the sights on our guns, take careful aim, and then let em have it, so that every shot counted for something.

I said to one of my pals that I was going to get a certain number of Germans. He grinned and asked what if they got me instead. I told him there was no shot they had that could hurt me, but they fooled me.

We went into the third line trenches the night before we went into battle and were on our feet all night. Tired? If I was I didn't realize it. I don't think any of the fellows did. We were to[o] excited about the big game the next day. At 6 the next morning we were taken into the second line of trenches. There were French and Americans in the first line trenches. Our officers told us we were going into battle. The Americans were going to try to stop the Germans at Chateau-Thierry. We were to take hill 204, I believe it was, and a stretch of woods to the right of Chateau-Thierry.

Before we went into the fight there was none of that movie picture stuff. Our officers got right down with us and spoke to us quietly and seriously. It was almost as if they were the fathers and we the children. They said we should be sure to wait for commands and to take care of ourselves. Do you think that made us solemn? If you do, you don't know the American soldier. We cheered and sang until they told us to be quiet.

Shortly after that the word came to go and drive the old Kaiser out of these woods in front of us. We had to cross an open field and we spread out so as to give just as little target as possible to the enemy. They got lots of our fellows with machine guns but when we came into the woods, the enemy beat it. They won't stand up to us man to man.

So far I had come through all right. All of us who were unhurt were laughing and joking when the Germans began to turn their long range heavy guns with high explosives loose on us. I remember we joshed about those shots too. One would say "That fellow can't spell our names" and another would answer "Yes, his shells can't hit us unless they have our names on the cover."

We were moving forward and I was near an old concrete wall in the fringe of the woods when a shell hit the wall and I dropped. For a minute I didn't know I was hurt. I felt no pain. I was never unconscious. I tried to rise and couldn't. Then I saw I was bleeding from cuts in the arm and head and had a very deep wound in my left leg just about the knee. I tried to drag myself and my injured leg, it felt as if it had weighed ten tons. My steel helmet had been knocked off I remember I took time to pick it up and put it on my head.

I called to one of the men that I was hurt and they got me back to a first aid place. The doctor asked me whether my leg hurt. I told him it didn't. I asked him for water, I was always asking for water. My wounds must have made me feverish. I kept drinking water and more water.

The doctor took two boards and tied them on each side of my leg as tight as he could so as to protect it when I was taken in an ambulance and bumped along the roads. I was taken back to a field hospital. The first man who saw me there was a major in the medical corps. He asked me whether my leg hurt much. I told him it didn't, but that I couldn't feel my toes. I said they must have tied the boards to tight to my leg that they stopped the circulation. You see I had no idea how badly I was hurt. I thought maybe some of the bone was splintered and that, at the worst I would have a game leg. They cut the cords that held the boards to my leg and the last I knew a wet sponge was quickly put over my face.

When I woke up the surgeon asked me how I felt. "All right." "Any pain?" "No sir." "Can you feel your toes now?" "Yes sir." He laughed and went on to the other men.

The third day I was there he asked the same questions and I gave the same answers. Then he didn't laugh any more. His face became very serious and he said: "I guess my boy I'll have to tell you now. You haven't got any toes. We had to cut your leg off above the knee to save your life. You've been very sick. You lost so much blood we had to transfuse some into you and we were afraid to tell you the truth for fear the shock would be to[o] great."

"Its all right, doctor. Its no use to worry. Its done. Its happened. I suppose I am lucky to come out the way I did."

One of the nurses said she wrote back to her folks at home saying our American boys are so splendid that even when they lose a leg they say to the doctors they are not much hurt. And say, I want to hand it to the Army hospitals. I had nurses around me all the time. You didn't have to ring any bells and wait a long time. They were right there. Annie on the spot. To attend you and the doctors were never far away. All the fellows said the same thing. They agreed we got wonderful attention.

And when I was lying there, you know what worried me? Not the future, I'll get a job all right. Not my folks back home. My dad wrote. "It doesn't make any difference about the loss of your leg. We will be ever so glad to have our boy back again after serving his country."

Not my best girl friend, she's blonde and blue eyed and that's the reason I didn't parlay vouz with those black haired, black eyed French girls. No my girl said she was glad I was coming home. What worries me is that I helped start the scrap on the Marne with the old Kaiser and now I can't be in at the finish.

And that is what is worrying every fellow you talk to here in the hospital. Everyone of them would have liked to get a few more Germans and be there when the end came.

Joseph Maleski.

When He Met His Maker

August 1, 1918
Sergeant Kenneth Pugh
U.S. Army Medical Service
A.E.F.
Somewhere in France.

Dear Mother:

I must tell you that I have two Pottsville boys in my hospital, Robert Hughes and Sampson Koch. They are both slightly wounded and are now convalescing, but there is another story I want to tell you and that is I was with a near Pottsville boy when he met his maker. His name was Sylvester Hoy of Port Carbon. He was badly wounded and on my tour of inspection

Going over the top—a scene that many a Pennsylvanian witnessed during the war, and many soldiers never wanted to again.

I noticed he was in bad shape so I stopped and started to talk to him. I asked him his name and he said Hoy, and the next question was as to the town and state and when he said Port Carbon, Pa. I put out my hand and told him I was from Pottsville. He seemed happy and relieved and we found out that each of us knew the same people. He looked weak and after consulting his chart I knew he would soon leave us so I made things as pleasant as possible. Rev. Carpenter, of Hartford, Conn. was with him also until the last. He fought hard but he was up against odds. He had a very nice burial and now rests in the American cemetery at Tours.

So you see it is a small world. No doubt I have hardened considerably since I have seen so many pass out but I did not want to see Hoy go because he was from my home. All is over and war is still on, so lets go get the Hun.

Kenneth.

They All Wear Big Boots That Weigh 50 Pounds

August 2, 1918
Pvt. Robert Simmons
Co. D 109th Machine Gun Battalion.
28th Division
A.E.F.
Somewhere in France.

Dear Mother:

I am in the best of shape, Brother Bill is still with me and he is fine and dandy, so don't worry about us. I guess that old town is deserted by this time.

We are having fine weather here at the present time. We are at a rest camp and just came back from the front lines. We were in a dug out that the Huns were in for over a year, and we raided it and cleaned them out.

They surely had it fixed good for we don't stay long in one place as we intend to keep the Huns on the run. They all wear big boots that weigh 50 pounds but that don't make any difference to us, we have their feet smoking. They are going that fast that we were after them on trucks. The Huns are cowardly at short range: they drop to their knees and holler "Kamerad" with both hands up like sheep but when your back is turned, they are dirty.

I just saw a few thousand of them pass through this village that the American troops turned over. They get them ten to one. The German's don't take any prisoners as they don't have a chance, we take them first. They are glad when they are taken prisoners. Their officers tell them that the Americans take no prisoners, just to make them fight. The Boche don't want to fight [when] he has to get out and do his part. If they refuse they are tied to the guns. I have a lot of experience in the big war but I don't think it will last long as the old Boche is being hard hit on all fronts. I would like to get a few thousand of those animals before I get back to U.S. In some places where the Germans have driven out the French, the people are coming back again but their houses are still shot to pieces. Brother Bill and I are with a fine bunch of fellows. They are nearly all from around home. I met Josh Joy the other day at a village close to where I am. He sure was glad to see me. He is with the engineers. I shook hands with a bunch of them, most of them were young fellows and they had me kind of mixed up for awhile as they all knew [me] and I could not think of their names. I guess you have read lots of the Marne River. Josh Joy and I had a swim in that river today, it is some river.

Robert.

My First Experience with Shell Fire

August 4, 1918
Pvt. Stanley Matthews
Co. M 112th Infantry Regt.
28th Division
A.E.F.
Somewhere in France.

I was poisoned drinking water on grounds where the Germans retreated and I was sent to the base hospital where I am yet

There sure were some bloody battles up where I was and they are still going on. The night of the fifteenth of July was my first experience with shell fire and I'll sure say it was a good one for the first time we wee digging trenches at night near the lines at 11:45, a few gas shells came shattering over our heads and we put on our gas masks and in another minute, we were all hurrying to the trenches waiting for our turn to get hit.

As they started sending over shrapnel, high explosives and gas which lasted from 11:45 until 6:00 in the morning, then it settled down and we started carrying our wounded to dugouts. They started in again but we kept on carrying them out. We lost fifty men killed and wounded but we were lucky at that.

The following day we started on driving and they are still going but I don't know how many of my company are left but I hope they all are. Here I was poisoned as we were going after them. I think I fell over from sickness and weakness. I was taken away by ambulance so I don't know how they came out. They will find out before this war is over that the Americans are not jokes. I am ready to go back to the lines now and will sure try to make up for what I lost. I started to write you but had to stop and pack up and leave so I didn't get a chance until today. We are having fine weather here but while I was on the line it was raining.

Stanley.

I Thought a Shell Had Come Through the Back Window of the Car

August 4, 1918
George L. Whitmeyer
Sec. 502 Ambulance Corps.
A.E.F.
Somewhere in France.

The talk is all over this country at this time [of] peace. Everybody is wondering if it won't soon come, and looking forward for this coming fall to end the Worlds greatest war. Yes we boys over here look for an end to come soon but even though we want the time to hasten when all wars shall cease and can hardly wait for that glad day to come, yet through it all, do we want peace? When the war is over and the boys are once more backs in the U.S.A., will we be satisfied if the war ends this fall or coming spring.

No not the boys who have sacrificed everything to come across, and have seen the ghastly work of the Hun. Nor will the parents, wives and sweethearts of the boys who have fallen on the field of battle be satisfied.

Can the sinking of the Lusitania, the blowing up of ships and factories, the sinking of the Tuscania, the hospital ships, the bombing of the Red Cross buildings where many of the wounded were being treated. The ravages of the Huns on the Belgian people, cutting off the breast of women, the arms of small children and the old and infirm who were unable to get away from their home to be left starving, the ruination of the French villages, the terrible things like the shelling of the church on Good Friday, during the three hours between 2 and 3,000 people were kneeling and saying "Father forgive them for they know not what they do." Can a thing like that be over looked?

We have them on the run now and will keep them going. Every day all along the front the boys go "over the top" and make great progress, so much so that they keep the Ambulance companies busy changing quarters. It's always move forward the boys have advanced.

Our Aviators are on the job and keep the Boche from making any headway in their observation and bombing planes. Are airplanes are getting through to Germany and doing excellent work and now the German people yell, "Why do they do such things to ruin our villages?" Yes why do we. Well because we are playing there own game, soon we will have them way back and out will come a peace proposal and we will give them peace? Yes perhaps we will for we are fighting for civilization, not for gain. But put yourself in our places, we leave fond parents, wives, sweethearts and friends, drill hard, work day and night, sleep in the open with clothes on, yes gas masks at the ready and gun for a bedfellow, move forward faster than supplies can be brought up and thereby get poor food, always on duty, in foreign country and must go through more hardships than people at home can ever imagine. See men fall at our sides, brought in moaning and asking for mother. Do we want peace—again I say no—Not one boy over here wants peace till we get the Hun back on their ground. Ruin their cities and have them starving and homeless, begging for mercy. Then and only then do we want peace.

Of course Germany has lost many men, but they are taught militarism from birth and have been practicing it for years. Man power is nothing to them, and if we have peace now, Germany will not be whipped, but will be getting extra breath, only to go on preparing for another war, a war on the east, they must be put down now so that ten years from now we won't have to take up arms again in the far east.

Every day we learn to hate more and more, but until yesterday August 3rd I always pitied the German wounded and gave them water and food always drove slowly so no jarring would hurt them, but hereafter I will hardly be blamed if I went over the largest bounces and tried to end them before they reach the hospitals. Every wounded German is brought in properly treated and evacuated to the hospital, there given food and attention till well and placed in a prison camp, given food, clothing and a little work and plenty of recreation while our boys are sent to hospitals then back to the fight.

Well about 4:30 p.m. Saturday August 3, I made a trip to the lines and got two Americans and one Hun, the Americans I put on the bottom racks and the Hun on the top away from the boys. That Hun had a rifle bullet through his thigh and was unable to sit up, although not badly hurt I started out and while driving along the road I heard a crash of broken glass behind me and I thought a shell come through the rear of the car so I ducked and thanks to my steel helmet I got a smack on the top and when I turned the Hun had a big trench knife in his hand but had missed me when I ducked, my machine swerved into the land along the side of the woods and stopped so I quick got off the seat and looked at the Boche and the way he had broken the little window in the front of the car to get me, then at the hat which had a nice shinny streak on the top where the knife skidded. Now the ambulance drivers are part of the Red Cross organization and are not supposed to be armed and the Hun dropped the knife on the seat and said "Kamerad" I thought how much he loved me, so I opened the rear of the machine, pulled out the stretcher out and made him roll over off the road and put the stretcher back into the car, dragged the Hun into the woods him crying "Kamerad" all the time: I only stayed in the woods a few minutes then backed the car onto the road and delivered my patriots at the hospital. When I got back to the dressing station the doctor asked me if the Prussian gave me any trouble. He said the Prussians were his worst to deal with and forgot to send a guard with me. I told the doctor I had no trouble but the poor Hun had died on the way in and I dumped him in a shell hole. The doctor understood me, so gave me two extra cartridges as souvenirs to repay me for the two I lent the Hun. I passed those woods twice during the night and I honestly believe I could smell a skunk.

Yes I guess we will be glad when peace does come, but lets up hold it with a glorious victory and the Boche begging for mercy.

George L. Whitmeyer

My Heart Was Bouncing Like an Old Vickers Gun

August 5, 1918
Lieut. Robert Mills
Royal Flying Corps
Isles of Wight.

My Dear Dad:

Trusting that I may not rile the wrath of our most noble and venerable censor, I take this liberty to relate a narration of our patrol of July—. The day was perfect and most of our machines of the War Squadron were out on patrols, when suddenly a pigonierre (messenger) dashed into the orderly room with a wireless message, stating that a hostile submarine had been sighted at —longitude —latitude —proceeding, etc. etc.

Immediately our famous bomb sprinkling patrol was ordered out to locate and destroy this monster of the deep, and within a few minutes we were under way. The weather was ideal. Visibility about eighteen miles, which is excellent, and the whole show was going like a dream. For hours we steered a due course cruising about 90 mph, constantly watching for this submergible custodian of Boche Kulture. But here our course suddenly changed to due south; for our bowgunsman had sighted this ghastly object. As we advanced, we flashed our recognition signal; awaiting their reply of identification, there was no reply. It was this mysterious raider of the high seas. With phenomenal accuracy our bombs were released with a vengeance and in an instant our objective was pulverized.

But lo and behold, this supposed to be pride of the German Navy, which disfigured the sea with its utmost impunity, was only a camouflaged launch. Our death deal bombs which had been released with the greatest caution and pride had only destroyed a suppositious float.

And the battle started. Their lure had been a success and from all the four corners of the sky came August and Heine and Fritz, until we were out numbered three to one. Twas then that we realized, we were playing the hazardous role of a fly caught in the spiders web. For we were in the inner ring of Christiansonn's famous circus.

There were only a few of us and we new it was a case of fight and shoot, as Quinlin never could —, for Mister Boche was showing his tracer affections all about us. They whistled and spluttered every where we turned. Our guns also spitting back streams of fire and white wax in colossal defiance.

Then through a cloud of smoke, I saw the first Hun descending in a nose spin and crash upon the water and immediately after, through the flare of an explosion, I saw the second black cross go down in flames and the smoldering debris floating about the sea.

My heart was bouncing like an old Vickers gun, and being accompanied by whistling projectiles and chronic cold feet, I nearly upset the good old ship, which the blooming beggars had looking like a sieve.

I was wondering how much longer we would last, when faithful old engineer came up from behind, just like a thunder storm in England, and bellered in my ear, with a frigid air, "Your petrol will only last three more hours sir!" Well I am wondering, whether it was his voice or the thoughts of being a flying target for one hundred and eighty minutes, that annoyed me, but I felt as tho I had lost my sugar card and Eddie had left me flat.

Possibly it would have been just as well, if he had mentioned this fact, for the next moment I felt a slip, yea, a wild side slip and I knew we were departing from our precarious position in the clouds, to one more appalling upon that glittering sea a few thousand feet below.

Our motors had knocked out completely, without the slightest provocation, [and] we were left helpless. Fritz followed us down with his insalubrious attentions, until he felt certain that we were going to crash. Then he left us and returned to the show above, only to meet his eternal doom, for several hours later as a destroyer was towing us home, we saw his wrecked machine floating on the water.

All was tranquil and unconcussive, there in that mass of twisted wings. We beat them at their own game! Christiansonn's circus is no more!

Your loving son,
Robert.

First Lieut. Robert Mills enlisted in December 1917 and trained at Benbrook field, Fort Worth, Texas. In March, 1918 he went to Beamsville, Ontario, Canada, and took a course in aerial gunnery. He sailed for England, May 1918.

He was stationed at the seaplane base at Felixstowe, near Harwich Harbor, England. He was engaged in the "silent navy" work, a series of brilliant strategic moves in and around the North Sea. Mills was in command of a 7½ ton flying boat, with a crew of seven and armed with 12 Lewis machine guns. The aircraft carried six 230 pound bombs and over 900 gallons of fuel. The aircraft had an endurance of over 12 hours' flying time. It carried two machine gunners on the top side, a machine gunner, observer, and bomber in the front, and two more machine gunners in the rear along with a wireless operator. During his flying career Mills lost 17 crew members.

During his time in the British flying service, over one year in all, he was shot down into the sea three times and was wounded during an engagement at Hellgoland Bight. He also took part in the famous raid on Zeebrugge and covered other well known German bases, including Borkum, Trescheklling, and Ostend.

August 6, 1918—Americans take Fismes on the Vesle.

August 7, 1918—77th U.S. Division crosses the Vesle.

The following account of the 28th Division's actions during the Vesle campaign is taken from the *Pottsville Journal.* It was written by G. Proctor and entitled "The Iron Division."

When the Hun grip was torn loose from the positions along the Oureg, he had no other good stopping place short of the Vesle, so he lit out for that river as fast as he could move his battalions and equipment. Again only machine guns and sniping rearguards were left to impede the progress of the pursuers, and again there were times when it was exceedingly difficult for the French and American forces to keep in contact with the enemy.

The 32nd Division composed of Michigan and Wisconsin National Guards, had slipped into the front lines and with regiments of the Rainbow Division, pressed the

The typical Pennsylvania soldier from the 28th Division, posing for a picture to be sent home to loved ones. The soldier in this shot has not been identified.

pursuit. The Pennsylvania regiments, with the 103rd Engineers and the 111th and 112th Infantry leading, followed by the 109th and then the 110th, went forward in the rear, mopping up the few Huns they left in their wake who still showed fight.

It had begun to rain again, a heavy dispiriting downpour, such as Northern France is subjected to frequently. The fields became morasses. The roads, cut up by heavy traffic, were turned to quagmires. The distorted remains of what had been wonderful old trees, stripped of their foliage and blackened and torn by the breaths of monster guns, dripped dismally. In all that ruined, tortured land of horror on horror, there was not one bright spot. And there was only one thing to keep up the spirits of the soldiers, the Hun was definitely on the run.

Drenched to the skin, wading in mud at times almost to their knees, amid the ruck of the armies' wake, the Pennsylvanians trudged resolutely forward, inured to hardship, no longer sensible to ordinary discomforts, possessed of only one thought, to come to battle once more with the hateful foe and inflict further punishment in revenge for the gallant lads who had gone from the ranks.

All the time they were subjected to long distance shelling by the big guns, as the Hun straffed the country to the south in hope of hampering transport facilities and breaking up the marching columns. All the time Boche fliers passed overhead, sometimes swooping low enough to slash the columns with machine guns and at frequent intervals releasing bombs. There were casualties daily, although not of course, on the same scale as in the actual battle.

Just below Longeville, the Pennsylvanians came into an area where the fire was intensified to equal anything they had passed through since leaving the Marne. All the varieties of Hun projectiles were hurled at them, high explosives of various sizes, shrapnel and gas. Once more the misery and discomfort of the gas mask had to be undergone, but by this time the Pennsylvanians had learned well and truly the value of that little piece of equipment and had imbedded thoroughly the doctrine that, unpleasant as it might be, the mask was infinitely better than a whiff of that dread, sneaking, penetrating vapor with which the Hun poisoned the air.

The objective point on the river for the Pennsylvanians was Fismes. This was a town near the junction of the Vesle and Ardre rivers, which before the war had a population of a little more than 3,000. A few miles west of Fismes the railroad divides, one branch winding away southwestward to Paris, the other running west through Soissons and Compliegne. The town was one of the largest German munitions depots in the Soissons-Rheims sector and second in importance only to Soissons.

Across the river was the village of Fismette, destined to be the scene of the writing of a truly glorious page of Pennsylvania's military history.

The railroad through Fismes and in its vicinity runs along the top of an embankment, raising it above the surrounding territory. There was a time before the Americans were able to cross the railroad, that the embankment became virtually the barrier dividing redeemed France from the darkest Hunland along that front. At night patrols from both sides would move forward to the railroad, and burrowed in holes, the Germans in the north side and the Americans in the south, would watch and wait and listen for signs of an attack.

Each knew the other was only a few feet away, at times, in fact, they could hear each other talking, and once in a while defiant badinage would be exchanged in weird German from the south and in ragtime, vaudeville

English from the north. Appearance of a head above the embankment on either side was a signal for a storm of lead and steel.

The Americans had this advantage over the Germans: They knew the Huns were doomed to continue their retreat, and that the hold up along the railroad was very temporary, and the Germans now realized the same thing. Therefore, the Americans fought triumphantly, with vigor and dash—the Germans, sullenly and in desperation.

One man of the 110th went to sleep in a hole in the night and did not hear the withdrawal just before dawn. Obviously his name could not be made public. When he awoke it was broad daylight and he was only partly concealed by a little hole in the railroad embankment. There was nothing he could do. If he had tried to run for his regimental lines he would have been drilled like a sieve before he had gone fifty yards. Soon the German batteries would begin shelling but he simply dug deeper into the bank. "I just drove myself into that bank like a snail," he told his comrades after. He got away the next night.

Corporal George D. Hyde, of Mt. Pleasant, Company E 110th, hid in a hole in the side of the embankment for thirty six hours on the chance of obtaining valuable information. When returning, a piece of shrapnel struck the pouch in which he carried his grenades. Examining them, he found the cap of one driven well in. It was a miracle it had not exploded and torn a hole through him. "You ought to have seen me throw that grenade away," he said.

In this waiting time it was decided to clean up a position of the enemy that was thrust out beyond their general line, from which an annoying fire was kept up constantly. Accordingly, a battalion of the 110th was sent over to wipe it out.

The Rev. Mandeville J. Barker, rector of the Episcopal Church in Uniontown, Pa. is chaplain of the 110th, with the rank of first Lieutenant. He had endeared himself to officers and men alike by his happy combination of buoyant, gallant cheerfulness, [and] deep Christianity. He went over the top with the battalion that attacked by night on the heights of the Vesle. It was not his duty to go; in fact had the regimental commander known his intention, he probably would have been forbidden to go. But go he did. He had an idea that his job was to look after the men's bodies as well as their souls, and when there was a stern fighting to do, he liked to be in a position where he could attend to both phases of his work.

The attacking party wiped out the Hun machine gun nest after a sharp fight and then retired to their own lines, as ordered. It was so dark that some of the wounded were overlooked. After the battalion returned voices of American wounded could be heard out in the no mans land, calling for help. Dr. Barker took his life and some first aid equipment and water in his two hands and slipped out into the dark, with only starshine and the voices of the wounded to guide him and between the two armies, attended to the wounds of the men as best he could by the light of a small pocket torch, which he had to keep concealed from the enemy lookouts.

One after another the clergyman hunted. Those who could walk he started back to the lines. Several he had to assist. One lad who was beyond help he sat beside and ministered to with the tenderness of a mother until the young soul struggled gropingly out into the great beyond. Then, with tears rolling down his cheeks, the beloved "Sky Pilot" started back.

But again the sound of a voice in agony halted him. This time, however it was not English words that he heard, but a moaning petition in guttural German; Ach Gott, Ach Mein lieber Gott!

The men of the 110th loved their "parson" even more for what he did then, he turned right about and went back, groping in the dark for the sobbing man. He found a curly haired young German, wounded so he could not walk and in mortal terror, not of death or the dark, but of "those terrible Americans who torture and kill their prisoners." Such was the tale with which his comrades had been taught to loathe their American enemies. Dr. Barker treated his wounds and carried him back to the American lines. The youngster whimpered with fear when he found out he was going, and begged the clergyman not to leave him. When he was finally convinced that he was not going to be harmed, he kissed the chaplain's hands, crying over them and insisted on turning over to Dr. Barker everything he owned that could be loosened helmet, pistol, bayonet, cartridges buttons, and other odds and ends.

"All hung over with loot, the parson was, when he came back," said a sergeant in telling of the scene afterward.

"The Fighting Parson," as the men called him, did not fight, actually, but he went close to it as possible. On one more occasion snipers were bothering the men. Dr. Barker borrowed a pair of glasses, lay flat on the field and after prolonged study discovered the offenders, four of them, and notified an artillery observer. A big gun casually swung its snout around and barked three times and the snipers sniped no more. Two or three days later, the regiment went over and took that section of German lines and found what was left of the four men. "The Parson's Boche," the men called them.

Toward the last of the action below the Vesle, a group of men of the 110th had established an outpost in a large cave, which extended a considerable distance back in a cliff, just how far none of the men ever discovered. After they had been there several days, Dr. Barker arranged to cheer them a little in their lonely vigil. The cave had been an underground quarry. The Germans had occupied it, knew exactly where it was and its value as a hiding place, and kept a constant stream of machine gun bullets flying past its mouth.

For three weeks it had been possible to enter or leave the cave only after dark. Even then it was risky for the mouth of the cave was only fifty yards from the German trenches and sights and sounds could be heard [*sic*]. After dark the Hun fire was laid down about the entrance at every suspicious noise. Sometimes the men inside would amuse themselves by heaving stones outside from a safe position within to hear Fritz turn loose his "pepper boxes."

Despite these difficulties, Dr. Barker got a motion picture outfit into the cave and gave a show of six reels to the men stationed there, after which the Y.M.C.A. men entertained them with songs and eccentric dances. Men who saw that performance, in the light of torches and flambeaux, will never forget the picture.

Toward the last there were sounds from the farther interior of the cave, and two American soldiers walked into the circle, blinking their eyes. Nobody gave much attention to them, supposing they just wandered away, a few minutes before until one of them interrupted a song with the hoarsely whispered query: "Got any chow?" Ah go lay down, was the querulous reply of the men addressed. "Aint yuh show? Shut will yuh." "Gee but I am hungry," came the answer. "I need some chow," We been lost in this doggoned cave for two days."

Investigation developed that he was telling the truth, and Dr. Barker produced from some mysterious horn of plenty some chocolate, which the famished men ate with avidity. With the natural, healthy curiosity of American youth, they set out to explore the cave and became lost in its mazes. Only the noise and lights of Dr. Barker's concert led them out.

Soldiers of Pennsylvania Dutch descent had amazed the Germans more than once not only by understanding the conversation of the enemy, but by their intense anger, almost ferocity which they displayed on occasions when confronted with the intolerable thing called the Prussian spirit. Offspring of men and women of sturdy, free minded stock who fled oppression in Europe, they flamed the spirit of real liberty lovers when in contact with the Prussian.

A little group of the 11th ambulanciers when carrying back the wounded met a German major who was groaning and complaining vigorously and demanding instant attention. The contrast between his conduct and that of American officers who almost invariably told litter bearers to go on and pick up worse wounded men, was glaring, but finally the bearers good humoredly decided to get the Major out of the way to stop his noise. He was not wounded severely but was unable to walk, and they lifted him to a stretcher with the same care they gave all the wounded.

Promptly the major began to upbraid the Americans, speaking in his native tongue. In the language of a billings gate fishwife, or what corresponds to one in Hunland, he cursed the Americans, root, stock and branch, from President Wilson down to the newest recruit in the army.

Thomas G. Fox, of Hummelstown, Pa., one of the bearers, understood his every word and repeated the diatribe in English to his fellows, who became restive under the tirade. At last the major said: "You Americans think you are going to win the war, but you are not."

That was too much for Fox and his companions. "You think you are going to be carried back to a hospital, but you're not," said Fox. Whereupon the litter was turned over neatly and the major deposited, not too gently, on the hard ground. For some time he lay there, roaring his maledictions. Then he started to crawl back, and by the time he got to a hospital, he had lost some of his insolence.

I Could Sleep on a Cart of Rotten Eggs, and Wouldn't Mind It

August 7, 1918
Pvt. Harry H. Leiby
Co. C 103rd Engineers
28th Division
A.E.F.
Somewhere in France.

Dear Sister:

Hello; how's the weather over there? I am fine and hope you and hubby are the same. At present we are having wet weather and the mud is fierce. I should know because I laid in mud and water all night, up at the front. This is some country and very picturesque, but "America for me."

Very often you see us galloping around here with our packs on. Everything we own or need we carry on our backs, so we sure do make a limit to it.

Say, aren't they having some drive? They're driving Jerry that hard he don't know which way to turn and he sure does leave some paraphernalia behind.

I sure have had some real beds over here. Do you know I could sleep on a cart of rotten eggs and wouldn't mind it. Once in a while we get a chance to live high, second story of a barn. I am so used to rolling up my pack, I very often do it to pass the time.

Do you know Sis, it's a wonderful thing to find yourself whole after being in a barrage! Then is the time you know there is a God to take care of you and you thank Mother for teaching you how to pray. It is an awful predicament to lay behind a tree or in a small hole with the shrapnel shells bursting all around. Whiz Bang-Whiz Bang they say and as you lay there you wonder if any have your name on it.

I haven't told you about the pullman cars we travel in. When you sleep you rest your head on the floor and have your feet in the air. They look something like our box cars, and not as neat and smaller. Your meals are served by the Red Cross along the road and they deserve all the help they can get, along with the Y.M.C.A. their services are wonderful.

Your Brother,
Harry.

What the Engineers Did Since Leaving Home

August 8, 1918
Pvt. Bertram G. Dunlop
Co. C 103rd Engineers
28th Division
A.E.F.
Somewhere in France

Dear Sir:

Just read a few of the papers dated June 22nd, and they sure were interesting. Any news from home is always welcomed by the boys.

I will try to give you an account of our trip since we left Camp Mills, L.I. May 18th. We left camp at 11:30 a.m. with a few people watching us as we passed the gate to the camp. After a few hours ride we arrived at New York and went aboard the Washington Ferry boat. Then an hours ride down the river, passing under the Brooklyn Bridge and given cheers by the people of New York. The fellows working at the many wharves yelling "Get one for me" Good luck and many humorous suggestions. At four p.m. we went aboard the boat a large English vessel, the first time in New York harbor. We spent the next four hours loading the boat. At six p.m. the vessel was towed out to Sandy Hook harbor. We were left there for the night.

Some of the fellows felt sorry for that they could not enjoy one more evening in New York, but that was because we could see the many lights of New York City. The evening was spent in singing songs, and one fellow telling his pal of what good times he had [for] a few hours at home.

Sunday morning every one was up bright and early, after sleeping in hammocks about four feet from the floor. One of the fellows fell out of the hammock and there sure was some noise. About 70 fellows in one room and each one trying to upset the one next to him. We had very little sleep that night. At two p.m. we sailed. Almost all the fellows on the boat were on the deck getting a last look at the Statue of Liberty.

We saw a whale that night, and went to bed early. The boys did not mind it until we were out about two days, them some of them got sick. You can imagine how they were kidded by the rest of the fellows, but then some of the fellows that were kidding those that were sick went under.

Well by the time that we were through with them they would have given their last cent to be back in New York. Next we had boat drill. Each man was sent to his bunk and assigned to a section; then when a signal was given he marched to the upper deck and stood opposite to the boat he was assigned to. We had a boat drill every morning, and in the afternoon we had rifle drill. The evenings were spent on the upper deck singing and dancing.

One feature of the English was their tea. The fellows could not understand why they only got a cup of tea and some cheese for what should be our supper. The fifth day out we had rough weather. Almost all of us were sick that night on account of the ship tossing about in the waves. That night I was put on guard with orders to shoot any one that showed a light on deck. Well, it sure did rain that night. The next night the Y.M.C.A. man had a show on the boat.

There was an Englishman on the boat and he sure was a Christian. Sunday went to church, which was held on the deck. The seventh day out we entered the danger zone and here we were met by em [deleted] The day we entered the Irish Sea we were in it about three hours when the engineer of the boat blew the signal of a "Sub" about…. Here we turned in and after the whistle blew it gave four short blasts and we heard the report of a cannon, Well, those that were below thought the boat was struck by a torpedo, but it was the gun on our boat firing at the periscope of the sub. All of the fellows rushed to the starboard side to see the sub. Our boat fired twice, and the boat in the rear of us fired once, and the shell gained and burst in the air. Some of the shrapnel landed on our deck. The dirigible made a wonderful nosedive and dropped a depth bomb.

Well that sub had no chance at all. He did not even have time to come up. All he showed was his periscope and then when he knew we were ready for him he went down. It sure did cause some excitement, but we did enjoy it. There wasn't any sleep on board that boat because we were nearing land and the fellows were sick of seeing nothing but sky and water. And when the Irish coast was sighted we sure did make some noise. It sure did look beautiful. We sailed up the coast and landed at [deleted]. We went ashore at 2:30 p.m. and marched up the streets of [deleted] and crowds of people cheering and weeping [and] every house had an American flag and English flag waving. Had a six-hour ride on third class passenger cars and enjoyed coffee and sandwiches by the Red Cross. We passed through some beautiful country; all of the houses built on the same level and the rural scenery was magnificent.

We were taken from the train at two a.m. and then marched through the dark streets of [deleted]. It seemed strange not to see a light in the houses. Here we slept in barracks until seven a.m. Then we had some more English tea and cheese. At two p.m. we went aboard a boat and had a queer feeling when we were given life preservers that were still wet and was told they were used three days before. We crossed the channel without incident and landed at [deleted] marched to a rest camp. Here we saw English girls driving ambulances. We were at a supposed rest camp, but while there we had very little rest. We were given tickets for meals and if we happened to lose the ticket we were out of luck for a meal because no one was allowed in the mess hall with out the pink slip. Here we turned in our barracks bags and extra clothing. We hiked three miles through deep sand and were issued British rifles. We were also given gas masks and sent through a gashouse to try the masks. We were at [deleted] for three days and then received orders to roll packs and after a hot tiresome march we were put in the French cattle cars marked 8 horses or 40 men.

Some how 40 of us managed to get in the car after walking on other fellow's fingers, arms and legs. We passed through the city of [deleted] and saw some buildings that had been ruined by bombs from aeroplanes. Along the route we passed a number of German prisoners. We rode for four hours and at [deleted] received orders to hike to a small village four miles distant. We sure did sweat on that hike and went up some hills as steep as Seventh St. in Pottsville. We reached [deleted] at five p.m. and were billeted in barns outside of the village. We were there over night and sure did enjoy night's sleep. Everyone was dead tired. Next morning we had to roll packs and pitch tents in a field near a French church. Here we were among the peasant people of France. No matter how small the village may be, one can always find a church there. The people are very religious. Here we could hear the big guns sending shells over to Fritz. While at [deleted] we were under English training and we sure did drill. Every morning we went to drill at eight o'clock and drilled until 12. Then we went back to camp and had English stew. We played games with the gas masks on, so as to get accustomed to them. Had these quick thinking games. When the sergeant says O'Brady says attention, we stand at attention then when we would just say attention he was sure of catching some one asleep. While there we saw two air raids. Saw one plane drop in flames. Went back to camp and had the 12th meal of beef stew, then hiked 12 miles to turn in English rifles. We sure were happy when we received orders that we were transferred to the French army. Next day we saw some British rifles drilling. They were good, but the Americans were just as good. Next we rolled packs and hiked to [deleted] and again went into the cattle cars, and the car that we were put in was much smaller than the first one we were on. We rode all day and passed through some ruined cities, and towards evening we passed through [deleted] city about the size of Reading. It was being shelled by Germans and no one was in it. We passed that night in misery. About half of the fellows fell asleep and the other half had to stand.

Well those that were left standing were out of luck, at least for 10 minutes then they got sore at seeing the others sleeping and they tried to find room to either lie or sit down. They began to move around and after stepping on some hands legs and heads they wakened everyone in the car. There was a riot right there; everyone had a grouch on, and felt like cleaning six Germans. After ever one was settles one fellow got a cramp in the leg. Well he moved and that wakened three others that were resting their heads on his leg, and once again every one in the car was arguing. No sleep that night. At [deleted] we were ordered from the train and saw a house ruined by a plane. But the Boche plane was brought down by an American flyer. I have a piece of the German plane. We billeted on a French farm and slept on a bunk that had been built by German soldiers, and I sure did sleep that night. I swore that if I ever met the Boche that built that bunk I would shake hands with him. Next day we hiked 12 miles and billeted in a barn near a large lake, where we could take much need bath. Here the fellows that missed the boat at Camp Mills were transferred back to the company. They were glad to get back and the whole company was out to greet them. Here we could see the flashes of large guns at night; saw quite a few air battles. We were there for three days and hiked another 12 miles to a large city, and once again billeted on a farm. A tired company of soldiers crawled up the mountain that night. We had been marching since four o'clock and had to hike up two miles of mountain road before we could rest. The fellows stuck right to it and when we reached the farm house more than one fellow crawled up the steps and went asleep without unrolling the packs. Every one was dead tired and all the German shells Fritz sent over did not waken us.

The first day when the shells whistled over the house we felt queer, but after a while we became accustomed to it. Next night we were given tools and sent out to dig trenches. We had to do all our work at night, as if we were seen working by day we would have been shelled. Fritz sent a few shells over that night, but they were high over our heads, and did not bother us. We were working about a week and enjoyed it very much. We had very good eats and plenty of time to ourselves, but could not get a sheet of writing paper.

One morning about three o'clock we had finished our work and were just falling asleep when Fritz sent some gas over. We were ready for him, as we always slept with our gas masks in alert position. He (Fritz) sent some sneezing gas over it is harmless, but if a fellow gets some of it he has to sneeze; that is Fritz's chance to send some poisonous gas over and the fellows can't keep their masks on because of sneezing.

We had it once again while we were eating our supper just before going to work. Then one day we got orders to move and hiked back to [deleted] and waited until 11 p.m.; then we were put on large motor lorries and rode all night over roads that were full of shell holes. We passed through about 10 shell-ruined villages. At six a.m. we got off the trucks and hiked about five miles and sleep in woods.

Here we saw five Boche planes swoop down on a farmhouse and drop two bombs on it killing one Frenchman and a fellow from company B of our regiment.

Some of our fellows fired at them with their rifles. They waited until chased by a squad of French planes and we saw a Frenchman bring down one of the Boche planes in flames.

[Whole sentenced deleted.] That sure was some awful night. They shelled us for four hours, but we were sent there to help the other fellows and no one in the company even thought of turning back. We had a [deleted] here our infantry captured some Germans and used them as litter bearers. I suppose you have heard of it. Every one in the company worked hard, and next day the fourth platoon brought a meal up to us through a heavy barrage and up a steep mountainside. Next day we were relieved, as we had taken our objective and captured a number of machine guns.

From there we hiked to another front and were ordered to a very important town to build a bridge across [deleted]. We reached the top of a hill before dark and we could see the [deleted] and the shells from our guns exploding down in the valley.

We started down and about 300 yards from the river we were halted by a French guard. Our Captain told him where we were going and the guard told us that the Germans were at the town that we were to occupy. Well it was getting pretty hot right there, so we went back about 25 yards and the company was scattered among the buildings of a small town.

We were there about one half hour when Fritz started to shell the town. Our Lieut. found some dugouts or rather wine cellars and we were taken to them. I being in the first platoon went with the Captain and was in a wine cellar six feet below a house. Talk about being comfortable! Some German soldiers had been using the cellar for their headquarters and they had everything fixed up great for us. Feather beds, chairs and tables that they had taken from the homes. Fritz sent quite a few shells over but they did not bother us. We had to stay in the cellar all night and the next day received orders to come back to headquarters: but while in that town we could not even put our heads out doors, as the planes overhead and the Germans being on a hill they could have seen us. The next night we moved out under cover of darkness.

We got out without a man being scratched. We went back to a small village for a rest, and were there two days, and then brought to another part of the front, filling up shell holes in the road. Now we are back in the woods with eight large guns just across the road sending shells over to Fritz just as fast as they can. Today we were in the woods making barb wire stakes and were in some German dugouts.

They sure are being driven back: did not even have time to bury their dead or take their wounded with them. The Americans of the [deleted] are bringing in prisoners every night; 50 passed here last night. One fellow in our company who spoke German asked one how he liked the war. All he said was "Finish." Some of our doughboys found a German chained to a machine gun and the gun was chained to a tree. The Allies sure surprised them. They expected to go through to Paris, but by now they have changed their minds.

Well I hope this will pass the censor. I was going to write long before this but could not get the paper. Since we have been on this front we can get the paper from the Y.M.C.A. trucks which run up almost to the front. There isn't any trenches here. Its all open warfare and traffic along the road here has it all over Fifth Ave. Motor trucks motor cycles, wagons, bicycles and all kind of carts.

Just brought some more prisoners up and we almost scared them to death. Nine marched up the field and just about 500 fellows were waiting for them. One fellow saw them coming out of the woods and gave a yell. They all raced across the field to see them. Imagine being a prisoner of war and seeing a mob racing a cross the field towards you. None of the fellows hurt them, but they sure were sad, hungry looking bunch. Well, it is getting dark, so I will have to close.

Letter continued from August 8.

Well, I suppose I may as well tell you I was going to keep it quiet but what the dive! Nothing serious I'm in the base hospital in [deleted] a little gas, but mostly exhaustion from loss of sleep and overwork. I do not think I will be here very long. I guess I will begin where I left off.

The next night we were sent out to work. It had been raining for a week and the roads were terribly wet and muddy. We left the dense woods at 10 p.m. stumbling over trees and roots, each fellow having a hard time to keep from falling and at the same time trying to keep an eye on the fellow in front of him. We reached the road and each fellow was given a pair of wire cutters. Well, then we [k]new we were going to do some barb wirework.

We hiked or rather slid along that road for a mile, then turned off into the woods and again passing a number of shell holes and dead horses, also German graves. We were thankful when the big guns would bark as, when they did we could get a glimpse of the path for about 30 feet.

After hiking through two acres of woods, we came upon another road. Here the Artillerymen were trying to move the guns up to a new position. This road was awfully muddy and slippery and eight horses hitched to one gun. It made us feel good to hear the men talking to their horses as they stumbled along through the inky darkness. Such words as "Come on Prince! Getting to it." "Pull it out old boy!" "Come on Dick. Get it out of here." Etc. while others were cursing all the Germans under the sun.

We walked along this line of artillery for about an hour, then came the motor trucks moving along slowly. Talk about your traffic on Broadway! It has nothing on the roads of France.

Well, we finally reached our place of work and after carefully examining the ground we were to work on we started. Each fellow doing his part that had been laid out for him. Then those that had finished help[ed] others that could not work as fast. It certainly was beautiful not thinking of the dreadful work the artillery was doing. To see the spray clouds go up from the line, first a single light would shoot into the sky and hang there for a few seconds as though suspended by an invisible wire, then it would break and a thousand shining stars would float towards the earth, lighting up the ground around for a mile.

Then to see the red very lights shining, it looked just as though the moon was coming up just over the horizon. All the while the cannons firing as fast as they can fire. Next we heard the hum of the aeroplane. As it came closer we knew it to be a Boche plane, not one but four. The order was given to lie flat on the ground. We waited until he was well past us then started on the work again. We had been working for about ten minutes when we heard an awful noise from the direction we had come. We had been in France too long not to know what it was, that was making the racket. We knew that planes that have passed overhead were at their work of merciless destruction and killing. We were stopped working just before break of day and returned to camp. Just before entering the woods we had a little fun, well, it looked funny to us.

The road being very muddy everybody was doing his level best to keep on his feet. The Captain was in the lead and was looking for the path entering the woods when Zip! Both his feet were out from under him and he landed in a nice wet muddy sloppy shell hole. Well he crawled out of it and was just taking his first step when down he goes again. Well, we fellows in the lead were snickering and almost bursting trying to keep from laughing outright when he fell the first time but when he went down the second time it was to[o] much for us. We just couldn't stop laughing and that made him sore. He sure was some picture, standing in the middle of the road giving us a lecture and all the fellows along the line laughing at him.

We made our way back to the dugouts and slept until noontime. When we were at mess we heard what damage the planes had done. Some one in the woods struck a match to light a cigarette. That was what the Boche wanted. He knew that there were soldiers in the woods when he saw the light, well he bombed the woods and got about 30 fellows.

The following night we received orders to move. We rolled wet packs and hiked through a number of villages destroyed by shells. We hiked until about 10 a.m. next day. Then we were given orders to dig in. We dug in the sides of a hill, each fellow taking a partner and building a home in the ground. At night it rained as usual. We made ourselves as comfortable as we could and got about two hours sleep between gas alarms. The Boche is a dirty mean sneaky fellow, first, he sends high explosives over and after about 20 of them have burst around us there was the odor of explosive in the air. That is just what he wants, as good many fellows think the smell of explosives is gas, then when they find they are mistaken they remove their masks. That's just what Fritz is waiting for. So he sends in a few more explosives over and with them a few gas shells. But, after a few days you become accustomed to the different gases.

Well, I am away from mystery. We were in dugouts on the side of a hill that was almost straight. Well, talk about your cliff dwellers of New Mexico, we had had it all over them. A photographer from the front took a picture of the hill. I suppose it will be in some of the papers, anyway we told him to put it in and he said he would. We were in the dugouts for two days, almost having a good time. We were only annoyed by shells around meal times. It seemed that Fritz knows what time the American Army eats its meals. Anyway, every time we lined up for mess, he would send over a few shells just to make the meal warm for us. Of course they did no harm.

One night at 6 p.m. we received orders to roll packs. Well, we rolled them and had them rolled about a half an hour when an other order came to unroll and stay there for the night. Everybody was happy and went to bed feeling fine. 11 o'clock and almost all had been asleep when the Captain yelled everybody up and roll packs. Well you can imagine our feelings, I'm not saying much but I sure didn't blame the others much either.

We rolled our packs, of course, slid down the side of the hill. The road was one whole line along the mountain side, nothing but mud and water and more mud. We hiked for about 10 minutes and I hiked no more.

The next thing I remember I was in a dugout on a stretcher. A few minutes after that I was on an ambulance going to a dressing station. Here I was given a tag, put on another ambulance and hauled to a field hospital. Here I was put in bed for about six hours and slept the whole time. Then in an another ambulance and hauled down to an evacuation hospital where I was put in another bed [and] lost all my clothes my helmet and gas mask. The evacuation hospital is where all the wounds are operated upon. All pieces of shrapnel removed. Here about six hours and then hauled to a station where I was for about three hours. Then put on a brand new Red Cross train. Talk about a swell car. Each car painted olive drab with a large Red Cross on it. Inside everything is painted white and has berths three high and 12 rows, 16 beds in a car. I cannot tell much about my ride as I slept all the way. We reached [deleted] at daybreak and were taken into a large room at the station. Here the gassed and wounded patients were weeded out.

A real live American woman asked me if I was gassed or wounded. Well, I guess she thought I was crazy because I just opened my mouth and looked at her. It was the first American female voice I heard in two months. I suppose she thought I was shell shocked, any way she sent a medical man over to talk to me. I told him I wasn't wounded I was sick. So they took me off this bed, put me on stretcher, put the stretcher on a baby cart and wheeled me about a block to an ambulance. Three other fellows and myself were put into an ambulance and we started off for a ride around the whirly city. Well, to go through here in ambulance is a cure for any sick man.

We had a good driver and he left the doors in the side of the ambulance open so we could see the people as we passed them. It's a wonder the driver didn't get seasick for the way we went zigzagging around the city, up one street, and then to our right, then left, then back in the direction we came. And every person we passed took a look at the occupants of the machine and tried to keep on walking at the same time. I had often heard that the French girls liked the American soldiers to smile at them. Well, I tried it on one girl. I suppose she was going to work. Well, we were just passing a corner when I smiled at her and waved my hand. She kept on walking but had her head turned towards me and was returning the wave when she walked on a man's heels that was going in the same direction as she, but was much slower than she. I just caught a glimpse of them jabbering to each other. That was enough, you could imagine what they wee saying.

Well we reached the hospital, which was once a large hotel. It is situated on a high hill and from my room I can see all over the city. It sure is great. Just one week ago I was telling some of the fellows how I could enjoy a nice bath, a meal and then jump into a spring bed. I got my wish.

Well I suppose I will close,
Bert.

Glad That I Got My Gas Mask on in Time

August 9, 1918
Pvt. Harry Keller
Co. C 103rd Engineers
28th Division
A.E.F.
Somewhere in France.

Dear Parents:

Just a few lines to let you know I am in the base hospital with a few slight gas burns, which I received on August 5th,when a mustard gas shell burst about ten feet from my dug out. I am feeling fine and getting treated fine, believe me. I do not think that I would have been burned, if it were not for the fact that my clothing was wet from the rain. Mustard gas hangs to the clothes and whenever a person perspires or is wet, that is where it burns. I am just glad that I am not burned as bad as some of the boys that I have seen. Also glad that I got my gas mask on in time. When a person gets burned with this gas they take him to a first aid station and he has to discard everything he owns because it is more or less saturated with the gas and the clothing are of no use any more. After they strip a person they give him a bath with some sort of solution and believe me I got one of these baths and I needed a bath badly.

After I had my bath, at the dressing station, I was put on an ambulance and taken to a field hospital where I was given another bath and there I stayed over night and from there was put on a hospital train and brought down to the base hospital where I am now and getting along fine. I hope to be out soon. I would have not gone to the hospital but some of the fellows thought it best that I do so.

Harry Reber was bunking with me at the time and he got more of it than I did. Quite a few from the company got some of the gas. The burn is somewhat like the burn of a stove or steam. I have been over quite a bit of the battlefront where the drive took place and had quite a lot of experiences. I saw quite a few German prisoners that were captured in the

Another job of the Pennsylvania engineers was that of digging trenches. During the war they helped repair and dig many new trenches.

drive, and also quite a few German dead compared to the Allies.

Your loving Son,
Harry

I Shot a German Sniper the Other Day

August 10, 1918
PFC. Mearl Sinton
Co. K 112th Regt.
28th Division.
A.E.F.
Somewhere in France.

Dear Mother and Father:

Just a few lines to let you know I received your kind and welcome letter two weeks ago. I am feeling fine and hope you are the same at home. It is pretty hot over here. I don't get much time to write, I am always on the move. It is pretty tough over here, a fellow got to keep his eyes open all the time in order to escape the enemy's shells that they are sending over here thick and fast. I got a taste of their gas the other night. I don't know what a good night's rest is anymore. We did not receive any pay for three months.

I shot a German sniper the other day. He was up a big tree when I got my eye on him and he came down very fast. The drinking water is not very good here. One day we hiked through mud up to our knees. Sometimes we get plenty to eat and others not enough. I wish you could send men a Pottsville paper. I don't know what a paper is anymore. The Red Cross gives us literature. We sure are doing some great fight for the French.

How is the big league base ball team. The other day took a bath in a tin can. That was the first bath for two months. We sleep with our clothes on. Don't know what it is to change clothes any more. I received a letter from Uncle Howard a few weeks ago. He said that he is in a good outfit. Goodbye to all and kisses to all and don't forget Woodrow.

Mearl

Snipers would observe the enemy trenches for days at a time without firing a shot, noting the exposed positions and daily routine of the enemy. They usually worked from behind cleverly concealed positions: some used trees, tying branches around their bodies; others lay on the ground covered by grass or other debris; others crawled out under the cover of darkness, covered themselves with mud or dirt, and then lay still for hours waiting for their victims.

That Was My Third Time Over the Top

August 11, 1918
Pvt. Charles Evans
Co. M 58th Infantry Regt.
4th Division
A.E.F.
Somewhere in France.

Dear Mother:

Just a few lines to let you know I am getting along very well. On August 4th I was hit by a piece of shrapnel, on the jaw, as I was going over the top. I didn't get hurt very bad, any way I can say I got a few Germans for what they did to me. By the time you get this letter, I will be out of the hospital and with my company again. I don't know where Gilger is. I don't know if he is with his company, or if he is wounded. The Red Cross certainly treats a fellow good over here.

That was my third time over the top. I got a few Germans every time I went over. I guess old Fritz knows it by this time. Well I don't know much more to write, so I think I will close, hoping to hear from you soon.

Charles.

"Well, What Is Your Trouble Lad?"

August 13, 1918
Sergeant John T. Duffy
Co. D 103rd Engineers
28th Division.
A.E.F.
Somewhere in France.

My Dear Father:

We are all proud of the splendid work done by our officers and men in this great drive and it is a pleasure to know that our officers are recommended for bravery, which has been earned by their good work. I happened to be close to Lieut. Powers, who was in the thick of the fight, and his skill and bravery were an example for every man to follow and he has earned the recognition which brave men deserve.

Now that I am well again I want you to know of some of my experiences. I was brought down from the lines in a side car of a motorcycle and I was turned over into the hands of our genial Major Moore, I want to describe his abode, where he labors for the relief of stricken humanity. The building is a very old one, in fact at any point you can see the starry heavens and his only light at night is a candle on his operating room would remind you of the old log cabin days, made famous by writers of fiction when they wished to weave romance about a character of olden days. Picture this abode and then amid the shelling and the bombing of the Boche night raiders, you can see the ambulances stop with their loads of wounded or gassed heroes and they are brought into this little hospital behind the lines. I have sat in this room and I have seen them come in and a greeting from the Major of "Well what is your trouble lad?" and then with a hand that can only be credited to a clever surgeon, he performs the necessary operation, to relieve the distressed one and then a hasty order of bandages or dressings, and so it goes on through the long hours of the night and stretches away into dawn. The Major's bed is a crude affair and he sleeps Ala American style, nothing off but your iron hat and he catches his sleep between ambulances or when time permits.

I have seen Lieutenant Murphy at work he is another that deserves great credit. He has worked at one stretch for ninety two hours and this is a Corps that deserves great commendation. I know of three members of the Corps that have been recommended for the Cross of Honor. And this is a branch of service that is sometimes forgotten when the hero stuff is painted. If you could see a gas attack and see men working under shell fire that would make you think of Dante's Inferno, going about dressing wounds and carrying men back. I know you would feel proud of this arm of the service. The quietness and the completeness of their work is carried on in such a manner that sometimes they are forgotten by the writers but I have seen them at work and they never hesitate about performing their duty, regardless of what their chances of coming back are.

In our last big drive I have seen sights that awed me and as I have told you before we have entered towns that the Hun evacuated just a few hours before. The men who fought in this great drive are worthy of the name of Spartans because they took places which seemed almost impossible and the great American Infantry cannot be beaten anywhere.

I do not want any credit myself because I was only a rivet in this great machine but I am proud to think that I was in the drive. If anyone thinks that this is a place for fun, he does not want to come to France, because over here this is a mans job.

The boys who go out on the line, the boys who build bridges and the medical men back of the lines, all working without thought of hours, and the last named object to relieve the distressed and make the journey further back more restful. When the history of this war is written to those in charge of writing may only appear the big events, but do you know, Dad, that there are heroes never mentioned, who are performing their tasks without murmur and accepting all living conditions as though they always lived them. To those men I give great credit and I shall always speak of with pride, because I have seen them at work, and by their deeds ye shall know them. I send best love to all and remain, as always your loving son.

John

There Was Machine Gun Snipers Picking at Us All the Time

August 13, 1918
Sergeant Harry Lankert
Co. C 103rd Engineers
28th Division
A.E.F.
Somewhere in France.

Dear Sister:

Received your letter, Ruth, and was more than glad to hear from you. We are having a mighty tough time of it over here. I wanted to write a week ago but we were sent up to the front, to build bridges, one of the worse jobs there is. Here is my personal experience on this job. If I had plenty of paper, I'd write our experience since we landed, as it is I'll have plenty to tell when I return.

The 103rd Regiment of Engineers failed trying four nights to throw a bridge across the—River. Out of our regiment—company got one over, D company tried and failed; that is were Stanley Dengler was killed. So our company and part of B went out to try our luck. We got to the river without losing a man. We had to work under constant continual shell fire, which is something that know one [*sic*] knows anything about, except those who are caught in a barrage. And those who live through it will never forget it. There were machine gun snipers picking at us all the time. Well. We were within an hours work of completing the bridge when, we could not finish it. Next night the Captain sent me through the town down to a different bridge to see if we could repair it. Well, the Hun excused me from the shells, but dear, oh dear, how the machine gun bullets would flatten against the walls of the houses. After crawling, rolling and darting from one house to another I finally got down to the bridge and found out we could fix it if we could get the men there to work. My trip back was just a bit worse. One sniper had me in the doorway of a house and every time I would move he would greet me with at least fifty shots, to me it seemed like a million. I was afraid to take a different road for fear of getting lost and for that reason I did not go through the house to the next street. I kept quiet for about 45 minutes then made a grand rush up the street and he never touched me. We had a fellow show us a different road to the bridge and when we got within a 100 yards of it, two other fellows and myself crawled to the bridge to measure the thing. We just got her measured when four shells hit on both sides of the bridge. Then a sniper sends up a rocket and lights things up like day for 10 or 15 seconds, but we remained quiet and I guess he never saw us. We got back to the company and made—for the bridge. Every one grabbed hold of it and we took it out and put it up and no one was hurt. On our way back we were about a mile from the bridge when the Huns laid down an awful barrage, mostly high explosives. We were caught in it and well, I dare not tell you the rest, but I am now about two miles from the bridge sitting in a hole in the ground shaking hands with my self and sending a prayer of thanks to the good Lord. "Coaley" Frey and I are here together and about every three minutes a shell comes our way and we both try to see how far we can stick our noses in the ground trying to duck the pieces of flying shells. Take it from me, on the line is [no] place for a non believer. Every man sends his little prayer very often.

As I have only two pieces of paper I'll have to send a line to mother and you might tell her I had but one letter from her and one from Earl, none from Dad. I am in good health at present and hope this will find all of you the same.

Brother Harry.

It Was My 23rd Birthday, the 8th of July

August 14, 1918
Pvt. James Groody
Co. B 112th Infantry Regt.
28th Division.
A.E.F.
Somewhere in France

Dear Mother:

I wrote you several days ago. In my letter I told you I had just come from the front after being three days face to face with the Boche.

At the time of my writing, I also explained to you that owing to my trying experience, of these days, of constantly being on the alert, without sleep, and with only one meal, it was really a fact that I was in the same condition as most of the boys said they were, namely, "All in." Therefore that would explain the briefness of my letter. But since that time although only a few miles from the guns of "Old Jerry," as the English say, I feel more like writing than I did at the time above mentioned.

If God grants that I survive this great conflict, which I earnestly pray he will, the day that I first entered the line will not be hard to recall to mind, for it was my 23rd birthday, the 8th of July.

It was on that day real early in fact in the dark hours of the morning, that our battalion got orders to advance through a town until we reached the banks of a small river, and there set up our automatic guns, and secure different positions necessary for us to be in so as to take a good stand in either of the three situations, (namely an attack, a defense, or in support.) if the occasion arose for us to be there if things were going to happen, as we had a slight warning as they were as soon as the day light appeared, oh well things did happen. But first I want to tell you about the town through which we had to pass in order to get to our battling position.

The name of the place by this time to you people, who read the newspapers would sound as familiar as Tumbling Run, or Garfield Square, for it has been talked of and written of a great deal in the past few weeks owing to it having been the scene of some rather great battles and in which some of our boys have received serious wounds, and a few have given their all for Democracy.

A photograph of no man's land that separated the Allied trenches from the German trenches. There were thousands of miles of trenches in World War I.

It is notable for the fact that it has changed hands several times. In as many days. But the night I went through, our boys were holding it, having finally captured it that day. After some skillful manuvering, with a few loses, for keeps. But even after the Germans had done their usual "dirty work" after being forced to flee, set part of it on fire. But what I want to tell you most was the beautiful sight of the flames, leaping from the interior of the stone buildings. Stone, yes. For all the buildings here in France are stone. At least I have yet to see my first frame building.

I'll say for myself after having crossed over the English Channel have passed through the greater part of this country, France, mostly via the hike road, especially in this present drive we had to do some old time "Georgia" hiking to keep up with Fritz, who is some speed king, when it comes to retreating. He having since July 16th passed through about 30 towns to the rear. And as we boys of old Pa. were continually behind him, that lends proof to my above brag that we have seen most of France.

But to get back to my story of passing through the burning town. One of the boys from Pottsville who was near me at the time said, "This is real. The movies have nothing on it" and I agreed with him, for the buildings were then burning furiously all around us, and the heat was so intense that at times we had to run past certain parts, in order to avoid casualties. The running part was very difficult for the fire had burnt down several telegraph poles, strung thickly with wires, used for German communications, before the town was captured by the Americans. The wires were then laying in the street through which we had to pass. And many times the boys became entangled in them, which made progress difficult. But we finally got settled in our position and awaited orders, which came about day light. The orders were cross the river and clean out the machine gun nests in different houses, barns etc. Well, we did it. It did not take so very long for when we got in among them, throwing smoke bombs, hand grenades, etc. it did not take them long to come out of their hiding places. They soon came running with that old cry of theirs. "Kamerad Kamerad Kamerad." In all we captured 57 prisoners. At present we are waiting to be relieved for a period of ten or twenty hours, in which time we will go a good many miles behind the lines, to have a real rest.

So do not worry about me, for I am all right and in the best of health. I will write often when we are here. I saw the letter of mine that John had printed in the paper. Sending my love to Dad, Sis and brother Jack, and also my love to you.

I am your loving son,
James.

August 15, 1918—Yanks land at Vladivostok, Russia. The Allied forces claim they have taken 73,000 prisoners and 1,700 guns in one month's time.

Fighting on the Marne with the Pennsylvania Boys

> August 16, 1918
> George Whitmeyer
> Section 502, Ambulance Corps.
> A.E.F.
> Somewhere in France.

Things have moved so fast in the past few days I have been unable able to even send a note, but have kept a diary in hopes that I would get time to write a letter. However when I did get time off I was so all in I slept every minute of spare time. The following is copied from my diary since the drive began, and it has been some drive, too, believe me.

On July 20th, went on duty with the New England Division and all was quiet till three p.m. when a terrible barrage started by the whole Allied armies, our barrage by field artillery being some strong. Then a few minutes later when the ground ahead of our infantry had been bombarded good to get the Hun out of the way, and away from their machine guns our men started over the top, and then the work of the ambulance started. We worked all our machines, 20 in all and worked all night long in a terrible rain, and all day Jul 21st, then about five o'clock we had all the wounded from the field and returned to our little farm house and packed our clothing and started after the boys into the territory just taken from the Hun.

We advanced about eight miles, then established a new base for our machines and a base hospital dressing station till the base hospital could advance. We scouted up the road and then ran into the second lines. Then found out where they were taking their wounded and started them on their way to the rear. They did not have so many, so by daylight we had cleared all the places up. We stopped for breakfast, then back to the lines, but in the meantime the boys were waiting for dawn, so they went over the top again, and we had plenty of work all day, and with each trip we had to go farther and farther forward as they certainly were making some headway.

At one place we could command a good view from the hill, and could see the Huns going for all they were worth and our boys not so very far behind them. At six p.m. they halted and dug in for the night, which gave the Boche time to get their artillery into line and fire on them, so we had to go up to the lines under heavy fire with dressings and get the wounded. The roads were terrible to get over. It started to rain and when it got dark we just crawled over the roads, being pulled out of ditches by the men along the road.

Our artillery then came up and got into position for the morrow, and our advance guards and machine gunners started out for their posts in front of the infantry. There they ran into an ambush and Co. A of the Yankee Division was almost completely wiped out by the Hun shock troops, so those who were not wounded were killed out right, and only 30 some got through their fire. I had just come in from a trip and the lieutenant told me to call for four machines to go to headquarters and that I should take the lead and get the guide on my machine to the place we were going for wounded men.

Well, I started out, and one of the men stopped after we got near headquarters saying he had trouble with his machine, he then got on with another man for company, letting his machine along the road. We got to HQ and their [*sic*] the lieutenant of this ambushed company got on the machine and told us we weren't going up to the front behind the machine gunners but in front of the front line of infantry, and if we wanted to have cold feet it was to be then and not when we were on the way. Well we all said we would take a chance, so off we started, and the man who dropped out first and got on with the other man, got the other man to drop out, so that left two of us to go after the men.

We finally got to the front lines and were stopped by the outposts, but when he was sure we were Americans and we talked U.S. such as "What the hell do you mean by stopping an ambulance," etc. he left us pass, then it was into the open fields and out on to a little patch of woods, where the machine gunners had an outpost. We got there by the best of luck, after backing and twisting around shell holes, and to our disappointment the machine guns were not there but had moved back to the infantry lines, as it had gotten too hot for them in those few woods.

So the lieutenant and we two drivers grabbed a litter and started to the front of those woods where the company had been ambushed, and we had to duck to the ground to let a German patrol go by, then the lieutenant said stay here until I get back to the infantry and get a guard for us, so we fell back to the woods and waited ages, but only 40 minutes until he was back with ten infantrymen as guards.

We finally got all the men we could find and made three trips to this place, then our artillery started in on a barrage to drive the Hun from their positions, and we had to leave that ground as some shells were falling short. We had too many men for the ambulances, and we had to take the men, so while we were considering what we would do the Boche started a barrage and shells started to fall all around us. We just packed the men in two on a litter, and some hanging on the side of the Ford, some on the fenders and off we went irregardless [*sic*] of shell holes, and by more good luck made the front lines and back to the hospital with our loads.

There we reported and our names were taken by the Colonel, and my lieutenant was tickled skinny with our work but gave us rats for being such fools as to go out in no mans land for wounded when we did not have to. It seems that the two men who had dropped out had come back with both machines and to save their faces said their machines could not stand the work, and reported to the lieutenant where we had gone. In all it took us three hours and ten minutes to do this work, just one trip but never again will I consent to go into such little hell. Went to sleep at seven o'clock and slept till two, then back on duty again.

At 11 o'clock coming from the front, I passed the 28th Division of Penna National Guards going into the lines. I stopped and asked them where the Pottsville boys were, and they reported that they had all been split up, but most of them were in the 112th Infantry and that was on the road behind them. I had to turn off the road before I came up, with the boys as I had a load of wounded, and when I came back they were not around.

So our boys went into the lines on the night of the 23rd and the morning of the 24th of July. They made an attack at daybreak and carried the lines away back, making good headway. We kept going all day moving forward at nightfall and had covered seven miles that the boys had gained during the day. They kept the ambulances jumping to keep up to them establishing dressing stations.

July 25th at one a.m. we moved farther ahead and established another field hospital and I am glad to say not many Pennsylvania men have fallen, they with the Yankee boys from New England have the Boche on the run so fast they will kill the Hun by running them. They captured a supply train with all supplies and over 400 horses. Many big guns and machine guns, just turned them around and are using them to good effect on the Boche.

The Germans are certainly leaving everything behind, and this is the Crown Prince's Army. Wonderful boy he must be. In one place we came to supper was still on the table of their Headquarters and officers horses in the stable, another place they found truck loads of brass they had taken from the clocks and farm implements. All this was left behind, so you can imagine how fast they have to go to keep ahead of our boys. I bet the Hun thinks those hawg fed boys of the eastern states are all marathon runners the way they keep them going.

When I returned in the evening I learned by official bulletin of the ambulance service of John Crane's death and Walter Lecher being severely wounded. I know, it certainly makes a fellow think when he is driving alone on these roads at night, who will be next. However, it must be, and we try to pack all our troubles and smile.

July 26th. Was sent out about ten miles back of the lines to follow up the 104th Infantry, who had just come out of the lines, and to stay there with them till further notice, as they were going to be relieved and it is expected that Section 502 will go with them to get organized and repair our machines, as most of them are down and out, and we only have seven men in our company driving now, five killed and 32 sick or wounded, so we don't soon get relieved by headquarters we won't be able to be relieved at all, as the whole company will be nit.

Am now with the 104th Infantry just laying around taking life easy, and hope I am left here until I get rested up and the section gets relieved. Will do all I can to go to see our boys, and if I once get them located I'll manage to detour around their way and as we drivers cooperate with the Red Cross, will see that they lack nothing in the way of hot chocolate and cigarettes.

George Whitmeyer

The Pennsylvania Boys Are Doing What She Has Done in All Wars

August 16, 1918
Wagoner. William T. Knight
Co. D 103rd Engineers
28th Division
A.E.F.
Somewhere in France.

Parents:

Just these few lines to let you know I am still kicking and well and happy, and hope this will find you all in the best of health and happy. But I guess you are happy in the states for the work our boys [are] doing over here. They sure are doing wonderful work here. And you can bet we are right in the big stuff. We were not over here any more than three weeks when we were in it. And the Pennsylvania boys are doing what she has done in all the other wars before this one. I think she has her name on the front page of history in this war already. But it sure is a hard job. We have a tough army to beat but I think Americans are a little tougher than they are. We licked the best they had; the Prussian Guards, and you know what they are cracked up to be. But they all look alike to our men. I met an infantryman the other day and asked him how he liked to stand up against them. He said they are all Germans to them. He said the bigger they come the harder they fall. So you see with that kind of spirit it won't take long to beat them. All we need is the people at home to keep things moving the way they have been and we will do the rest over here. You know its in the states where the war will be won. We wouldn't be much use over here if we didn't have the eats and ammunition to finish the Boche. So lets hope they keep the good work going for a while. For its up to America to win the war.

Those poor people over here sure have suffered. You don't see many young Frenchmen around here any more. They sure do love their country and flag. They would do anything for the American soldiers. I didn't learn to speak French yet, but I am able to get along making signs to them I didn't see any French people now for over a month only soldiers.

It sure is awful the way the Germans have wrecked the towns and villages they have retreated through since we are after them. What were once big towns are now only piles of stone and twisted Iron. They didn't as much leave a small shanty standing in some towns. In one big town we chased them out of they smashed all the furniture and pictures with axes, and mirrors in all the houses slashed bed clothes and everything they could cut to pieces. They are more like wild beasts than men. I would rather give up two lives if I had them than have an American family live under German rule. They know we have them beaten, and they don't care what they do now. They don't like to show themselves when the Americans are around. For as soon as they do they are knocked off, for the Americans sure can shoot straight.

After you get near the front line and hear a few shots you get used to them. If Fritz don't send them flying around your head every day there is something wrong. We sure were kept busy since we are here. This is worse than when we were training at Camp Hancock.

William I. Knight.

August 17, 1918—Three million men are now under arms for the U.S. with 1,450,000 men in France. Three hundred thirty-nine German airplanes are shot down in one week.

The "Old Keystone State" Has Reason to Be Proud

August 18, 1918
Col. George C. Rickards
Commander 112th Regiment.
28th Division
A.E.F.
Somewhere in France.

My Dear Wife

I have just come through hell, with all its horrors. I have won a victory that is the talk of the Corps and for which I and my command have been commended by all, from the Corps commander to brigade commander.

With my regiment and a battalion of the 111th in reserve I accomplished in a day and night what two brigades had failed to do in five days. I cannot write of it now it is all to vivid in my mind. I am unhurt, I have a number of men killed or wounded, as was to be expected. Killed three of the enemy to one of us and took many prisoners. I had none that I knew of who were captured.

I have a German officer, a prisoner, sitting with me now. Had others, but I sent them to division. Will send this one in few minutes if I don't kill him. On the night of August 16, the Boche went after a field hospital that is situated about a mile from where I am now, about it, but by some kind Providence they dropped five or six bombs in and not one exploded. There were between 400 and 500 wounded and about 10 women nurses in it at the time. It is a very unusual thing that shells and bombs do not explode, perhaps on an average of one out of five, but to have the whole lot fall is a strange thing and hard to account for. A great many of the Boche explosives are failing to explode now. Why we do not know, but we do know that we are mighty thankful for it and hope that the percentage will continue to get larger as time goes on.

The old Keystone State has reason to be proud of her troops. We have just come out of a very tight place. I have never been in hell and have prayed all my life, and continue to do so, to be kept from it. But that place can be no worse than what this regiment has been through in the last week or more, and came out with honor to every officer and man, and a higher place in the estimation of those higher in authority.

We have lost many of our comrades, but the proportion is about one to eight, that is, for every one of our boys that the Boche got he had to give up not less than eight of his. We have a lot of wounded but the Boche has more. We took a lot of prisoners and munitions, the Boche got none from us.

May the God of battles continue with us until the final victory, which will break forever the power of the Kaiser and give to the world a peace that shall last as long as the foundations of the world may stand. We should all like to be home, but this work must be done first and we ask the prayers and support of all good people that we accomplish this mission in the shortest time and then return to God's own country to enjoy the quiet and peace of home and loved ones.

George C. Rickards.

The Dough Boys Say the Engineers Have It Soft

August 22, 1918
Pvt. Hobart S. Wilson
Co. D 103rd Engineers
28th Division
A.E.F.
Somewhere in France.

Dear Friend:

You state you work 14 hours a day for 7 days. Good! You will soon be up to me. Two meals in sixty hours with one canteen full of water for the same period.

Just now I am sitting on a chair (?) on the side of a valley and with a pair of field glasses around my neck to look for Jerry—Wow birds. I have seen some fine air battles with fatal results for one side or the other. Just at present, Jerry is getting very inconsiderate as to where he shoots some of his big stuff.

The Dough Boys used to say that an engineer never gets into the fight and had it soft. Well. I think they were right about the fight part as we don't get in any of it. We just lie still and wait for the next one to make a direct hit on you. Some soft? I have seen houses knocked down on the top of a wine cellar I was in. I was chased through a yard by a "WoW" bird with a machine gun. Saw the tiles knocked off the type of a wall on top of me by a "Whiz Bang") and the latest and closest was a six inch shell hit three feet from the foot of my dugout, that was two feet deep with a door on top with dirt on top of that. It made a hole eight feet across and five feet deep. The roof fell in and dirt came in covering me up to the knees and the fellows in the next dugout were covered up to the shin and had to be pulled out. Due to kind providence and the fact that I was below the surface with a cover that broke the force of the concussion, the worst I got was a bad scare and a headache.

This country was made for fighting as it is full of hills, valleys and rivers in the right place to be defended by the party there first. The houses are of stone with thick walls that withstand a shock that if the same were to happen in New York City, the buildings would be falling for a week. The country without a doubt is the most beautiful country I have ever seen and it does not take more than a glance to tell just where Jerry had been.

Your Friend,
Hobart.

The origin of the expression "doughboy" is disputed. The first time it was used in reference to the American soldier was during the Mexican War 1846-47, where it was used in reference to the infantry. It was then used sparingly all the way up to World War I. Some of the theories as to the origin of doughboy concern the way soldiers cooked their rations using flour. The button theory relates to the fact that American infantrymen wore coats with large round brass buttons that vaguely looked like the flour dumplings eaten by the soldiers. One other theory is that during the Mexican War soldiers made so much dust while marching in the arid areas of northern Mexico that the soldiers looked like the local adobe buildings, and adobe sounded like doughboy. The American soldiers were also known as Yank, short for Yankees, or Sammies, after Uncle Sam. But the one thing that remains is the World War I American soldier will forever be known as the doughboy.

Last Night I Stepped on a Bunch of Rats

August 23, 1918
Corporal L. F. Krantz
Co. B 320th Mortar Battery
A.E.F.
Somewhere in France.

Dear Sister:

You say the weather is hot over there. It is awful cool over here and plenty of rain. It rained last night something awful. I thought old Bill threw a shell into a cloud. It was a very dark night. I nearly broke my neck several times going through the woods. I always carry a cane to feel my way. I told you I was made a Corporal and it is up to me to relieve the man at the guns. I go around and waken the men to go on guard and believe me, it is some job. They sleep in many different places so I must find them.

Last night I stepped on a bunch of rats and they gave a yell. Of course you know what I did. As a rule, a Yank will take it calm and pull out an automatic and look for trouble. You can never tell whether it is a German or a rat for we compare the German to the rat. They crawl along the ground in the same manner. They also love a hole like a rat. The first thing they do is beat it in a hole. I think they laid in their holes long enough and for the last time for the Yanks are like cats and have them moving in all directions.

I wish you were here in this moment. An air battle is over our heads, shells flying every way. It isn't very pleasant to be under it for the shrapnel flies in all parts of the field. They say it is the best thing to stay in one spot so I think I will continue with this letter. Shells are passing over head and as long as they keep going they won't move me.

I suppose the rats are in their holes for there is an awful noise. We have a cat, but she has no chance here for they are like jack rabbits. At night they run over our bunks and scare a guy. The other night, one of our boys got bitten on the nose with one. He got up in the morning and had a nice mark on his nose, so we doped it out, it was a rat. Between rats, cooties and Germans it keeps a guy busy. Last night I went to bed (we call it a bed) and slept fine. I believe it would have taken all the shells old Bill had to waken me. They told me a bunch of shells came over but I never heard them. I was out one night until one o'clock and saw some bust. My Lieut. gave me a Springfield rifle so I expect to do some sniping. I would like to have old Bill for a target. I would pick his whiskers off one by one.

I am in perfect health and can eat and sleep any place. I can sleep on a wash line and cover myself with a shoe string.

L. F. Krantz.

August 27, 1918—The United States forces take Bazoches, three miles west of Fismes.

August 28, 1918—General Pershing praises American troops.

One of the First American Boys on German Soil

> August 26, 1918
> Private Joseph Cookson
> Co. A 61st Infantry Regiment
> 5th Division
> A.E.F.
> Somewhere in France.

Dear Brother:

Well kid since arriving in these "Napoleon Bonaparte" diggins I traveled from east to west and from north to south. I have been in Belgium, Switzerland, and have the honor of being one of the first American boys on German soil, for which I am to get a silver bar on this occasion. We are known all along the front in this sector as the "Wildcats Playmates" since we went over the top without a barrage.

Its real funny to read in the papers now of some of the boys writing home, saying they can hear the big guns rumbling—well the worst is yet to come, believe me. I'll never forget my first experience in the front line in the latter part of April. It was a dark, cold, rainy night and the Hun trenches were only 70 yards away. I wasn't afraid, but Oh, Boy, how I wished I was back on dear old Centre St. The rain was dropping from the trees and if I am not mistaken the trees were walking all along the front line. There were two little cats in front of my trench, and I thought they were Huns. Well, I started some noise with hand grenades and naturally the other boys thought it was the Hun coming, so they all opened up. No one was ever so glad to see daylight as I was and then discovered the cats blown to pieces.

Well, kid when are you coming over the big pond? I would like to see you in this big pastime that I volunteered for, but look out for "Subs" and the only thing you want to surrender is your meals—I'll say I did.

The atmosphere is fine (wess paw) as the French say. We just arrived here for a well deserved rest, but expect to be back where the fun is in a few days.

A very dear old friend of mine from Buffalo is pushing up daisies now all on account of a dirty Hun, but my bayonet fixed him. It was either him

Three Pennsylvania officers pose with some captured German officers and enlisted men, 1918.

or me, kid. I haven't seen to[o] much of their dirty work with their hand grenades up their sleeves and if you take your eyes off of them it means "Bye Bye World." I had a bullet shot through my helmet, and thanks to the guy who invented steel helmets, Kid I could tell you different things, but I doubt if they will pass the censor.

I am in the best of health even if I have cows in the next room of this Hotel De Barn and pigs under the steps. Well I must stop trying to talk to you on paper, as it is almost time for chow. The cooties keep us busy at all times. They don't bite they just grab hold and pull.

Remember me to all the folks and my friends, and write often and tell mother not to neglect to send me the papers. Will close, with love to Mildred.

Sincerely,
Joe

By order of General Pershing:
To the Third and Fourth Corps, comprising the 1st, 2nd, 4th, 26th, 28th, 32nd and 42nd Divisions of the American Expeditionary Forces.

"You came to the battlefront at a crucial hour for the Allied cause. For almost four years the most formidable army the world has yet seen had pressed its invasion of France and stood threatening its capital. At no time has the army been more powerful and menacing than when, on July 15, it struck again to destroy in one great battle the brave men opposed to it, and to enforce its brutal will upon the world.

"Three days later, and in conjunction with our Allies, you counter attacked. The Allied Armies gained a brilliant victory that marks the turning point of the war. You did more than to give the allies the support to which, as a nation, our faith was pledged. You proved that our altruism, our pacific spirit and our sense of justice have not blunted our virility, or our courage.

"You have shown that American initiative and energy are as fit for the tasks of war as for the pursuits of peace. You have justly won unstinted praise for our allies and the eternal gratitude of our countrymen.

"We have paid for our success with the lives of many of our brave comrades. We shall cherish their memory always and claim for our history and literature their bravery, achievement and sacrifice."

August 31, 1918—1,533,000 United States troops in France.

7

September 1918
"On to Cambrai"
Is the Cry

September 1, 1918—Yanks take Voormezeele in Belgium.

Make Knots, Kid!

September 1, 1918
Pvt. Jack Scheibelhut
Co. D 103rd Engineers
28th Division
A.E.F.
Somewhere in France.

Dear Dad:

I received your letter today and sure enjoyed both of them. It is wonderful to receive mail, it makes a fellow feel great.

I slept in quite a few dugouts and believe me, I would sleep in them if they were rotten, because they are safer than standing outside and letting that "dirty Dutch, rat" spit at you.

I got your letter on the 29th of August. Some time it took to come. I'll say Dad, don't worry about the Huns getting me, just you keep your spirits up. I'll do the rest. If you want any souvenirs from old Fritz, I can get any amount of them.

We have a chaplain here and we have mass every morning. This morning we had a mass in an old church that is in half ruins, quite a few shell holes in the sides, it was wonderful. I am at Battalion Headquarters, just now and that is in a small town so we can go to church. We had a choir composed of the sing and whistle of Fritz's shells. They were dropping a few hundred feet away but no harm was done. Dad, that is the best thing about the shells, you can hear them coming, they whistle and sing through the air and all you must do is duck and lay flat and if some distance from you, get up and run for a dugout or shelter.

Over here, we say when you run from them, "Make Knots, Kid," and you can tell the world we do. Dad

When I get back you will have to beat pans and get the loan of a cannon, so I can go to sleep. I'll take a pick and shovel, go out in the back yard and dig a dugout for myself, then I feel at home. I often wonder how it feels to go to sleep with everything quiet and in a nice soft bed.

There was an air battle going on just a while ago. That is some excitement. Those "Birds" do some awful stunts when they chase a Hun. Talk about speed, they can go 125 miles an hour without any trouble. The best kind of fight is when there are about twenty or more at it in the air. That is some sport, everyone waiting for the Hun "bird" to bite the ground and when they fall they make about 400 miles an hour, some speed coming down.

An air raid is a great sight at night, especially the first one I saw. It was in a town we billeted at while going through France. The first thing we heard was the alert, that's an alarm given to the people to get under cover. We all stood out to watch it instead of getting under. The big powerful search lights play a steady stream of light on the plane and the aircraft guns hammer away "for fair." You hear the sing of the shells going up and burst. The Huns dropped a few of his compliments, a few hundred yards away and they made some noise. The next day we went to see the damage done. After we saw a hole it made, we changed our minds about looking at them. I don't go looking for them now. I saw quite a few of them and was not very far away. Now when I hear our friend coming with a load he wants to get rid of, I just beat it for the nearest dugout. There are wonderful tales to tell of this year. I could entertain you for a year.

Fritz is dropping a few now but they are falling in an empty field. He can drop them all day there is nobody home. I like to watch them burst when they are far away. I don't know what they look like before they "spit" because I have never had the heart to look at them when they are close.

Well, Dad, I think I have said quite a bit and will now close with love to you and Sis, I remain

Your Son,
Jack.

Brave Pennsylvanians in Battle

September 4, 1918
Special War Correspondent
Raymond G. Carroll
Philadelphia Public Ledger.

In a letter dated September 4, 1918, Raymond G. Caroll recounts thrilling deeds performed by Pennsylvania soldiers at the battle of Fismette.

Fismette is a village across the river Vesle from Fismers, France. The stone hedge road a continuation of the Fismes main street. Three miles west ward is Bazoches town. Both places have been scenes of desperate battles between American troops and the courier attacking German picked shock troops intent upon teaching a lesson to the newcomers of war.

During the preceding month the towns of Fismette and Bazoches changed hands several times. Ceaseless enemy shells, machine gun, and rifle fire have been encountered by the intrepid American soldiers. Especially has it been so at the approaches to the bridge and on the bridge itself.

Numerous deeds of heroism are recited. Sergt. Ralph E. Ord. of Dravosburg Pa. and Sergt. Alois J. Guenther helped to clear Fismette of snipers. At one time they rescued a wounded soldier by crawling along on their hands and knees and thus they hauled him up into the American lines. They also rescued several others by dragging them from the shell swept area, where these men had fallen wounded grievously.

Private Fred Ott carried messages between Fismette and Fismes five days swimming the river under fire and avoiding wire entanglements in its bottom. Private Mike Fisher, of Pittsburgh fearlessly and safely crossed the shell and machine gun swept bridge while carrying messages and escorted over the bridge, one at a time, 25 wounded men. Fisher seemed to have a charmed life.

Sergeant Tom Cavanaugh, Pittsburgh, organized a strong point at a bridge across the Vesle, controlling the approaches. He also volunteered and stood in the open doorway in Fismette under enemy fire and directed to safety the American wounded.

Captain Edward H. Lynch of old Company B 6th Regt. Chester Pa.

seeing that his lieutenants, Glendenning, Pittsburgh and Fitzgerald, New York City who with a detail of the company were making an attack were in danger of being out flanked by a German machine gun unit, that had gotten around to their rear unobserved, single handed advanced with his automatic gun blazed away and killed six of the Germans before they got him. The Lieutenants and men hearing the shots in their rear took a safer position and thus were saved from annihilation. Lynch was 31 years of age and was elected Captain of Co. B just before the company went to Mexico's border. He hailed from Sharon Hill. A dispatch from Chester said that he was the most popular commander the company had in 50 years.

Seven officers and men performed a fearless feat in holding the left of a sector during the German frontal attack beyond Fismette lying for twelve hours in shell holes in the open under a hail of bullets and other projectiles, and at the same time pumping into the enemy lines a hail of deadly bullets, preventing repeated attempts to out flank.

In desperate fighting on another section of the line, one company of Americans is reported to have trimmed an entire regiment of Germans.

Lieut. Robert B. Woodbury, cited for bravery at Fismette, was a member of Co. D 103rd Regiment of Engineers and won the promotion to lieutenant by personal qualities. He is still a member of the law firm Woodbury & Woodbury of this city and is married. He was appointed a lieut. in a Chester company of the former Sixth Regiment. Lieut. Walter Ettinger, cited for bravery with Lieut. Woodbury, according to a dispatch from Chester, is from the Southland, and had been assigned to duty at the Remington rifle factory near Chester before assignment to the company.

Valiant Comrades of Co. H 112th Regt. 28th Division

> September 4, 1918
> Special War Correspondent
> Raymond G. Caroll
> *Philadelphia Public Ledger.*

Lieut. Horst Lutz, captured in a ravine by American troops along with another officer and 60 German soldiers, evinced admiration he felt for an American officer and a body of fine soldiers who held forlorn hope in Fismette a village north of the river on the south side of which is Fismes, by inquiring whether this officer and his men had escaped. Then under the spur of the Intelligence section he revealed something that led to full disclosure of the facts.

Lieut. Lutz led one of the companies that led a fierce attack on the 190 American soldiers and six officers who held the thin line of khaki, a half circle around the outskirts of the town. Tuesday, August 27, tiny Fismette once more was a bloody cockpit when at 11:35 o'clock, the fury of the German barrage broke upon it without the slightest warning. It was a concentration of fire from a wide range—gas, shrapnel, smoke bombs, machine gun spray all were used. Overhead airplanes dropped torpedoes and now and then swooped low through the air and swept the trenches with machine gun fire.

Soon came the rush of German infantry. Not an American wavered. Officially it was reported of this fight, "Some in American uniform ran among our troops shouting further resistance was useless, and one of the officers advised everybody to surrender. Out of our men only two officers and about 30 men retreated, fighting and firing and reaching the northern bank of the river."

The soldier who spread this report is believed to have been a German in an American uniform. Far inside the American lines a German soldier named Max Kau of the 463rd German Infantry was shot and mortally wounded by American soldiers. He had lived in the United States for many years. The man was well stocked with food. It is altogether probable that the man who shouted surrender in Fismette was another German soldier spy.

No surrender was the motto of Lieut. Turner and his men. "Surrender Hell, I should say not." Shouted Lieut. Turner, who was a grizzled sergeant of the regulars before he was promoted to a lieutenancy some months before this and assigned to the 112th.

"We will fight it out," said he to his men. This was in the dim light of the early day of the 28th. By 8 a.m. he and his men were at the point of a salient and almost surrounded. They commenced to drop back dealing out death in defiance as they moved. By 9:00 o'clock they were near the river Vesle north bank. Within 100 feet of the battered Fismette bridge they dropped into a shattered stone house and began to pump streams of missiles at the following but wary Germans, who had a dear dose of their medicine. Their fusillade was described by the German Lieut., as a fearful and veritable blaze of fire, filled with shot.

The Lieut. Then had with him six intrepid soldiers, Sergeant Richard Moore and Private William Fileshifter, of Ridgway, on the edge of oil country, Pa. Privates Frank Incoushi, Port Carbon, Pa. And O. H Hunt, Logan W.Va., Private Ralph Letcher, Pottsville Pa., Private Douglas Hunt Factoryville, Pa. Private Stanley Savage, Pottsville.

Private Letcher said, "Lieut Turner told us to stick until reinforcements came across the river. The heavy barrage laid down by the Germans prevented that. In an adjoining building a machine gun was kept popping away, and that helped us, but at 10:30 a big German shell smashed the building and we heard the machine gun no more. We should like to know if our brave and unknown supports got away.

"The Lieut. encouraged us at every emergency, advising us to keep cool and fight on. We had three Springfields and two automatic platoons. Men from our other platoons crossed the river, some swimming and others crossing the bridge by jumping over the broken parts.

"At 11:30 the Lieut. Shouted 'You men clear out, I will stay awhile and follow later'; he had seen it was useless to hold on. We refused to go. So he started with us making a bluff that he too would go along. When we got to the river edge he wrote his wife's address on a piece of paper and gave it to me. In ten minutes he was across the river and directing us how to get out of the ruins of the river front in Fismes and get into the dugout further back, from which we later crossed the Vesle and recaptured Fismette."

Savage said, "I got a few Germans and I am going to get some more." Savage was reared about the coal mines and is not afraid of anything human. Frank Inoushi is a typical Schuylkill lad, not anxious for a scrap, but dangerous if he gets in one. Letcher he is a devotee of baseball and athletics, a typical Pennsylvania lad.

I Surely Did See Enough Huns Already

September 4, 1918
PFC Raymond J. Ruppert
Co. D 103rd Engineers
28th Division
A.E.F.
Somewhere in France.

Mr. Frank Muehold:

Just a few lines to let you know that I am well, and that I arrived in France safely and have been in the big drive, but am still among the living, for I don't think that old Kaiser Bill has any shells with my name or number on it. I hope that he doesn't for I sure do want to get back. And take it from me I'll never leave again in a hurry unless I have too. Well, I surely did see enough Huns already, and I don't care if I ever see another one for I am well satisfied. I am back of the lines now with Captain Reese he is an instructor at one of the schools, so I am taking care of him and he surely is some Captain, and say the boys surely do like him for he [*sic*] like a father to them.

We are just having an awful thunder storm and at times when it thunders I don't know whether it is a cannon or a shell bursting. I have a little poem here I want you to read.

A disabled German tank in the American sector of trenches in 1918.

In Memory of July 15, 1918

*Twas in the year 1918
On the fifteenth of July
And in the early morning
When dawn came through the sky
The guns roared like thunder,
And the shells came on so fast.
The shrapnel flew around us
The earth seemed to be shaking
Whenever a shell hit the ground
Sent dirt and shrapnel flying
For many yards around.
The flashes of the cannon
Told us that they were near,
But we held the front line trenches
And showed no sign of fear.
They killed and wounded many,
My best pal seemed to fall,
Not knowing when my time would come
Or I would hear death call.
The sky begins to brighten
The daybreak is at hand,
A day that to us was heaven
Since we saw into "No Mans Land,"
The barbed wire completely shattered
In pieces everywhere
The trees were cut to kindling,*

> *And shell holes everywhere.*
> *If you raised your head above the trench*
> *To look around and see,*
> *A bullet would just skip your bean*
> *From a sniper in a tree.*
> *The day it brought no ending,*
> *We thought it time to rest.*
> *But the shells still dropped around us,*
> *As we carried off our mess.*
> *In order to get water*
> *On the ground we had to crawl,*
> *Make our way back to the trenches*
> *As we hear the big shells fall.*
> *If the champion "Negro Dodger"*
> *In the states I used to see;*
> *Was dodging high explosives,*
> *He'd have nothing sure on me.*
> *We gained a reputation*
> *For sticking to our mission,*
> *And we are known the world over*
> *As the "Corking Iron Division."*
> *They sure did send them over*
> *A hundred at a time*
> *And all the shells in Germany*
> *Just dropped around our line.*
> *That night I'll ne'er forget.*
> *And I'll picture in my mind*
> *The special shell with my name on*
> *The Kaiser left behind.*

I am glad that he did leave mine behind if there is one with my name on it. I guess the people in the states were surprised to here we were in that drive. Well the only place I want to see here is Paris, and if there is any way to get there why I'll be there.

Best wishes to all as ever,
Ray J. Ruppert

The shell with Ray Ruppert's name on it found him on September 4th and ten days later on September 14th he died of his wounds.

September 5, 1918—The American troops reach the Aisne line; Germans burn supplies along the entire front.

September 8, 1918—British regain positions lost in March; Yanks cross Aisne canal.

I Would Fill My Canteen with "Dew Lay"

September 8, 1918
Corporal Frank Miller
Co. F 348th Infantry Regiment
87th Division
A.E.F.
Somewhere in France.

Dear Mother:

I was unable to write before this on account of our moving around. We were moved to the rear of the lines for a rest after spending about seventy-five days on the front. It certainly feels great to be back around civilization again and where we can go to town and buy things. Also to go to the Y.M.C.A. and hear music and read magazines. I don't know how long we will be back from danger but I hope it will be a few months. While we are back here we must drill at work at that, it's peaceful. We were out to drill this morning for the first time, but the rain chased us to our barracks. I guess we will go out this afternoon again.

On the fifth of September, we were in a pretty hot place doing some work under shell fire, and when we were finished and on our return, the Boche saw us and started to shell us again. I got a slight shrapnel wound in the left leg but my gas mask saved me from a bad wound, as it is I was lucky. My wound is pretty well healed up already. It was not serious enough to go to the hospital.

This is the third birthday spent in the army. The next one will be at home. I had sometime this birthday. I took a bath and washed all the clothing I owned then searched for the many friends we carry with us. After that was done, I went back to my bunk which was in a straw heap over the top of a cow stable. Nearly every morning I would hear the madame come out to milk the cow. Of course, I would get up and fill my canteen with "Dew Lay" ([as they say] in French). Believe me, I still love milk. I wish could be back home and get some of that cream before going to bed like I use[d] to. We are having an awful spell over here just now. I hope this rain will break it up, its to[o] hot to drill. I guess it will soon be cold, then I can make use of the sweater. I think it will come in good use this winter, France is a pretty cold country and fire wood is scarce.

We are expecting our July pay one of theses days, then we will be rich again. We have two months coming, I think they hold one month from us all the time. If the Hun keeps retreating so fast, we will be in Berlin by spring time. I hope they are out of France by the time we go up to the lines again, because I don't like to be in a village working while the snipers keep you ducking their bullets and blowing houses apart. I suppose the people at home have heard the casualty report from both companies. I don't think I am allowed to give a list of the wounded.

Your loving son,
Frank Miller

September 13, 1918—Seven German divisions are reported trapped at St.-Mihiel.

September 14, 1918—St.-Mihiel salient smashed in; 16,000 prisoners, 443 guns taken; Yanks in cannon shot of Metz.

Three Cylinders Is Rather Unpleasant

September 14, 1918
Lieut. Robert H. Mills
Royal Flying Corp.
Strand, London
England.

My Dear Brad:

Am enclosing some newspaper clippings to let you know what the people thought of the Yanks doings over here yesterday (Friday the 13th). This old town went wild and last night as the news was coming in, it seemed as though peace had been declared. Everybody was cheering! The Yanks are certainly "top ole" (Ace High) now, both there and in France.

In the last three days I have had the extreme pleasure (?) of taking three new machines each day from here to… And returning in old ones (for repair) is awful. Going over it is ok but coming back on one, two and never more than three cylinders is rather unpleasant and I am glad I only had to do three days of it (as I was a nervous wreck), but as I am now considered an expert on crippled machines, I might get more of it (lets hope not).

With kindest regards to all I am.

Yours,
Robert.

September 15–25—Yanks extend line westward past Verdun to Vienne Le Château.

If the English and French Would Fight Like the U.S.

> September 15, 1918
> Pvt. M. E. Hanner
> Co. D 304th Div. Supply Train.
> 76th Division
> A.E.F.
> Somewhere in France.

Dear Abe:

This is some country over here. I have not seen any of our fellows since I came over here. This is an experience!

It is pretty cold over here just now and I guess it will be cold this winter. I think before Xmas this war will be over and we will be home by spring. Our boys are doing some wonderful work if the English and French would fight like the U.S. boys this war would be over in a short time but they fight one day and rest a week. They are so far behind the times its not like the U.S. Just the way you see pictures of towns shelled to pieces that is the way they look and some are not that good.

I am feeling fine and do nothing but eat. It is such a dreary climate rains every day almost. The sun hardly ever shines. No place like the U.S.A.

> M. E. Hanner

There Were Many German Dead About

> September 20, 1918
> Sergeant A. Judson Hanna
> A.E.F.
> Somewhere in France.

The Germans as you know, had started their great offensive which was to end the war. The Americans had driven them out of Chateau Thierry and some miles north of that the Huns made a stand. Their guns stood almost wheel to wheel over some miles of the front. When the big barrage began the guns swept a whole valley from end to end, including some half dozen towns. The shells fell with surprising regularity some dozen yards apart, even closer in places. You can imagine the result. All the roads were swept. Where dugouts were available the men used them but there must always be a certain amount of traffic supply trains, ambulances, and couriers or runners as we call them.

The shell that killed practically all the personnel staff landed in the court yard of a large house, where the staff was engaged in removing its valuable records to a safer place. The shell fell on the little group, killing the lieutenant and eight men.

When the fire slackened about noon of the 15th, and the Germans attempted to follow it up with the infantry, they were hurled back by our troops and have been on the go toward Berlin ever since.

There were many German dead here and about, especially one hill where the Americans attacked them with the bayonets and the fighting was ferocious. It would surprise you to know how courageous our boys are, many of whom are mere lads, just of the draft age. The German dreads the bayonet. It seems that he abhors the use of it even by himself. The majority

What the American sailor looked like during World War I. This sailor has not been identified.

of the dead Hun did not have bayonets on their rifles. Yet they had plenty of time to resort to bayonets had they so wished.

Two middle aged Huns were found on there [*sic*] knees with clasped hands and an American bayonet through the body of each. They had evidently been caught, and feeling death near, had taken each others hands. One of our men was struck by a piece of shell while marching in line. He walked deliberately out of line, and down beside the road, as though merely weary, and died a moment later, with a smile on his face. One Hun was plugged as he was climbing out of a trench and there he was found one hand grasping the top of the parapet, one leg up, like a figure in marble.

Yesterday a company of French men passed us for their fighting line. It was a sight that stirred my heart. Not a man I think was under 45 years of age. Some were gray-bearded, many were bald. The going was hard for the old chaps; you could see the terrible weariness on their faces. They had just negotiated a long steep hill and there wasn't a smile on a face. I was glad they were going to rest. But France has youth yet. I saw some of them on my way up, travelling to the training camps. Their cars were chalked up with "Vive la classe 1919" and "A bas le Boche."

For three nights it has been quiet, no air raids even. These are particularly annoying. One simply has to lie doggie, helpless for a time, and wonder if the next bomb will light on his particular house or barn.

Some men who went through the big barrage still show the effects of it. Let a door slam, and a big healthy man will jump as if stung. Last night we had a band concert to cheer the men and make them forget if possible. I was sitting next to a friend who seems perfectly capable in every way. He had started to light a cigarette when the band struck up. The man jumped violently, dropped the match and looked around dazedly. It were all laughable were it not for the memory of those times.

One of our men, an unusually jolly fellow, has been sober since the big action. This is the reason: He had taken refuge in a dugout and was standing there when a shell crashed through the corner, just missing his waist. The shell dug into the opposite wall and the man waited for it to explode. Second after second passed. You may possibly imagine his horror, expecting every instant to be blown to atoms. As the seconds passed and there was no explosion, the man turned mechanically and went to bed. The next morning he remembered the shell and on examining it found it was a dud.

Another of our men were lying in a field under a small tree. The shells were landing all around him. One finally struck within a few feet of him covering him with dirt. He waited for it to explode, knowing the uselessness of trying to escape, and trying to prepare his mind for the bumping off of his body. Those seconds of agonized waiting for an expected tragedy may change a whole mans character. This bomb was also a dud, but the man today goes around with a strained face and seems always listening for something.

Judson.

He Laid Down His Life for the Flag

September 23, 1918
Private John G. Bolton
Co. A, 108th Machine gun Battl.
28th Division
Somewhere in France.

My Dear Mrs. Bolton:

Your letter of August 19 received today and the contents have impressed me very much as I feel the loss of every man in my company as if one of my family. Your son, Private John G. Bolton, was killed instantly in the battle of the Marne early in the morning of the 15th of July. He was buried where he fell by his comrades. His platoon was not with the company that morning it having been detached and sent to the support of an infantry detachment.

His personal effects consisted of the gold ring and 90 francs that were turned over to the effects depot and in due time will be forwarded to his nearest living relative.

They did not find any bible, which might have been in his pack, which was lost in the engagement before he was killed. As far as I know your son was true to his God to the end. I can say that he was a good soldier and was the first man out of my company to lay down his life for the flag.

As to the place of burial I am unable to give it to you for military reasons, but his grave is marked appropriately and I doubt not that after the war is over our government will convey the remains of the brave boys that fall fighting to their native country, which we all love so well.

In conclusion I will say that your other son is a good soldier and trust that he will be spared to return to you. We can only trust in the Divine Providence and look to him who doeth all things well. The boys who are here are the finest there are in America and it makes me shudder at times to see the wounded and dead, but such is war. May the people of America pray that this war is soon over and that after it shall come a lasting peace.

Captain Ralph C. Crow
108th M.G.B.

A strange occurrence happened in late September of 1920. The family of Private John G. Bolton read in a local newspaper that instead of his body lying in one of the national cemeteries in France, he was alive and well and working in Allentown, Pennsylvania, and was expected to come home soon. Just how the news of his being alive originated was not known. The true story of Bolton's death was related to his mother by Corporal Wenrich who was with Bolton when he died and saw Bolton get hit. He also personally helped in his burial. On July 15th Bolton was reloading a machine gun when a piece of shrapnel struck his dugout and caused his death. The shrapnel caused two wounds in his head. The dugout in which Bolton was killed was the only one that had not been completed among a number of dugouts. It was not deep enough and was not finished when the Germans attacked.

September 26, 1918—Yanks begin Argonne offensive.

September 27, 1918—Americans and French open new drive and American troops drive over seven miles on the first day. American troops take the Argonne with a rush that surprises the French.

September 27–28, 1918—Yanks advancing in Argonne take 16,000 prisoners.

By the Time You Get This We Will Be on German Soil

> September 27, 1918
> Pvt. Clyde Storch
> 103rd Engineers Train.
> 28th Division
> A.E.F.
> Somewhere in France.

Dear Father:

I am still alive and well hoping this letter finds you the same. We are still giving the Boche all he can take. We are on a new front now. We chased the Hun from Chateau Thierry to Fismette so now we are starting them out on this new place again. I only expect to be on this front for awhile then we go to another and start them on the run again. We expect to go to Italy from here, that is where they send the divisions for a rest as there isn't much to do down there but I guess they are waiting for the 28th to raise a little hell. I don't believe it is so bad in Hades as we are making it for the Hun. It sure is good to lay in your bed at night and listen to our boys sending the Hun a couple thousand shells over and read in our newspapers of the planes dropping tons of bombs. The British captured 55,000 prisoners and we have taken 9,000 on this front

So far and they are all old men or just kids about 16, no middle aged men at all. We are driving at his strongest point now. When he loses here and our attack proves a success we will just cut his army in two. They are now shelling a German town. By the time you get this we will be on German soil fighting. Our Dough Boys from the 28th don't wait till there is a barrage to go over the top like there is supposed to be, but go over without. The casualties on our side are very few. You can gamble that this is going to be over by Xmas. The Germans were taken by surprise on this front, we advanced 7 miles in two days. I haven't heard now how far they have gone today yet. The Hun used to rule the air but he is sure out of luck now. He is done in the air and on the ground, very few of his planes get across the lines any more. If you can get a war map you follow us up and

I will try to tell where we are. We are driving at Metz now a place the Hun
has held for three years.

Clyde.

September 29, 1918—The 27th and 30th U.S. Divisions in Hindenburg line
smash the Hindenburg Line.

8

October 1918:
Unconditional Surrender
Demanded

October 1, 1918—1,976,000 United States troops in France.

October 2, 1918—2nd and 36th United States Divisions on Rheims front.

October 3, 1918—Fearing the Americans drive into the Alsace, the German army has evacuated Flanders and the entire Western Front. Americans reach last German defensive line near Verdun.

October 4, 1918—Argonne advance resumed; 5th United States Corps takes Gesnes.

October 5, 1918—2nd U.S. Division takes Blanc Mont (Rheims sector) Front.

October 6, 1918—GERMANS ASK UNITED STATES FOR ARMISTICE.

October 7, 1918—1st U.S. Corps takes Chatel-Chehery.

October 8, 1918—United States refuses armistice. 2nd U.S. Division takes St. Etienne. Allies have penetrated to the rear of the Hindenburg line.

October 9, 1918—3rd U.S. Corps takes Brieulles in Argonne; 36th U.S. Division crosses Aisne. The American and British armies have broken through the German line. American forces are driving everything before them northeast of Verdun.

October 10, 1918—Allies take Le Cateau. Yanks have cleared the Argonne.

October 11, 1918—U.S. transport *Otranto* torpedoed. German army is still in full retreat. American troops are held up because of slow supply system.

October 14, 1918—1st U.S. Corps takes take St. Juvin. 5th U.S. Corps smashes Kriemhilde line.

October 15, 1918—President Wilson in his reply to Germany's peace proposals, says: "Unconditional surrender by Germany to the Allies is the only means of ending the war."

October 17, 1918—Germans are evacuating Flanders in haste. Flanders roads are filled with German prisoners.

I Came Out of the Attack Without a Scratch

> October 17, 1918
> Captain John Lesley Ryon
> Co. H 371st Infantry Regiment (Colored)
> 93rd Division
> A.E.F.
> Somewhere in France.

Dear Father:

We have just come out of an attack which was very successful and in which we suffered terribly. You no doubt have read the capture of Refout and Monthois. We occupied Monthois but had to retire because the Division on our flank were behind and we went too fast for our artillery. It was very exciting and terrible of course. I sent Mortimer a copy of the message from our Division Commander complimenting us. We now enjoy the highest compliment paid to French troops. "The Army Reserve Attack Troops" purely shock troops and very likely will never hold a sector again.

I have about 80 men in my company. Have lost two officers and over 100 men. We gave boche hell while we lasted. At one time during the attack, while my company was in support, the Battalion went too far to the left. My company then was the strongest so we went ahead and filled the gap. We were fired on at point blank range by Austrian 88's the worst gun the German's have. 155's and 77's and the machine gun and rifle fire was withering. I lost two officers and 75 men in less than five minutes. We advanced to the crest of a small hill. I could see the boche pulling out a big gun not more than 200 yards in front of me, and boche officers standing on a hill

American heavy artillery going into action. Many Pennsylvanians served in the artillery regiments during the war.

directing artillery fire not over 500 yards from me, and German troops marching over the next hill on several roads in columns of squads. I could not move. The fire was terrible, and one by one, we crawled to a railroad cut to our left and joined what was left of the Battalion. Major Greennough and his adjutant had fallen. That night, I took command of the battalion and commanded for three days.

I came out of the attack without a scratch. Our casualties were very heavy, and I had a very warm time. The regiment has been cited, and we have been awarded very fine privileges. We now are straight shock troops and will hold the sector no more. While the loss in my company was very large we fared the best in the regiment. Lieutenant Nesson and Lieutenant Williams fell wounded. We were nearly five days and nights without food or water and suffered from gas and exposure. We drove about 18 kilometers and at all times were at the apex. I have seen very extraordinary things and tell you some hair raising stories when I come home.

Everything looks bright now and the war is doing better than ever before, and looks as though the finish is in sight. We have had very delightful weather lately and have certainly taken advantage of it. It was impossible for me to write during the attack, of course and even now we are very busy so it is hard to get letter writing. I haven't had my clothes off for 18 days and consequently I am physically very uncomfortable but mentally very rested. I did not have my shoes off for 11 days. Can you imagine that?

As soon as I get the paper work up in the company and finish the literature on a number of dead men, I am going to get a complete new outfit. I am well but very tired. Yesterday we traveled over 200 miles. It looks like another attack as soon as we are replaced.

Love to all,
Lesley

October 19, 1918—U.S. rejects Austrian peace plan.

I Have Been Over the Top Now a Couple of Times

October 19, 1918
Captain Harry Cooney
Company K. 314th Infantry Regt.
79th Division
A.E.F.
Somewhere in France

Dear friend Bob:

Well, "Old Top." I am pounding away once again and its you who will stand for the "bull" this time so brace up for I just feel like throwing it for now for we have just landed back from the big show where we have been since it started Sept. 26th. We are now about ten miles from the front of today and still can hear those big boys pounding away for they never let up day or night, but even tho we are so close to it, they are not bothering us as they have moved the largest and only the heavy field pieces are on our front. They only have a range of about twelve miles at the maximum. Of course, we get a few bombs every clear night, which is very seldom for we have very few clear nights over here. Yesterday was the first that we saw the sun since October.

I have seen about all there is to see "over here" for I have been "over the top" now a couple of times. The fact of the matter is it has been one continuous "over the top" since Sept. 26th and believe me boy, I have had my share. They can't call this off too soon to suit me, its just hell and the worst kind of it, but then I am glad I have seen it for it is something that each fellow must see to appreciate and all I could say would not let you see things the way they are. Just try to picture all the worst kinds of hell that you can think of and triple it and then perhaps you have a faint idea of what it is like.

My outfit suffered very heavy casualties, for I only have 137 out of 250, of course most of them are injured. I only lost two officers out of five which was extremely lucky and personally I have nothing to complain about for I suffered very little outside of the many things that one can expect in times like these. I got an occasional taste of gas but it did not put me out any time and I think that if they give us a couple of weeks in this area to recuperate that I will be ready to go at them again. We have got the whole business on the run now and I believe we will keep them going at least. I hope so, for that is the only way it looks to me, but until they chase old man Bill, we could make it just as hot as it is possible to do. We captured quite a few in our drive and those that we could talk to said it couldn't last much longer and they seemed glad to be with us. Most of them are young fellows, all the way from 15 to 20 and some old men about 45. We ran into some Prussian regiments which put up a good fight and in most cases, they would fight until we killed them, but others would give up mighty easy after they saw we would take some of their comrades prisoners, they would come out and surrender. I suppose the poor devils do not know what they are fighting for. They have good outer garments but their underwear is made out of paper and very poor. They seem to be well fed as all the dugouts that I went into were well supplied with eats and everything else and all the prisoners had some food with them. It is nothing unusual to find a big piece of weiner-wurst stuck in the lining of their coats in the hope that we would overlook it. I always left the poor devils have it.

I ran into "Shea" who worked on the road at the same time I did. He is a big buck private in the 315th Infantry which is in our division. We were hiking after the show was over, that is, we were relieved and he saw me and hollered at me and we had a chat for about 5 minutes. I didn't know him at first, he looks smaller than when I last saw him. I also met Fisher who worked in Divies at the time I did. He is also in the 315th Infantry. I met him when we were getting the hell shot out of us. He looked pretty low at the time, but I guess I looked just about as bad for none looked as though they would like to work at this job for life. I only talked a few minutes with him as I was too busy about that time for I had someone else besides myself to look after.

I must ease off for I have a hundred and one things to do. Now this coupon is an extra one that I managed to get a grip on so if you want to use it. I will appreciate it very much as chocolate is very scarce and what we get is without sugar and only 10 cents for our usual 5 cent bar, so you can see at a glance the reason for this unusual request.

I fear that Pershing was wrong when he said Hoboken by Christmas, I think that this maybe over at that time but never Hoboken, probably Easter.

Captain Harry H. Cooney

October 23, 1918—United States rejects new German peace plan.

October 24, 1918—Yanks advance to line of Bantheville.

October 26, 1918—German losses are 50,000 in the three day drive by the Allies.

I Killed One German with My Automatic

> October 26, 1918
> Corp. Paul A. Staller
> Co. A, 108th Machine Gun Battalion
> 28th Division
> A.E.F.
> Somewhere in France.

Dear Sister:

Wish to say that the boys in our company are in very good health for what they were going through for the past couple of weeks. The first day of the drive we went over the top without any breakfast and nothing in sight looked like eats. We kept it up all day and never thought of eating. Our captain did all he could to get us something to eat, but you could not keep track of us, as we were all scattered. Two squads went into one bunch of infantry and the rest went with the other companies. From the third day we began to get two warm meals a day and after that we had more than we could eat. We boys certainly must take our hats off to the captain. He certainly did all he could to keep us supplied with everything necessary. He went to the trouble to get each man an extra pair of socks, so we could change when we got wet feet.

At one time we had to run and had to leave our gun behind. That time I found that I could really run. I used to hear the bullets strike the stones in back of me and we told a Major that the Huns were breaking through, and he sent some infantry into town and there certainly was some fighting done. The next morning we took up another position. It was a strong point and we were one hundred and ten men and the following morning the Huns with two battalions had us surrounded. We surely mowed them down. We only had two killed in the whole fight. I killed one German with my automatic. I missed on the first shot but he took an awful spill the second one. The spare men that we had took the wounded Hun's guns and shot the Huns down. My corporal ran out over the top after them and I saw the Hun's bullets strike in the bank in front of the gun, but that wouldn't worry me as long as the gun was going. We fought about one and one half hours, then they retreated again. The closest call I had was a bullet which took a small piece out of my coat. As yet I have been uninjured. William Wike, one of my comrades, was wounded, but now he is getting along fine.

Your Brother,
Paul A. Staller

October 31, 1918—Turkey surrenders. United States has 1,977,000 troops in France.

9

November 1918: The Armistice—the Eleventh Hour, the Eleventh Day, the Eleventh Month

November 2, 1918—American troops northwest of Verdun are ahead of schedule. The Germans are still putting up strong resistance.

November 3, 1918—Austria surrenders to Allies. 37th and 91st U.S. divisions reach Audenarde.

November 5, 1918—3rd United States Corps forces passage of Meuse.

November 6, 1918—Yanks occupy Sedan. Hun retreat line seized; Germans get Foch's truce terms.

November 9, 1918—Yanks fight through Meuse hills to north of Metz. Revolution in Berlin.

November 10, 1918—Kaiser and crown prince flee to Holland.

November 11, 1918—GERMANY SURRENDERS.

Company photograph of Company C, 103rd Engineers, from Schuylkill County, Pennsylvania.

Tonight We Are the Proudest of Men

November 11, 1918
Sergt. Joseph Duffy
Co. D 103rd Engineers
28th Division
A.E.F.
Somewhere in France.

Dear Father:

This is the day for congratulations, for this is the day of Victory, not only to the American people but the world at large and long before this letter reaches you, the glad tidings that came to us early today, will be known and that is that Germany has signed the armistice. To say that is welcome news would be putting it mildly, for it was received here with out burst of enthusiasm. We had sort of expected it from day to day, for we learned conditions and knew that it was only a matter of time. And if Germany hesitated it meant for the American army, on to Berlin, for there surely we would have gone, wal[l]oping her right and left and in the end, she would be completely trimmed.

When Germany started this awful war they evidently had one idea in mind and that was that they were the only nation in the world and with their bullying methods thought they would conquer everybody, however, they soon began to realize that it was all a dream when their masters became interested.

How pleasing it is to realize that the 28th Division went in at the turning point at Chateau Thierry, on July 15th, continuing in the midst of it ever since and now when the climax comes, we are still on the fighting front. Naturally every state will take pride in the work done by their troops but when the history of this great war is written, we believe that our division will receive due credit for the great sacrifices made. For no matter where they have been, they have always proven that they were made of the right kind of material and Jerry is well aware of this fact from the start. By their heroic work, the boys made a great record and we feel that the State at large and particularly our people at home will be greatly pleased when they learn the true state of the work done.

While we realize that peace has not been declared yet it is only a question of time but when this will happen, no one, at this writing can tell, but we look on the bright side and trust that it will not be long. When we take into consideration the short time that America had to prepare and take a real active part in this wonderful conflict, it is surprising how successful we were. This vandal, who thought that he had everyone buffaloed, sure struck a snag, when he came in contact with the Americans, for the Americans have beaten him every time they met.

Tonight we are the proudest of men and give thanks to God for our safety and all are proud to be permitted to take part in this wonderful conflict and we hope and trust that the day is not far distant when all, who are spared, will return safely to their homes.

Today, our boys got a Boche moving picture machine and at this writing are busy making announcements of the wonderful work the outfit has done and if you were to hear the cracks that are made you would call it real fun.

We are all pleased to learn that the influenza is checked at home and that the town is getting back to its old time form. I am sending you a paper which will give you some idea of what they think of the Kaiser over here.

Isn't it strange that the end came at the eleventh hour, eleventh day and eleventh month? Am enjoying good health and trust all at home are the same.

Sincerely,
Joe

All fighting ended at 11:00 o'clock a.m. on the 11th day of November 1918. Under the terms of the armistice the Germans were required to withdraw from all occupied territories, retire all their armies to the east bank of the Rhine, provide all Allies with bridgeheads beyond the Rhine, and give up enormous amounts of military equipment which would preclude their continuing war effort.

The actual armistice signed by the German representatives was completed at 12:00 o'clock midnight. Washington made the announcement to the American people at 2:45 a.m. The next morning there was great rejoicing everywhere in the country. People paraded throughout all the Pennsylvania cities all day long.

When Germany signed the armistice she was required to surrender to her foes the following:

160 submarines	*30,000 machine guns*
50 destroyers	*3,000 flame throwers*
6 battle cruisers	*2,000 airplanes*
10 battleships	*5,000 locomotives*
8 light cruisers	*50,000 wagons*
5,000 long guns	*10,000 motor trucks*

A Mysterious Calm Seemed to Prevail

November 14, 1918
Major John Moore
Medical Department
103rd Engineers
28th Division
Somewhere in France.

There is hardly any doubt but that you folks knew that the armistice was signed as soon as we did, but we had the opportunity of being over here and seeing the last minute fighting, and it certainly was something awe inspiring, for the guns seemed to thunder more fiercely than ever on the morning of the 11th from up until eleven, then everything quieted down and a mysterious calm seemed to prevail entirely out of calling with what had been going on but a few minutes before. It was only then that we really began to realize that the big show was over and would soon be a thing of the history and wonderful memories. Our boys went over the top on the morning of the 11th and we had quite few a casualties in the Division in consequence. Why they should have sent over an attack when everybody knew that it would be over by 11 a.m. is something I cannot comprehend, but I feel that it was orders and to prevent the Hun from pulling over any tricks at the last minute. A few minutes after eleven, when the firing of all kinds had subsided we soon saw the Hun approaching our lines and soon they were over with our boys saying how glad they were that it was over and "to hell with the Kaiser" and asking for tobacco and cigarettes. Exchange of souvenirs then began and such a scene one could hardly believe with two bodies of men, who but a few minutes before were killing one and another but that is what really happened and it was something most extraordinary and worth seeing.

Can you picture the wild enthusiasm and excitement of the French, well they ran about hugging the American troops and shouting " Vive la France" "Vive America" and laughing and shouting in a manner that was almost indescribable, but it certainly must be the most wonderful relief to the people of France to know that after four years of fighting and suffering that the beggard Hun had been licked so badly by the Allied Armies and was on his knees asking for mercy and relief. It is not strange that now when it is over we have started in and fed them after all the bluster and talk. What a mighty nation they tried to impress the other nations of the world they were. It is always thus with anybody who shouts that they are superior to anybody else, and I guess it will take the German nation a hundred or more years to regain the respect of the peoples of the world.

It surely is almost impossible for us to realize that no more will [we] experience the whizzing and explosion of the big shells, see the numerous air battles hear the hum and whiz of the machine and rifle bullet, and the relaxation from the terrible nervous strain seems to effect everybody the same for we are now all full of smiles and it is rather hard just to picture the feeling of how it effects one.

Can you picture what it means to have real lights again, fires burning any old time, the shutters no longer closed to keep out any light, the going about without gas mask or helmet, and walking and going any old place without the feeling that a shell may drop in on you or about you in any minute? Well if you can then I am sure you can about imagine how we must all feel. The Division Headquarters was all decorated with the flags of the Allies, and electric lights, for they carry with them a portable electric light plant for the purpose of lighting up the General's Headquarters. They had one of the Infantry bands giving a concert from 4 p.m. until late in the evening, so that it was a real nice holiday for everybody.

The Colonel decided we would have a little celebration of our own at Headquarters and we had our electric lights going in force. A special dinner which consisted of cream of tomato soup, roast lamb, massed potatoes, sweet corn, asparagus, peas, salad al la American, coffee, lemon merangue pie, cigarettes and cigars. We even had an orchestra for one of the officers happened to know there was a colored regiment of road building troops and he rustled up a few band men, a snare drum and bass drum a trombone and a baritone. Well they couldn't play so well but it was music of a kind that made your feet want to wiggle and the antics of the bunch were so ridiculous that I had pains in my jaws from laughing at their antics and music.

Last night Miss Wilson, the President's daughter was at Division HQ to sing for the boys, and it was pretty nice. She is going from one outfit to another singing for the boys and told the boys she and the people from the

States would do anything in the world for our boys and then the boys yelled and cheered for further orders.

Am sure everybody back home will have a real Thanksgiving day for there is lots to be thankful for. Hope you will have a happy Thanksgiving. We will be marching that day and will be lucky if we get corned willy and hard tack, but will be hoping for something better. Hope you escaped the Spanish Flu and are now feeling fine again. Hope things are fine at home and everybody is well. Guess the boys called for the draft will be happy now that they will not be called. It has been very cold over here, but the past few days have been fine.

John Moore

Influenza Is a Dream Compared to This

November 16, 1918
Private J. F. Curran
Ambulance Co. 29
5th Division San. Train.
A.E.F.
Somewhere in France.

Dear Sister:

This peace sure is some great stuff, and I sincerely hope that it will last forever, for it sure was a rough game right up till the last minute. You should have heard the big guns roaring over the final and finishing touch to this man's game, in which I said my prayers more than once. It was no joke at any time. You are all wrong about our transportation. They were not Lizzies, no, poor old stiff helpless G.M.C's, but they are gone now. I guess when we leave here for somewhere in God's country I will have to hot foot it. I sure hope it will be soon as I am well pleased with what I have seen of sunny France, with its rain, mud and fog. I would like to go into details in explaining to you the many beautiful sights and scenes along the Mouselle, [Moselle] Meuse and Aisne rivers. But sights that will most likely live forever in one's mind are the sights one sees on the front. To my mind to witness the passing away of some chum or pal are the sights impressive and will live long in one's mind. Influenza is a dream compared to this, shrapnel, machine guns and bombs, or in other words the hell that so many human beings have endured since this dirty muddle began in 1914. We Americans have only known a small portion of it, yet I thank God that it is over, as will many thousands of others, and you can bet those square headed Huns will long remember the smiling Yanks.

Jerimiah.

Go Tell Your Captains We Will Not Go Over This Morning

November 16, 1918
Private James Kelly
Co. K 146th Infantry Regt.
37th Division
A.E.F.
Somewhere in France.

Dear Sister:

I was on the front lines when "Peace" was declared. We were to go over the top at six o'clock in the morning on November 11th and I was at battalion HQ as a runner and at four o'clock, our Corporal called the runners as there were eight of us from four companies, two from each company. My partner, a fellow from Ohio by the name of Snyder got up and all the boys were just going to growl when the Corporal said, "Its good news boys." They were all up in a moment and he said, "go tell your Captains that we will not go over this morning and probably there will be no more fighting, after today." And believe me, I did run with that message and we were only back with that message when there was another one that after 11 o'clock there would be no more fighting and that our kitchen would be across the river with eats. And that was very good news. The Kaiser and his family had left Berlin and there was a riot in the city.

Tell John that I have been over the top several times. But poor Reilly got his the second time we went over. We left France after Reilly and some more of our boys were injured, we left for Belgium and believe me, the Belgians are some people. They are more like Americans. We were the first American soldiers in Belgium and the people could not do enough for you. This is a pretty country. It is mostly all level and believe me, we did chase the Huns and keep them going until the finish.

Well, we did not wait for the old fellows to come over here and finish this war but got right into it and cleaned up the Huns on our last drive. We killed quite a few Huns and took many prisoners and guns.

On November 13th, we had a little feast on the peace terms; there were fourteen of us at battalion HQ and we ate turkey, two chickens and all that went with it. We also had some drinks including wine, beer, milk and coffee so you know just about how the boys feel at this time. I think we are going to see Brussels before going home and see the King and Queen of Belgium.

James

I Looked Up and His Nose Seemed to Be Pointed Right at Me

November 20, 1918
Lieut. Robert Brigham
Co. G 314th Infantry Regt.
79th Division
A.E.F.
Near Gilerey, France.

Today was quite a banner one for mail, received a lot from home folks. Then a lot of mail came addressed to me from lads of the company who were wounded at Montfoucon in our big scrap on Sept. 27th. I wrote to you last week telling you about the last and final drive up to the 11th hour of the 11th day, the one day in my life that I shall never forget as long as I live because it was not only my savior but the savior of thousands of other men on the front line.

Our company and part of our division is doing patrol duty on the front established on the day of the armistice. Although today the Germans are 30 miles back of the Rhine, nevertheless the last front line has to be patrolled and out posted by our men. Our orders are to collect and send back to higher authority all allied prisoners of war returning from Germany. They are coming back on foot in large groups, day and night and have to be properly conducted to their own authorities. It is most interesting to question them. The Russian is not very talkative but very happy in his simple way to be out of the Hun's reach. The French come in tens and twenties with all kinds of uniforms, from the Hun cap down to Turkish breeches and American shoes. They are a motley group and all are happy and smiling to be home. God only knows what these French people have suffered and what hell these prisoners have gone through at the hands of the Germans.

Food shortage seems to be the problem in Germany now. The prisoners most of whom have passed through my post have been working 12 hours a day in the ore mines of Alsace. They are paid poorly and are required to mine so much of the metal every day. When they come out all evenings, if they have not measured up to their quota they are strafed by the unter officer. The German officer is a dirty dog. I have seen evidence of his damnable work in places where the company has been. In one of my P.C's I found hanging on the wall of the dugout a large club like with seven rawhide tails dangling from one end. This is the way they discipline friend and foe.

I'll tell you an interesting experience that I had and one that I shall never forget as long as I can remember. You have heard and read of towns being raided by the Boche planes at night and of the deadly work of machine guns that they carry in their combat planes. The morning of the 9th of November, we had advanced our lines half way up the slope of 319 and were stopped by Boche machine guns that held the crest and sides of the hills preventing our advancing any further. We found cover in some trenches for one company but the other three companies of the battalion, including "G." were forced to huddle quite close together and hug the sides of the hill along a three foot terrace containing some brush. We had to keep right here for about five hours because the Boche were dropping gas and G.I cans, (the Yanks epithet for high explosive shells.) right at the foot of the hill we were on, and their was no going back until he at least stopped his shelling or until we could move back under cover of darkness. Of course the officers and battalion commander held a council of war to determine the next best thing to do. We determined that we would never go that hill by lying right there and that our only way to take it was to call on our artillery and have them lay down a barrage and so pummel up the crest of the hill, that the Boche machine gunners would be glad to haul out. Then and only then was the only time we could take it, so word was sent back to the artillery in Bois Belleau to give us one hours artillery on 319 and then we would take the hill. Our position was only about 200 yards from the crest where they would lay down the barrage. So we had to get up and move back to get out of our own artillery fire. We had then plenty of time to get back, so no one was in a particular hurry. I came up from seeing the Major and was explaining to the company what our plan of action was, when who should come over the hill but a Boche plane. Well he just flew around us once or twice doing some stunts and it really seemed as though he was trying to show us how clever the Huns are in handling their Gothas. We knew that he was photographing our position and getting all the dope for his own artillery. We knew what that meant. It meant so damnable shelling … when we should move back down the hill. Well the Boche flew from flank to flank once or twice and then disappeared around the side of the hill into his own lines. My own plan of action for old "G" Co. was now fixed and certain. I was going to move out as fast as I could maneuver the men back beyond the railroad. I had just gotten the men on their feet and given directions and the other companies were about ready to move also when that damn Hun came back and this time very low, so low that you could see the supports of the machine gun in the rear of his plane and could see the gold on the officers cap, about 200 feet high. The moment he reappeared, of course we all looked up, elegant target for him. Well, he just rained machine gun fire down on us and there we were with no cover and groups of ten and fifteen men together. He went back twice along our battalion, first shooting from the gun in his rear, the gunner standing up and traversing his gun back and forth, up and down and spraying us with bullets.

Emptying his rear gun, he pointed his machine, nose down and shot his forward gun rifle into our company. I'll never forget it. I looked up and his nose seemed to be pointed right for me and I just had enough time to think and a horrible feeling came over me, for I knew at such low position, he would get all of us and then I thought of our trusty little automatic Brownings and I called so loud as my scared voice would allow, "Cut loose on him, men," and the lads sure did and such fire as our 16 guns gave him! Splinters shot from his planes and propeller and he was so surprised at the unexpected fire that with a hasty salvo of fire that killed two of my men and wounded several others and killed a lieutenant of "L" company, the Hun beat a hasty retreat for home. So endeth one of the many little tales that I have to tell and thank God I am still alive to tell them.

I must get some sleep. It's now nine p.m. quite late for us in the army. We move south 120 miles near Chattlion sur Seine where I went to school last August. There we live in comfortable French beds again and enjoy the pleasures of France with no war to disturb our equilibrium.

Bob.

It's a Great Game and We All Liked It

November 22, 1918
Lieut. Douglas Crater
Royal Flying Corps
R.A.F. Station, Felixstowe
England.

Dear Bob;

Now that the war is over, everything is going along smoothly. I must tell you of a very peculiar coincidence. While in Texas U.S.A. training in the British Royal Flying Corps, I chanced to meet a young fellow from Pottsville, Bob Mills do you know Him? Well, when we left there in April,

I lost track of him and then sailed to England in July. Upon arriving here I was posted to seaplanes here at Felixstowe. After being here about three weeks, one day while walking down the road, along came an officer. I didn't recognize him at first. As I neared him who was it but Bob again.

It sure was a happy meeting, we had a long talk of days gone by. I inquired where he had been, answering me, saying he had just returned from hospital, being partly mended up from his wound. He felt fairly well, but after a few days he had to return, to be dressed. I then inquired around the station about him, and was informed he was one of the best pilots around the station, until being mixed up with a flock of Huns one day and shot in the leg. They say he had been in quite a few scraps, being extremely lucky in all but this. He came back a few days later, and after resting or rather being off duty for a week, he resumed his piloting duties. Since then, he had been shot down out of control a couple of times at sea, but being fortunate enough to be picked up by our boats, after being out a few hours. I have heard him say, that he was sorry now, for he wouldn't be able to get another crack at the devils.

We see lots of them just now, for they are turning over their submarines to us now, and for the past three days, they have been coming in our harbor. Upon arriving here, their crews are taken off not allowed to land, but put on our ships, and taken back to Germany immediately. We fellows fly right over them as near as possible, getting a good look at them. Happy looking devils too. All seem very contented. We aren't doing much flying now, but it's a great game and we liked it while the war was on, but now we want to get back. Have had some very lucky experiences my self, but have gotten away with it so far.

Douglas Crater.

Life in the Ammunition Train

November 23, 1918
Private George A. Crawshaw
Truck Co. A 103rd Ammunition Train.
28th Division
A.E.F.
Germany.

Dear Father:

We are now and have been for the past few weeks quartered in German Barracks near a small town named Savonneres, which is on the Metz front, about midway between St.-Mihiel and Hendicourt.

Private Frank Reith (center) and two unidentified Pennsylvania soldiers who served in the 3rd Infantry Division as ammunition truck drivers pose after the war in Germany.

A week before the battle of the Marne started on July 7th, our camp was moved to the rear some distance, as it was thought the Germans might be able to break through. A detail of the trucks was then sent to the front to have ammunition for our infantry and our engineers who were just moving up to the lines. I was lucky enough to get on this detail.

Our job was to have our trucks loaded at all times and when we got a call for ammunition to deliver it and beat it back to camp for a new load. They told us the 28th Division was highly honored by being placed with the Iron French Divisions, defending Paris. We, therefore, felt highly honored, but began to feel the trip here beginning to slip, as it was a good place to get bumped off. We pulled into a town named Pargmy les Phuys and decided that we had never seen a more peaceful place. Some of our artillery was firing there, but we never heard a sound of the Germans.

The only disquieting thing about the place was that the civilians all seemed to be in a terrible rush to leave. We then pulled our trucks into a patch of woods and settled down for our most peaceful week in France. We had nothing to do but enjoy ourselves and consider the many advantages the army offered a man. Of course, our artillery was firing, but we soon got used to that. We had never seen a dugout or thought of the necessity of having one, so were quartered in our pup tents.

On the night of the 13th our artillery fire gradually increased in volume, until it was one continual roar, but we just thought the French were beginning to celebrate the 14th, Bastil[l]e Day.

About 12 o'clock whirr Bang, yea, All of the German artillery opened up at once. They were using shrapnel, which bursting about 150 feet in the air at first, but gradually got the range and began digging holes in the ground near us with their "Nail Kegs." Mike Brogan, Fat Ormsby and myself were all in a two man pup tent, Fat immediately began to smoke cigarettes. Mike and I covered our faces with our helmets and made a poor bluff at sleeping. Not having anywhere else to go we stuck to the pup tent. Morning came after about 16 hours and we did not mind the shelling so much then, besides the shells never hit anybody and at last we got up nerve enough to go and look at some new shell holes along the railroad. This proved a very wise move as was shown when a nail keg came howling over and splashed us with dirt. We showed speed for our tent and strayed no more. Now we began to see why we were there, as the calls for ammunition came thick and fast. At first the Doughboys came with limbers and carried it away by themselves but the limbers got badly used by the shelling along the roads, so our trucks started to make the trips. This was rather contrary to precedent, as Packard trucks were considered too valuable to be used as kindling wood. I was again fortunate to make the first trip. Five of us started out with a load of rifle ammunition and suffocating bombs. The rest of the crowd shook hands with us when we left. We got the load up to the infantry o.k. and better still got back o.k.

After we took the ammunition up to the 109th Infantry we went back to camp for another load and were much disappointed to find another truck was already loaded and ready to go in our place. It had been reported that we hadn't gotten through, so the truck was going to make another try. Anyway they sent that detail and kept us back in camp, to our great disgust. That advanced detail of ours followed up the infantry to the place the Germans made a temporary stand at the Vesle River. I have always been sorry that I was taken off that advanced "eschalon" [*échelon*] as the French called it. The trucks left behind had quite a job on their hands moving the dump, as the advance from the Marne was very rapid. We would just about get settled in one place when we would get orders to pull up stakes and advance. Each move meant about eight trips for each truck, so it was rather wearing work. We first crossed the Marne at Chateau Thierry and camped in the woods near Le Charmel, right in the spot were the American Doughboys showed the famous Prussian Guard just why the Americans carried bayonets. Incidentally the Americans very rarely got close enough to the Germans to use the bayonet. Chateau Thierry was rather badly shot up, as were all the towns along the Marne, particularly Jaulgonne. The valley of the Marne is certainly pretty, and here we saw the most beautiful scenery which we have seen so far over here. The 103rd Engineers distinguished themselves by stopping the German drive, and our 109th doughboys are the boys who took Chateau Thierry. All of the 28th Division Infantry Regiments, the 109th, 110th, 111th, and 112th made wonderful records in this later engagement. While we were in the woods at Le Charmel we spent our spare time gathering up German ammunition and taking it to a safer place. There were immense stores of German shells here, and they were very good targets for German artillery and airplanes. Some of these shells were so heavy that it took five of us to lift one in a truck, and fourteen of them made a good three ton load.

Our next camp was near Gouzencourt, where we dug our dugouts and your ring was made. About that time the Germans made a stand at the Vesle River and our artillery and the rest of the ammunition train caught up to us. Our work now commenced in earnest, as the artillery went into action at once. Our job was to keep them supplied with 75 mm. (3 inch) and 155 mm (6 inch) shells and powder. This was rather exciting work, as we had to sneak up in the night, when the Germans weren't firing, and get rid of our load and beat it while we were still healthy. This was kept up until the drive from the Vesle to the Aisne started, when we got all excited and began to haul rocks up to the batteries in broad daylight. This drive was mean while it lasted, but luckily was only short. The 28th Division moved out of the sector on Sept. 13th, as did all the Americans. We were relieved by the French colonials. We moved to the Argonne sector next, moving to with in three kilometers of the front. At the Argonne we began hauling rocks for the drive of Sept. 26th We hauled about as many as we could, which was some. The lines in this sector were stationary for years and we saw the last word in trenches, dugouts, and barbed wire entanglements. We had our bunks made up in the dugouts right in the midst of the artillery shells of all kind, shapes and sizes.

The night of the 25th was a memorable one. We knew what was coming, but had no idea of just how strong it would be. Our barrage started at 11 p.m. on Sept. 25th and they say it was the heaviest of the war. It sure was the most noise I had ever heard. The German reply to it certainly did tickle us. They tried to answer feebly at first, but soon were absolutely drowned. I am glad I wasn't on the wrong end of the barrage.

Our company was given the job of following up the advance of the artillery with 75's and this proved to be an impossible job. The roads we had to go over had been in no mans land for four years, and had been soaked by recent continual rains, so our trip was just one succession of stops, first getting stuck in a shell hole and then sliding off the road entirely. After two days and nights of this stuff we were obliged to unload and crawl into a side road in order to open the road for the other traffic, which we had held up all the time. The road we got into proved to be a trap, as we couldn't get out the way we got in on account of the fierce traffic jam, and the only other outlet was an impossible hill. The difficulty was solved by tying two towing ropes to the front of each truck and dragging them one by one up the half mile of hill by mule power, we being the mules. We then began hauling over another road through Nuvilly and Varrenes, but the traffic on this road was also something fierce. It was the only road through for miles and was blocked by two immense mine craters and was mined in places beside this. At first it took us from 24 to 48 hours to make one trip, but the thousands of American engineers soon got it in shape, so that in a week [we] were able to make the same trip in hours.

The division was relieved on October 10, but we didn't leave this sector until the 23rd. This was the meanest engagement which we were in, on account of the miserable weather and a country as much from the Fritzie shells. We spent the last few days in this sector, we were under a roof for the first time in France.

George

A Big Fritz Shell Landed, Right in the Middle of the Cave

November 24, 1918
Sgt. Charles Dougherty
Ambulance Company 637
Service Unit.
A.E.F.
St.-Mihiel, France.

My Dear Dad:

Well, dad its all over but the shouting, and I for one am not sorry. Enclosed you will find a copy of our section citation from the French to English translation. That entitles us to have the French War Cross, the Croix de Guerre painted on our cars.

In the last offensive, Dad we went into the lines on Sept. 27th at Chauing, from where we began to advance. Our division took La Fere, which was the first place we took that Fritz had held for years. We continued right ahead until we hit the town and were [there] on the 11th of November when the Armistice was signed. I'm "all in" this last attack; we were in action about 45 days and gained about 655 kilometers that was giving Fritz a chase, eh?

Our first Sergeant has been away at school since the 20th of October, and I have been filling in his place. Then the Lieutenant has been sick nearly as long, which gave me a lot of work and I certainly have been busy.

During the last couple of days of the war we are very fortunate. One night while a couple of the fellows was asleep in a cave, a 210, a big Fritz shell, landed right in the middle of the cave, but it did not go off. That sure was luck, wasn't it? A couple of the fellows were cut up by bricks and rocks but that was about all there was to it.

I am going to tell you the names of the battles I have been in. June 9, we were caught in the German advance near Montdidier. That is where we got the citation. In July we were with the Americans between Chateau Thierry and Soissons. In September we were in before the city of Noyon, which our division took. Then this last affair.

We are nearly six kilometers below Belgium and I have been over there. Well Dad lots of love to all will close.

Your loving son,
Charlie.

The Citation
Section Sanitaire American 637

"Under the command of the American First Lieutenant MaPherson and the French Second Lieutenant Huret, it showed during the days of the 9, 10 and 11 of June, 1918 the best qualities of cold resolution, of high feeling of duty and the most noble spirit of sacrifice. After having lost eight cars and three men in the bombardment of Cuvilly, it continued to come and take from the first line, under fire of the enemy machine guns, the wounded to be evacuated. It only retired on the formal order of the Medical-Chief, and continued to maintain its evacuation service during the first three days under the most perilous circumstances, exposing itself with out count up to the extreme limit of the forces of its personnel."

Editor's note: Sgt. Charles Dougherty received the Croix de Guerre for gallantry.

Dougherty Charles E. 10050
Sgt.
Section No. 637 Ambulance Service.
FRENCH CROIX de GUERRE
with bronze star.
December 20th, 1918.
General Headquarters French Armies of the East. "A very zealous and devoted non-commissioned officer. He gave the measure of his valor and displayed courage and coolness on August 30th, 1918, in going out to pick up the wounded at an advanced regimental first aid station over a route in view of the enemy and notwithstanding a violent bombardment."
Residence: 142 W. Railroad St. Pottsville, PA.

We Crawled Through the Barb Wire and Into No Mans Land

November 24, 1918
Sgt. Burt J. Hasenauer
Co. I 18th Infantry Regt.
1st Division.
A.E.F.
Somewhere in France.

My Dear Parents:

Today is Dad's day over here. Every soldier is supposed to write a letter to his father, so here is your's and mother's. It was on the 13th of June at one o'clock we left New York harbor for France. We were 15 long days on the water. On the fifth day out at sea a woman was discovered on our boat. I suppose you have read of her. Her husband is in my company. We landed at St. Nazaire on the morning of the 28th day of June, 1917. After staying there a few days, we left in box cars, forty men in a car. After two days riding we landed at a small town by the name of Houdeisin court were we trained until the later part of September. We then went to the Luneville sector in Lorraine. We stayed there until December and then we came back and hiked to the Toul sector. We went into that sector about the fourth of January and stayed until March 5th. About the 18th of February I was given a seven day leave to Aix le Bain [Aix-Les-Bains] with 11 other boys from my company. We returned about the 26th of February and were only in the trenches one night, when 1500 of Hindenburg's travelling circus came over on us and killed six of the boys that had been at Aix le Bain with me, and captured one and I was slightly wounded in the right side. That was the first of March. That was a German raiding party. They were all large men. Almost all of them over six feet or taller. But they paid the price. They left ten dead to our one. It was several days later I was picked up with a number of others for a raiding party. It was 2:30 a.m., March 4th that we crawled through our barbed wire and across no mans land into the German barbed wire and laid there until 5:30 a.m. when our lieutenant signalled for the barrage and for an hour it was roaring hell. We went to the third line of trenches and captured nine men. (That was all we saw) While on our way back I fell and hurt my side, causing my wound to bleed, but it did not amount to much. It was only a small one. That was my last day on the Toul front. We were then brought back in automobiles to a town called St. Amand. We stayed there for a week and then boarded a train and rode to Paris. We hiked from there to Cantigny, a distance of 160 miles with a 120 pound pack on our backs and sleeping in the streets, fields or any place we happened to be. We stayed in the trenches 23 days. Then came out for four days. I lived on one box of hard tack. Our slum wagon was blown up nearly every night. After six days rest we went in a fight again and over the top and after the battle the roll of my company was called and my squad of eighteen men was finished. Three of us answered. Three nights later I was sent with a detachment to the rear to get ammunition, when we were on our way back, I was put out of the game. I woke up next day in a French hospital. From there I was sent to Paris.

Burt.

That Was the Day We Thought
It Was Up with Our Squad

November 25, 1918
Pvt. George Hartnett
Co. B 108th Machine gun battle.
28th Division.
A.E.F.
St. Aigan, France.

Dear Father;

Having permission to write you a little of our experiences, I thought it would interest you to know of some of mine. When I left the states, I arrived in Liverpool, England, after a pleasant journey over the pond. From Liverpool we went to Folkstone and from there we went to Fort Dover. Then we crossed the channel and landed in Calais, France. We went to Genevic and went in training on the Vickers Machine Gun, that was the last week in June. The next week we were rushed to the Marne. On July fourth we were living in hopes of having the day off, but early that morning the Germans made an attempt to cross the Marne, so we were ordered at a place called Conde. The last four squads of our company were transferred to the 109th Infantry from July 8, to 20. On July 15th, the Germans crossed the Marne. We were in positions at Monte Therrie and in the great battle, we lost a number of boys among them John Bolton, from Haven. On that day, also Muck Boyer, he being a member of the Machine Gun Battalion of the 109th Rgt. We left that afternoon for a place called Conde De Forest. From 12 o'clock Sunday night to 11 o'clock Monday night, we were under the biggest barrage the Germans ever sent over. It was our first time under fire and believe me, it made us fellows realize for the first time what war really was and what we were up against, and it put the Yankee spirit in us, that helped win the war. The town was soon in ruins, churches and buildings crumbling to nothing. Fritz certainly did send over some gas and all kinds of shells. In a place called Chirrey on July 19th, I met the boys from Company C engineers. Our battalion also saw service in the big drive at St. Agana and St. Eugene.

We had it easy at Chateau Thierry as often times we got close by the lines and did not use our machine guns. From there, we moved to Death Valley, where we had bum luck being heavily shelled and the German airplanes bombed us at night. That was some terrible thing to see after they were through. We lost heavily in life, horses and a number of mules were killed that used to draw our gun carts. From there we moved to a place called Fismes and used our guns nine days in succession putting a barrage on the Huns. On Sunday morning at 4 a.m. I put over 7 boxes in 15 minutes, each box containing 288 shots.

On September 2nd we left for our last drive on the Marne, and Chateau Thierry, and on the seventh day of September, when the French took over our positions, we were holding the front lines at a place called Fismette. On the fifth, we took a big rail head. The Huns fought like fury on that drive, and after that they lost heart and courage. After that we heard we were going to get a long rest.

Our squads were in bad shape. We needed drivers so I was chosen as one, as you know a number of our drivers were mustered [mustard] gassed, so you see that was a new line of duty to us machine gunners and seemed strange. On the 11th of September, I left with the wagon train for twenty-eight division, which was over five miles long. It took us nine nights to reach our place at the Argonne woods. We would rest at day time and travel all night until the next day. I was then sent back to my company and reached them on the 21st of September on the third line of trenches. From there I was sent to first squad. On the 26th of September the big drive started. All our big guns and also the French guns started to fire. The earth certainly did rock and fire. On our front alone there were 1600 of those big guns roaring. We did not get into action until September 27 in no mans land. On the 29th of September, Fritz had us in a trap and we started to fall back, but believe me, the next morning he got his. We then made some counter attacks and made big gains. That afternoon we went 300 yards ahead of the front lines to a quarry. In that party, there were two guns, one of our company, 2 from company C, 4 squads of engineers from the 82nd Division and 8 squads of infantry of the 110th. All went right until 5:40 the next morning when the Germans sent a bomb over. It missed its mark. We then knew that they were commencing and had us surrounded. When they got close enough our orders were to fire. There was a whole division of Germans, and dear Dad that was the day we all thought it was up with our crowd. Our orders were every man fight to his last. Our wires were all cut so that we could not get help from our other troops. But we certainly did some fighting and in two hours, there were not many Germans around. They went after us three times but we always made them fall back. After that short battle, the field was covered with the German dead, and we took 13 prisoners, all of them old men.

The Major and the Colonel of the 110th Infantry took our names and said we saved the day. The 13 prisoners certainly did look at the few Americans who had defeated their division. I forgot to mention I saw Muck Strauch while he was running one of the tanks.

The place we were in was some awful place, all wet and muddy as we had lots of rain while on the front. In the day time we had a little bread and some corn meal. In the night we all enjoyed a good feed. On the night of October first, we were moved to a place right near a cemetery. It was the best place we were in a long time, as it was high and dry. We went into action at 2 p.m. Oct. 3rd, tired and feeling in bad shape. At the time, the Germans were sending over a lot of shells and the one pounder's and the smell of gas was sickening and I think the smell from gun, did not know Fritz was gassing, until fell and left the line at 4 p.m. when I was removed to a field hospital. And on the 4th of Oct. I was sent down to the Base Hospital at Nevers.

While there brother Jim visited me and say wasn't I happy to see him, while there I also met a few more boys from town. From the Hospital, I was sent to La Guerchrie, and from there I was sent to a hospital at Grorsoure and remained there until the 27th and 28th of Oct, and then was sent to a field hospital at St. Amonda, I stayed there until I was removed here doing light duty, taking care of a billet. This is the famous town of St. Aigan. So I suppose I will stay here until I take a trip back to the dear old states.

George.

The Germans Gave Us Quite Some Trouble There

November 30, 1918
Corp. George N. Pyle
Co. C 103rd Engineers
28th Division.
A.E.F
Vigneulles, France.

Dear Father:

You will no doubt be surprised to get this, but I thought that you would like to have a letter from me. The censorship rules have loosened up a little so that now we are allowed to tell you where we are located. At present we are at a little town called Vigneulles. I do not know whether you recall the name or not, but it was one of the towns captured by the Americans in the St.-Mihiel drive on Sept 12. If you happen to have a map you can find it by looking directly below Metz and a little above Toul. We are about 25 miles away from Metz. We have made our longest stay here since we have been in France, and by this time we have things fixed up quite home like. We are living in the houses that are still standing, each room having a stove and everybody has beds or bunks.

This is the third front we have been on, the first one was near Chateau Thierry, and I never will forget the town of Fismes, where we had some exciting times. You can probably remember reading about that town for quite a long time. The Germans gave us quite some trouble there and didn't seem to want to leave it. After spending 70 days there we moved to the Argonne Forest where we started the big drive through there on Sept. 26. This was the first time I had an opportunity of seeing a real "no mans land," as this front hadn't changed for four years and there was a great system of trenches, dugouts and wire. The Americans never left the Germans stay in one place long enough to have trenches and dugouts.

It didn't take the Germans long to part from their trenches when we started our heavy barrage, which lasted for seven hours. Such a racket, you would think hell had broken loose. We were only there two weeks, during which we received special praise from the commander of our Corps. From there we moved to the Lorraine front where we had things a little easy, as there was no driving at this point.

Now that everything is over things are beginning to get more like our camps in the states. We once more hear the bugle which wakes us up in the morning, and calls in to drill. One of the changes is to see lights shining brightly from the windows and fires burning in the open, for unless you were far behind the lines, no lights were visible, everything black as ink.

It will certainly seem strange to walk around at night on lighted streets, we are so used to going about in the dark.

Thanksgiving was quite different from home, but while we had no turkey, we had quite a meal and at night we had a minstrel show where I played and we had quite a good time. Tonight there is a show given by the Y.M.C.A. I heard a funny thing which brought me back to old times. I happened to pass a house where the civilians had moved in and inside I heard a piano and woman singing scales and vocal exercises.

Yank has returned to the company and is living in my room. He is busy hunting souvenirs and he has gotten some fine ones. I haven't bothered with any as packs are heavy enough to carry with out souvenirs.

Well father I will close hoping that before many months pass, I will see you all. There is a rumor that we are going to move before long and if we do I hope it will be back and will be our first move towards the boat and good old U.S.A. As one of the actors in the show said, France is a fine country, to sail from.

With love to all.
Francis

James Eroh's War Story

November 30, 1918
Pvt. James Eroh
Medical Department
Hospital Train, Harvard Unit No. 59
A.E.F.
Somewhere in France.

Gassed and invalided home before his 18th birthday with a record of ten months Foreign Service, is the record, which the World War has made for Private James Eroh.

Arriving at Nevers, France the medical men were transferred to the Medical trains. Eroh being sent with the Harvard Unit, Number 59, to the famous million dollar hospital train, which was donated by the patriotic citizens of New England, and was the envy of every medical man in the service. The train consists of 16 coaches, ten of which were for the accommodation of wounded men, one for wounded officers, two kitchen cars, one pharmacy car, one storage car, and a clinic car which was in the center of the train so that operations such as amputations or other necessary work could be performed en route from the dressing stations and ambulances to the base hospitals in the western and southern parts of France.

Eroh was assigned to one of the cars on the train, there being 32 orderlies, three nurses and two doctors on the entire assignment. The headquarters of the train was in Paris, and it was from the French capital that orders were issued to make the trips necessary. The point of destination for the load of patients and the hospital [was] given to the commanding officer before the train left upon its mission of mercy. The cars were all prominently decorated with the insignia of the Red Cross, and inside were appointed so completely that 30 patients could be accommodated in each car, making a total of about 450 for the train. Some of the wounded and gassed patients [were] permitted to walk about the train or assigned to light duties during the trip. The train runs frequently to points within a few miles of the battleline and frequently makes trips to the southern part of France, which required three days. And two nights travelling. The trips were made by easy stages excepting upon good stretches of railroad, and movements during the big push were governed largely by the movements of the troop trains and supplies and the nature of operations on the front.

The first rip on the train was made on Easter Sunday when the train was dispatched from Paris to Toul sector where they loaded up the wounded and carried them to the hospital at Royette. The wounded men embraced all manner and types of injuries, from bullets, shrapnel, shell wounds, stone wounds from the high explosive shells, shell shock and gas wounds, but few bayonet wounds or other injuries resulting from fights at close quarters showing that the Germans had no desire to mix with the Yanks at close quarters and inflicted all their injuries at long range. Content to stay as far away from the Yanks and Devil Dogs as possible.

From Easter Sunday until Eroh was gassed at Chateau Thierry on August 22nd, Eroh put in six months of service on the hospital train during which time probably 15,000 of the Yanks and Marines were taken from the lines to points in the rear. Many of the worst cases treated were not those wounded in battle but those who met with unusual accidents which occur at the front. One of the worst injuries the Realtor saw were those sustained by a boy who had received them in an accident when he was run over by a lorrie.

Fortitude in the face of shrapnel and gunshot wounds was the most potent characteristic of the Yank, and no matter how badly or slight were the injuries the boys always measured them solely by the number of days, hours or minutes which would intervene between the present and the return to the trenches. Taken as a body the Yanks were the only soldiers who looked upon their mission in France as a serious pastime. They never failed to inject into the spirit of the thing some element of pleasure. They seemed to think that they were there for one single purpose and the more thoroughly and cheerfully they performed their duty the more pleasure they would derive from its performance.

Eroh made trips to many sectors of the front. His train took back wounded Marines from the Belleau Wood fight on June 6th to 8th, when the Marines of the Fifth Divisions and the 26th Regular infantry turned back the Germans from Paris and made conditions along that sector such that the big drive, which nwas commenced on the 18th by the 28th Division consisting of the Pennsylvania troops, became assured [of] success and the turning point of the entire war [was reached leading to the] subsequent defeat of Kaiserism and autocracy.

Eroh and his companions were standing near their train on a siding in a small town several miles behind Belleau about Decoration Day, when a trainload of the Marines pulled in on another track, en route to concentration points near Belleau. As they passed the outer sections of the hospital train, they exchanged greetings and shouted their home stations to each other as they do when strange troops pass each other along the line. Eroh shouted "Pottsville, Pennsylvania" in company with the others, and one of the Marines informed him that their Lieutenant was from there, and Eroh followed the train a short distance and was introduced to the young lieutenant, who was none other than Charles Ulmer.

A short time later Eroh read of Ulmers death in the Paris edition of the New York Herald, and had also learned of the Lieutenant's death from wounded Marines returning on the train returning from the dressing station ambulance to the hospital at Royette where naval patients are cared for.

He also heard from the Marines the story of their initial attack on Belleau Woods and how the Devil Dogs had attacked the square heads and drove them from the woods which lay a little to the rear. Eroh had a talk with Jacob Ulmer, [and] for the first time recounted what he had learned of his son's death from the officers of the command. It appears as though a number of men under the command of two lieutenants, of whom young Ulmer was one, had volunteered to take an important machine gun nest near the edge of the wood, which was raking the ranks of the Marines. The men were advancing under temporary cover and dodging from shell hole to shell hole and obstruction to stumps and everything which would afford a moment's protection from the rattling bullets of the machine guns when a shrapnel shell struck a tree almost immediately overhead and riddled the contingent. Donnelly, the other Lieutenant was wounded previously and while the wound was being dressed by Ulmer another shell struck and Donnelly was killed outright and Ulmer was so terribly wounded that he died the next day. He is now buried in the courtyard of a little Chateau overlooking the Marne where the hardest fighting the world has ever seen took place, and won the day for America. Of Ulmer's original command of 250 men only 40 were left on October 1st and all the officers were killed or missing.

Two trips later about the 20th, the train loaded up a number of the wounded of Company D 103rd Engineers who had been shelled by the Germans at Dorman's on the second day of the drive. The Engineers had gone out ahead to perform their work in conjunction with the Infantry when they were shelled by shrapnel and sustained their wounds.

Every where along the entire line of the western front the French people have the utmost respect for the Americans. One of the most admirable traits displayed by the Americans was their treatment of German prisoners, who were never treated harshly and whose severest duty was to aid in the burial of American dead. At the Marne river shortly after the big push in which the Pennsylvania Division earned the nickname "The Iron Division," Eroh saw the shallow portions of the river clogged with the dead who were killed in battle. They represented the dead of the German, French, English and American forces and bore silent witness to the terrific fighting which had taken place along the river.

While standing with three of his train mates near the train just behind Chateau Thierry in August a gas shell struck less than 20 yards away and before the men could adjust their masks they were caught in the fumes and slightly gassed, but serious[ly] enough to send them to the hospital. Eroh developed a condition of the lung which required an operation and he was invalided home after spending several weeks in the embarkation hospital.

The Hun and Boche Were Pushed, Chased and Defeated

> December 4, 1918
> 1st Lieutenant H. R. D. Schwenk
> 314th Infantry Regiment
> 79th Division
> Hill 361, 25 kilometers, N.E. Verdun.

Dear Mother:

Take a look at that heading. Wass densht from sell? (Poor German). We are still holding the hill and not being molested in the least, barring the cooties. It was an easy matter for us to come here after Nov. 11th and comfortably place ourselves, because the Germans did the exit stunt into Germany. Had we tried to rout the Germans from the fortified positions at the time when we were at logger heads with each other, sigh, quickly sigh. It would not have been a yell for more food or more ships, but a silent and solemn request for more men.

I am at a loss to know the exact cause for their willingness to suspend hostilities; at first, I thought it was the food question and no doubt it had played an important part. Yesterday Major Schoge and the Colonel autoed to Metz and claim that the food question in Metz is excellent and a far shot from expectations. They ate and ate at little cost, duck, chicken, turkey, potatoes etc. and could have done some drinking too, but they declined. Beer by the glasses at three cents, (our money). Major Schoge sized the place very carefully and thinks our troops would never have been able to take Metz, because of the strong fortifications.

It must be remembered that our troops did erase the St.-Mihiel salient; that they did meet and defeat the best troops of the Kaiser between the Argonne and Meuse and gain ground slowly at times but surely and finally on the east side of the Meuse. The Hun and Boche were pushed, chased and defeated from one fortified position to another, up and down hill he retreated with the Khaki clad boys close at his heels. This all done in a short period of time and what have the French said, "It couldn't be done," and did not tackle it, thereby allowing the damnable freak of human nature to live four years on his soil. The longer he lived here the harder it was to wrest the land from him, for he was continually making the place safer for himself by stringing barbed wire, planting concrete machine gun nests, and measuring distances from hill to hill and stronghold to stronghold. Ammunition! I can hardly believe he quit because of ammunition for the lowlands north and east of this hill is literally chocked full of ammunition of all kinds.

I was in one shed and noticed on the blackboard, bearing names, Bertha, Frederick, Albert, Minerva, Wilhelm and several others, and under the names were figures either showing what kind of ammunition shells were required for each gun or the amount needed. I stood alongside one shell and was surprised to know that I was taller than it. It only came to my shoulder. That's the kind the boys call the G.I. cans; they turn a street into the appearance of a dam. Because these G.I.'s were floating through the air nonchalantly it is necessary to list the names of some of our boys under the missing in action class. Of course the Boche had the same trying circumstances, and I know, for on two different occasions before the burial squad cleaned up, I saw the right wing of a German taken clean at the shoulder and again at the foot which was still covered by the shoe.

It seems to us the Boche were pleased when our artillery would kill his animals for it meant steak for him. By actual count, I saw five animals cut clean from the neck to tail on both sides and in two cases their jaws were broken and the tongues robbed as far back in the throat as possible. This appeared to us like a lack of food at the front, and if this were really the case what could have been the conditions in the interior.

Three weeks from today is December 25th and it will be December 25th with me no matter where I am. You people will be celebrating Christmas in a manner that I know something of. I will celebrate also but in a manner that remains to be found out. This makes the third consecutive Christmas season away from home for me, because of war and rumors of war; 1916 at Camp Stewart, Texas, 1917 Camp Meade, Maryland; 1918?

Dad's letter gave me the first inkling of Ivan's death. Then Lieut. Kaufman and I read the sorrowing news. The past two Christmas's were spent together and this coming one I will dwell with him in thought only. It hurts, it pains, it bewilders to realize this fact. It was his ill luck to make the supreme sacrifice, a thing we were all prepared to do and willing in a certain sense of the thought. Soldiering with him for several years and knowing him as I did you can feel assured he gave some account of himself before the damnable Hun caught him in the advance. As I said before, Bagenstose saw him carried by four men from the field of battle that is all the news I received until dad's letter broke in on me. I was hoping and praying that his wound would not prove serious but to no avail. He jumped into the front line on the night of September 25th and started forward with his platoon, no doubt at 5:30 a.m. Sept. 26th, the time set for the advance by the American divisions gathered between the Argonne and Meuse. This advance was pushed over country held by the Boche from the beginning of the war and he was sort-a-tamed by an artillery bombardment lasting from 2:30 to 5:30. The first several kilometers were easy sailing, the Hun occupying the trenches being scared blue and it was simply a case to drag them out of the dugouts.

As they advanced, the 316th on the left of the 314th, the ruined town of Malancourt came toview and the resistance stiffened, altho our troops forged ahead with few casualties. Passing Malancourt, the real fighting began. Montfaucon, a stronghold of the enemy was the first objective and lay a few kilometers ahead. Trench work well protected by barbed wire, and machine gun nests, so placed to cover every inch of the ground, were encountered and delayed the speed of our boys. Prisoners were not seen anymore. The few Boche left to protect these heights stuck to the finish and by this time the peaceful and law abiding citizens that formed the regiments of our divisions were hardened soldiers, hell bent for revenge and revenge was theirs. The Crown Prince viewed the battle of Verdun in 1916 from the heights of Mountfaucon, but not anymore for on September 27th, the 316th and 313th on the left of it and the 314th and 315th on the right, encircled it, and continued onward. The resistance was still stiffening and in the face of it our boys advanced slowly but surely. Our division was relieved on Monday, September 30th and it was on this day somewhere to the left of Natillois that Ivan was wounded. Several days later, I learned of this sad news through Bagenstose.

It is very late so will close,
Lovingly,
H. R. D. Schwenk

The soldier Ivan was 1st Lieut. Ivan Lautenbacher, a close friend of Schwenk's from their home town of Schuylkill Haven, Pa.

Men of the 4th Pennsylvania National Guard. A 1917 photograph at Mt. Gretna, Pennsylvania, prior to being amalgamated into the 28th Division, 103rd Engineers.

Bullets and Shrapnel Flew Like Hell All the Time

December 5, 1918
Private William Bartsch
79th Division
A.E.F.
Vitel, France.

Dear Sis and Bill

I have been in this town since November 24. Am feeling fine but have only gone into town once since I am here. This place used to be one of the Kaisers summer homes and its beautiful.

Sis, news is scarce and so are the girls around here and very few can talk English and then only a few words. I was in the last drive from October 26 to November 15 and it was hell, as one never knew when he would be knocked off or injured. Bullets and shrapnel flew like hell all the time.

Our company was in the front lines and we lost heavily. Our two Lieutenants were wounded, Major killed and three sergeants wounded and about 29 men in the company, so you can see how awful it must have been. Now I was one of the lucky ones when our sergeant called the role [roll] in the morning of Nov. 11 about 11:30 a.m. There was only 36 men and 11 other men that were on the ration detail for food and that made 47 men in the place of 107. Where the others got to no one knew till that very evening when a few more came in but not all.

We had to hike about four days and nights and sure did play on the able bodied men. Then once we had to do without anything from Saturday night until Wednesday night at 1:30 and we did not get anything hot until Thursday morning. Sis I am patiently waiting until it comes my turn to come home, but don't have any idea when it will be.

They are mostly all Phila boys in the division I am in. It is called the 79th or the Liberty Division but there are not many of the old men left and it had to be replaced once, as they lost so heavily. I have only seen one fellow from home. He is June Clay's brother.

The Red Cross sure did treat the Dough Boys fine. They can't do enough for them. This town is up near the Swiss border and has never been shelled. They say they never heard a gun shot since they are here, so see the town must be beautiful. There are about eight or ten buildings and all are hotels. They are made of stone and brick.

Well sis, I guess I will have to close as I have only been to town once and I don't know much news.

Till the next time.

William.

December 7, 1918

On this date, December 7, 1918, United States Army Chief of Staff General March announced the makeup of the Army of Occupation which would consist of the following divisions: 1st, 2nd, 3rd, 4th, 5th, 7th, 28th, 32nd, 33rd, 42nd, 79th, 89th, and 90th.

The makeup of the A. of C. was as follows: 1st to 7th, the Regular Army 28th, Pennsylvania National Guard; 32nd, Wisconsin and Michigan National Guard; 33rd, Illinois National Guard; 42nd "Rainbow"; 79th, Pennsylvania, Maryland, District of Columbia, National Guard; 39th, Kansas and Missouri National Guard; 89th, South Dakota, Colorado, Nebraska, New Mexico and Arizona National Guard; and 90th, Texas and Oklahoma National Guard.

General March revealed that a total of 5,326 officers and 135,515 men had been assigned for early convoy home while the grand total actually embarked to December 7, 1918, stood at 554 officers, 17,362 men, a few nurses, prisoners and civilians, eleven navy officers and 554 navy enlisted men.

Webb Miller, a United Press correspondent, wrote the following story about the Army of Occupation for a syndicated column picked up by many Pennsylvania newspapers.

The policy of the Americans in charge of civil affairs has been to impose restrictions only as it is shown they are needed, but they are prepared to impose and enforce the most stringent and drastic laws if necessary.

The German people make no attempt to fraternize and do not conceal the fact that they are glad about the American presence. On the other hand American rule has been extremely mild, with the exception occupying of public buildings, some coal and forage, part of the railway and telephones and the billeting of American officers with German civilians families.

During the occupation of some German villages and towns, the American soldiers are unaccustomed to German soldiers still dressed in field gray walking around or standing on street corners, while only weeks before they were meant to kill or be killed.

Military police are guarding bridges and railways and patrolling the streets of the occupied towns and villages. The hotels and restaurants and movies are thronged with American troops. The people never seem to get accustomed to the sight of the khaki clad columns flowing through their villages day after day. They appear to retain the bewilderment caused by the quick turn of events. Only a few weeks or months ago their reserve troops marched westward through these same villages to the front.

Adults stare, but covertly, at the dough boys as the latter go quietly about their business. Only the children are unable to conceal their sentiments, which mostly are some form of curiosity. They follow each column that marches by, some clinging to the hands of good natured dough boys, despite the admonitions of their elders.

A score of small boys, who looted a warehouse of a hundred shiny new dress helmets, did a thriving business with the Americans trading them for anything from a few marks to a slice of white bread. I saw an artillery man purchase three for half a loaf of bread. Another got an Iron Cross for some soap.

Every auto mobile is fringed with urchins, until the driver, fearful of their safety, shoos them off. Whenever a kitchen outfit is set up every child in the neighborhood gathers around, the troops tolerantly sharing their rations with them. At Bitburg, I saw a soldier, eating beside the road, give half his rations to three little girls. On the other hand the only hostile demonstration has been by the children, who threw pebbles and vegetables at American troops.

Officers billeted with families in small towns report that their hosts fulfill the requirements satisfactorily. Generally they utterly ignore the Americans presence in the house.

At Wittlich and Killburg I found a number of officers billeted with families who had lost their sons in the Argonne, where they fought the Americans. The houses were in mourning, but the people accepted the invaders presence stoically.

The proprietor of a hotel in Treves, which was taken over by the press section, was unable to conceal his interest in the quality and abundance of the food the Americans had. They furnished themselves from the regular army rations.

The principal hotel in Treves is filled with staff officers. They sat at one side of the big dining room, while pictures of the former Kaiser and Von Hindenburg stare down at them from the opposite wall.

On Occupation Duty in Germany

> December 12, 1918
> Corp. William J. Doyle
> Bty. E 12th Field Artillery
> 1st Division.
> A.E.F.
> Soldier Bill's Missive
> Bergbrohl, Germany

Dear Dad:

Well at last we've reached the Rhine, and your old son is still alive and well. Looking back at the whole thing, I've often wondered how I ever pulled through. We started at Verdun, a somewhat quiet sector, and then came Chateau Thierry, the tale of which is now a household talk. We were the division that stopped the Boche in his mad rush to Paris on July 14th, we were relieved from Chateau Thierry and hiked to Soissons, some fifty kilometers away, resting one day and went into position the night of the 16th. We adjusted fire the 17th and on the morning of the 18th saw the offensive in full swing. The morning of the 22nd our artillery regiment went in over the top with the tanks. On the 28th we were relieved and hiked back to the rear for a rest.

We held the lines of the Lorraine sector with out firing a shot for twelve days. Then came the St.-Mihiel drive, an All-American one, and we were given the squeezing point. We were again relieved on September 10th, spent a few days in rest and then left for Champagne front, Monte Blanca was our objective and we finally got it. We were twenty-eight days on the front before being relieved. After our relief was effected we made a two day hike to the scene of the American struggle were given the post of honor for the American drive and got our two days objective in one.

We were still on the Argonne front when the Kaiser called it quits and from then on we have been advancing the line until the present writing.

We have been with the French army the majority of the time while on the front. General Mangin, the one armed French leader, was our commander at Verdun, Chateau Thierry, Soissons and Champagne, and we have been called his favorites. The other drives were under the command of General Pershing.

At Verdun, Chateau Thierry and Soissons I was an observer with the infantry and had some real thrills. On the quiet Lorraine front I served as a kitchen police. St.-Mihiel saw me as a cannoneer, Champagne as a wireless operator and runner, and at the Argonne I also ran. I am at present attached to the Fourth Marine brigade as a messenger to our regimental headquarters.

The conditions here upon the Rhine are all that one could ask. Real winter has not yet set in, and we are enjoying almost autumn like weather. The river has over flown [*sic*] its banks due to the somewhat heavy rainfall of the past few days. I saw an accident the other day in which a German was killed. The casualty would have furnished a corking good editorial upon the rights of corporations to own public highways. A narrow gauge road running alongside the main road between two small towns was the scene of the accident. There are no guardrails, and traffic being heavy on both roads there is always the danger to human life. Such road would be prohibited in the states unless the corporation owning and operating it assured its hearty approval of safety first. In this country, however, everything tends to the idea or fact, rather, that "Might is right."

I am keeping like the Teutonic warriors of old "Der Wacht am Rhine," with great fidelity. So is the rest of the great Army of Occupation. As it will be a physical impossibility to bring the noble old river home with us upon our return, we can do with combined feelings of pleasure and pain the next best thing, carry along the fond remembrance of its many beauties in addition to harrowing memories of previous sanguinary events that brought us hither.

William J. Doyle.

Left Him Alone in His Glory

December 13, 1918
Pvt. Henry L. Minnig
509th Ambulance Regt.
Section 563
Ambulance Corps.
Army of Occupation
Rhineland. Germany

Dear Father:

It's about a year since I landed in France and until now have been unable to give any account of my experience and happenings during the twelve months. January 10 we landed at Brest after a voyage which kept us busy on the lookout and dodging enemy underseas craft. At the French port of landing we boarded a train and after 40 hours of travel detrained at Sandmourt Base Camp. There I was made chief bugler. We stayed at Base Camp two months until the middle of March when I was transferred to an ambulance repair shop at Chalone Sur Marne. Here I saw much of the surroundings, but as yet little of the front, the place I was longing to get to. On my first night at Chalone the Boche air raided the town causing much destruction. One bomb hit an ambri, killing 50 people. The boys of our park went voluntarily to the aid of the distressed. We worked all night in the face of a terrific barrage. One Boche bomb struck a house close to where we were engaged and the shock knocked us down and for a time made us helpless. We soon rallied, however and finished the eventful night. For our part in the rescue the commander of the army, Gen. Gouraud saw it fit to cite us individually.

A few days later an American aviator in the French service met death while operating above us. We organized a firing squad of ten, I sounded taps, and although far away from home, the brave Yankee was given a military funeral after the custom of his own land. We marked the mound with a tiny U.S. flag and "Left him alone in his glory."

My next service was with my captain and we drove along the fronts in the Champagne and Argonne sectors. Exciting times and narrow escapes were not uncommon but we came out all right after many heatless, sleepless and eatless nights. Bad roads and extreme darkness except for the intermittent light from artillery fire.

In the fore part of November, I was transferred to section 630 and ordered to Paris. I arrived at the French capital on the 11th in the height of the celebrating of the signing of the armistice. Such a display of wild enthusiasm I did not think possible. Pandemonium reigned throughout and as I had no knowledge of the cessation of arms you can imagine the condition of my mind. France "bled white" had outlived her four years of trial, and on this fateful day realized her hope and prayer of 47 years. The hated Prussian lay prostrate at her feet, and as I stepped from the train the sight of a doughboy uniform added increased vigor to the French cries of "Vive L France," "Vive L' America" "Vive L American poilus," filled the air. The women nearest laid hands on your son Henry and such effusion of hugs and kisses I did not think it possible to bestow. And during all the time I did not know what it meant.

At present we are stationed in a small town in Alsace, near Strasburg, about 20 kilometers distant from the Rhine. The natives speak German only, so different from the French tongue we heard so much of until now. But to us it is all Greek, so why worry? We are looking forward to happy days and the good ship that will bear us westward to the best country on God's green earth.

Sincerely your son,
Henry I. Minnig

We Have Had Many Hair Raising Experiences

December 16, 1918
Private George A. Tobias
Co. D, 304th Motor Supply Train.
79th Division
A.E.F.
Verdun, France.

No doubt you have had numerous letters from the soldiers of different organizations of the army including the Infantry, artillery, aviation and machine gun units, etc. but there is one which I never seen mentioned in you paper. I wish you would print a little article regarding our unit. I am a member of company D, 304th Motor Supply Train, 79th Division, which has made a record for itself equal to any other supply train.

We have been on three fronts, Argonne, St.-Mihiel, and Verdun, and have driven our trucks over roads that one would think impassable. We have kept our infantry and artillery supplied with food and ammunition and in many instances have had to take the supplies up to the front line trenches under heavy shell fire. The traffic up to those places makes Center St. look like a small country road. Our men have until recent drive been caught on the roads in dark rainy nights or stretches of 70 hours with hardly a bite to eat and no sleep, and besides taking up supplies have always brought back wounded men off the fields. We have had many hair raising experiences, for instance one of our trucks on returning from the front was hit by a high explosive shell and though the driver and his assistant were wounded and are both in the hospital at this writing they brought the truck back to the park and our mechanics had it in perfect running order and loaded with supplies ready to start on a return trip within two hours time. This showed that our trucks proved on equal basis with the shrapnel of the Boche.

Every man in the unit has been working with that "Do or Die" spirit of 1776 and has taken his chances behind the wheel. I have spoken of the truck driver running machines on congested roads and under all kinds of circumstances, but I wish to give some credit to our cooks. They have spent many a sleepless night preparing our hot meals for we men as we came in hungry and weary. The meals being cooked in old stables and houses that have been half blown down, with the rain running into their kitchens and about a foot of mud around the stoves.

We are driving the Riker truck made by the Locomobile people of Philadelphia, and they have proven to be one of the best trucks over here, in fact equal to the famous Liberty Truck.

I have been in the army for seven months, leaving my home town on the 27th of May and sailed for France on the 14th of July, having been in active service ever since I arrived here. I have seen many strange sights which I will never forget and have come through without a scratch though I have had many narrow escapes.

Respectfully,
George A. Tobias.

December 23, 1918—The location of all American Divisions from the 28th November to present.

> 1st—Canach, Luxembourg
> 2nd—Modernach, Luxembourg
> 3rd—Remich, Luxembourg
> 4th—Hayange, Germany
> 5th—Longuyen, France
> 6th—Ancreviller, France
> 7th—Euvekin, France
> 21st—Marbache
> 26th—Montigny-le-Rol, France
> 27th—Corbie, France
> 28th—Heudlcourt, France
> 29th—Bourbonne-les-Bains, France
> 30th—Le Mans, France
> 31st—Le Mans, France
> 32nd—Conesdorf, Luxembourg
> 33rd—Troyon
> 34th—Le Mans, France
> 35th—Larauville, France
> 36th—Tronchoy, France
> 37th—Oostroosebeke, Belgium
> 38th—Le Mans, France

42nd—Mersch, Luxembourg
77th—Les Vignettes, France
78th—Semur, France
79th—Vacherauville, France
80th—Ancy-le-Franc, France
81st—Wassy, France
82nd—Prauthoy
84th—Le Mans, France
86th—Le Mans, France
87th—Foulain, France
88th—Lagny, France
89th—Dentergham, Belgium
90th—Marville, France
91st—Dentergham, Belgium

Depot divisions locations.

41st—St. Aigan
75th—St. Nazaire, France
39th—Toul, France
40th—Revigny, France

Cootie Hunting Is Fun

January 5, 1919
Pvt. Allen Klahr
Battery B, 20th Field Artillery
Breshem, Luxemburg.

Dear Mother and all:

It is Sunday evening and for the want of something to do, I thought it best to write. It is raining now and a fellow can't move out anywhere. It is raining most of the time and life is pretty miserable. It is not very cold, and that surely is one consolation. We do not have heat of any kind in our room, so it is well its not cold.

There are a bunch of fellows around me talking about life in the woods and I am quite interested, as I prefer life in the woods, to being billeted in some town. I spent the greater part of my time in France living in the woods.

One of the fellows has just gone "cootie" hunting. There is surely a lot of fun hunting them, the more you find the more fun there is. About midnight is when you mind their company most and as to having close friends, they cannot be beaten. Once a fellow gets them they are hard to get rid of, unless he has about a dozen different changes of clothes, and a chance to take a bath everyday.

> Your loving son,
> Allen.

"A Runner" Tells His Story

> January 24, 1919
> Pvt. John Reber
> Co. C, 103rd Engineers
> 28th Division

John Reber a member of Co. C, 103rd Engineers in an interview to the *Call* newspaper of Schuylkill Haven, Pennsylvania, gave an account from which the following article is compiled.

Reber enlisted in Co. C on July 14, 1917. He was wounded at Fismes, having been struck on the right arm with shrapnel. This was on his seventeenth birthday, July 29th. He received attention at a Red Cross station and then returned to his company and work. On October 2nd, he was in a gas attack at the Argonne forest. He was sent to the hospital, put in a gas ward and then sent to an embarkation center and arrived home.

John was what is termed a "runner," one who carries messages, does scout work and all sorts of dangerous jobs. As such he was in constant danger throughout the entire time the company was near the front. At first there were four runners for the four platoons, namely, Lester Reber, John Reber, Jesse Wilson and Mugs Dewald. Lester Reber was made a male orderly. Wilson was gassed and wounded and Dewald was gassed, requiring John Reber to do the carrying of messages for the four platoons.

His first experience was at Charley where the company had built trenches and put up barbwire entanglements. The company was held in reserve in case the Germans broke through the first line of trenches. It was here that he was struck on the back by a piece of spent shrapnel. He was the first man in the company to be hit. The shrapnel dropped on his back from the air and was still hot enough to burn a hole through his uniform. This is how he discovered he was hit when the hot metal came in contact with his skin. The piece was but two inches long and all the men wanted to see it; even the captain made a big fuss over it.

The company was then taken to the Château-Thierry sector in trucks part of the way, and then they were compelled to hike it. They built in at a place called St. Agnes. They then hiked around for several days, as it appeared they did not know where to put the company. The Germans drove the French back from Dormans, six miles, and Co. C was ordered back to St. Agnes, which was on the right flank of Château-Thierry, and put in the front line, with the first battalion of the 103rd Engineers, namely Companies A, B and C and the 109th Infantry, in all about 3,000 men. In front of them they had at least two Prussian Guard divisions, about 20,000 men. These 3,000 men held this crowd back for three nights and two days and were then relieved by the French Blue Devils. Before they were relieved the 109th Infantry went over the top four times without the aid of a barrage.

This particular feat of the 3,000 men according to a French Colonel, who later addressed them, prevented the Boche from getting to Paris. Had it not been for their holding the Germans back at this point they would have been enabled to get around the right of Château-Thierry and would have surrounded and cleaned up the 5th and 6th Marines and the 2nd Engineers, who were in Château-Thierry and given the credit for holding back the Germans. The French were routed because they had been celebrating some sort of a national holiday on July 15th and were drunk with too much white wine. It was here that several soldiers of the 103rd were wounded and gassed.

They were brought back to their billets and remained for several days. At this place they also received the first meal they had had in three days; beef that was prepared the first day did not reach them until the third day and when it did it was simply rotten. They had no water except the rain they caught in their slickers or raincoats. This water had to be then strained through their handkerchiefs to get the sand out it and then was put in their canteens. At the billets then, they received their first meals, a good feed that Sgt. Brown had prepared for them.

They were then taken back to Charley again and they hiked for two days and three nights. When they were three miles from the place the orders were changed and they were rushed back to Château-Thierry and hiked to Courmont. There they again met the 109th infantry and saw Lieut. Woodbury. They had a hard time getting up; they hiked all day and night and worked trying to drag the teams through the woods and mud. The mud was so deep that the heavy wagons sank in to the axles in it and the horses up to their bellies. They had to chop down trees in the woods and throw them across the roads in order to bring up their trains. They had to hitch 12 to 15 horses to the heavy tool wagons to get them through and after working a whole night only got two wagons through. The next day they had to go back again and assist the other wagons to get them through the mud.

The company was sent out to fix roads. Sergt. Brown got a meal ready and Reber was sent out to look for the company. He hiked four miles to tell the captain eats were ready and the captain sent him back for the eats. The meal was brought up in the little "dinky" wagon and while being brought up the road was being shelled all along the entire length. Sergt. Brown and Lieut. Woodcock went along. Lieut. Woodcock was hit with shrapnel in bringing up the train. They had a hard time, as the place was full of barbwire entanglements and strewn with grenades. They had to pick their way through and had to be mighty careful not to have the horse or wheels strike any of the grenades, which were not exploded, or they could have been blown up.

When they reached the point where the company was supposed to be there was no company, they having moved ahead towards Courmont. They waited for orders and no orders came until the next night. Reber went forward to find out where the company was and on the way met Lester Reber coming to look for the grub. They then proceeded for a distance until they came to a clump of trees where they hid the wagon and carried the grub to the men.

All the while the Germans were shelling all about them. The members of the company who were lined up along a building were good targets for the battery of machine guns of the Germans. The men when they got their grub would go inside the building to eat it. A shell struck the building and took out the roof of it clean off. Just a moment before the shell struck, Raymond Mill had gone outside with his mess pans for grub. When it struck Mill turned right around and came in again without getting any grub. No one was hurt while they were feeding under those difficulties.

They then started to take the cans back to the wagon again and when they reached where they had left the wagon the driver was nowhere to be found. The Germans had spotted him and shelled him with both gas and shrapnel and he had had a hard time with the horses as they were frightened and became all twisted up in the harness. They finally righted things and when the cans were loaded on the wagon they made some flying trip back to the mess tent. Reber was slightly gassed on this trip.

Later the company began hiking toward Fismes. They dug in and remained in position for a day and then hiked on again. This hike took them all night and it should have taken but fifteen minutes if the captain had chosen the right road. The same distance was later covered in fifteen minutes by the company. That evening Reber counted 52 shells that were thrown by the Germans at the company. Only three of these exploded. This is explained by reason of the fact that the Germans were victims of the prisoners whom they compelled to work in the ammunition factories. The shells were filled with either sand or sawdust. Reber stated that oft times, it was told later, on the English front, these shells that refused to go off were opened up and were found to contain notes which read, "You do your bit, we'll do ours."

They then moved further towards Fismes and had to cross what was termed no man's land. The entire regiment was taken up to Fismes to try to put up a bridge but they did not get any up. Here almost the entire Company B was gassed. The orders were given to return to the woods outside of Fismes. In going back they made the trip in fifteen minutes when it previously took them all night to do it having at that time gone a roundabout way. When they got back the captain found out he had left some of his belongings up near Fismes. Reber was ordered back to get them. When he reached the spot he found that the captain had appropriated his, Reber's, shelter half, which was one half of a pup tent. After being missing for some time, Reber brought the belongings back to the captain safely.

The company was sent up to fill a mine hole in front of St. Giles. While on the road John Knarr, the wagoner, was hit on the head with shrapnel and had four horses that he was driving killed outright. He was taken to the hospital.

Company D of the 103rd Engineers, the company that had been at Fismes, were given orders by Major Bradford to retire to the rear because the town was being surrounded. They did so and when they assembled at the given point they only had about thirty men left in their company. Twelve of them were killed and the others wounded and missing. The entire company was scattered all over. This is the place were company D suffered all its casualties and all on the account of the orders given to retire. The town was in no danger of being surrounded. Company C was then ordered to take their places and went toward Fismes. The company was left just at the edge of the place and the captain, a 2nd lieutenant and three runners, Wilson, Lester Reber and John Reber went into Fismes. The courthouse was on fire and this illuminated the entire street near it. The place was still full of German snipers with machine guns and rifles. The captain had a map of the place with the location of the infantry battalion headquarters, which he was seeking to find marked thereon. He had the men hold his slicker or a raincoat about him while he attempted to examine the map by the aid of a flashlight. Just as quick as he flashed the light, a ray shown through or between the folds of the raincoat and just that quickly, German shells hit right above them. They moved to the other side of the street and the place was then showered with bullets and shells, but they finally reached the battalion HQ. Reber was then told to go back and bring up the company. He found his way back but only with and under great difficulty. The flare of the fire at the Court House lighted up the street and made it fine for German snipers to shoot at anyone who got in the light. At one place Reber happened to get in the light and that quick the bullets whizzed by him. He dropped in the mud on his stomach and lay there for a while and then attempted to get up, but as soon as he did another shower of bullets greeted him. He had to crawl on his stomach through all the mud and water of the streets for 150 yards. He reached Lieut. Woodcock and found that the other two runners had been hit.

Reber and the lieutenant began bringing up the company and after going but a short distance found they only had 6 of the company and the balance had dropped out in places of shelter. Reber then had to get out in the streets and in the light and the range of bullets and gather up the balance of the company. Finally all the men were coupled together again and started off.

In order to bring the company up to headquarters a sort of square in the town had to be crossed. The German snipers had this point well covered with machine guns and it was very dangerous to cross it. Reber was required to crouch near the point up against a building and directed the whole company across one at a time, telling them to beat it quick and what they were up against. The entire company was thus brought up to headquarters without any being hit. This was considered good luck by the company and as Reber stated, all of Company C was in good luck throughout the entire time when they were at the front as they were in so many dangerous places and under so much shell fire that it was remarkable they were not all shot to pieces. Also that it was through no directions or foresight of their commanding captain that they escaped.

Well, just as the last man got across the square the order was passed to Reber to take the company back again. The same difficulty and dangers had to be encountered again, but they finally got through the town. There was no commanding officer with them and they did not know where they were. They dug in along a railroad bank. Their captain, Captain Donnelly, was back in a dug out in the town with the major and the boys and they all had to look out for themselves as best they knew how. They all went to sleep while Reber went back to direct the captain to their location should he put in an appearance. He hid behind a wall to watch for the captain. He could get a range of the street he had to come down for a distance of several hundred yards. The Germans evidently had the place spotted as every time Reber took a peep to see if the lost captain was coming, shells were fired at the rock. Later they began to shell the place and he returned to the company. About nine a.m. the captain came along and joined the company and sent the company over the hill to where Company D was located.

A Company D runner, Lester Reber, John Reber and an infantryman, sent out to carry messages, heard a six inch shell coming and dove into a dugout. The shell struck near by and the three were hit but Reber escaped because he was at the bottom. The infantryman who was last in, was badly wounded in legs, arms and jaw, the Company D runner was wounded in the legs, and Lester Reber had the lapel of his coat taken off and was grazed below the eye. Just a little bit higher and he would have had his eye knocked out. Reber took the infantryman who weighed 200 pounds on his shoulders and Lester Reber took the Company D man and started to take them to a dressing station. The Germans had strung what was called hair wire, yet very strong, all over the ground and it was hard to walk. The wounded man could not lift his legs and his feet caught in the wire. They had a hard time for a while then Reber put the man on his back and carried him to the dressing station, after which he made eight trips through six inch shell barrage that same day.

Orders were given to put up bridges and volunteers were asked for. Enough were secured and they went up to the Vesle River and put three bridges across. They went back and were relieved. Coming back, Christ, Deer and Nandorf were injured and Baker was gassed. John was also hit with shrapnel. At the time Christ was hit he was lying on the ground adjusting the mouthpiece of his gas mask. A shell struck twenty yards back of him and the remarkable thing about that shell was it bounded backward and a piece hit Christ on the jaw. A fellow by the name of Hess shot himself in the leg at this time also. They were in no mans land and did not know when the Germans would pop up and always had their pistols out and cocked. Hess happened to put his pistol back in the holster. In walking along he tripped and fell and the pistol went off and the bullet plowed itself all the way through his leg.

Company C was relieved and had been in sort of a valley and located right in a dried up creek with the banks on either side of them. The place was called Longville Farm. The Germans, try as they would, could not reach them. The captain, however, was back five to eight miles, and in carrying messages from the captain to the company it was necessary for Reber to go through shellfire.

One time, to direct him to their headquarters an infantry runner was with Reber and a shell struck near them and the infantryman was almost blown to pieces. Reber picked him up and carried him back but when he reached the dressing station he was dead. Evidently the fellow had been dead when Reber picked him up but Reber did not wait to find out as the shells were dropping all around him. He was given another guide and went through. While lying at Longville Farm in the cut, they camouflaged the road by putting up canvas painted the color of the ground on thirty-foot poles, each piece being five feet long. The German observation balloons looking at this would mistake it. They were directed as to how and where to place the same by the Americans from airplanes.

Platoons were then sent to Fismes to keep the roads open so that the ambulances could get through and to watch the bridges. Lieut. Woodcock at that time was doing officer's work for the four platoons and Reber was doing all the runner's work. Reber would take the platoons up and remain with them and then take them back again and bring up the next. The distance was about eight miles. All this was covered on foot. In carrying messages from the headquarters to the platoons he either had to walk, crawl or sometimes he would be lucky enough to be given a lift by an ambulance, although very rarely as it was contrary to international law to allow any man on the ambulance with a pistol on his person. However, some of the divers would take him along occasionally. They were always under fire of snipers going into Fismes. When asked why the snipers were not dislodged he stated they never fired at an entire company, only at individuals or ambulances and they could not be located as they too were camouflaged. Some of the snipers, when they were located, would be painted all over, their heads, faces, and clothing like the leaves of a tree.

In telling how the Americans would locate the snipers, Reber stated that at night they would watch the fire from the rifles and then set up a stick and another in front of it and would then move them until the second stick would be in line with the flash. When daylight came they would be able to tell by looking over the sticks, the trees in which the sniper or snipers were. A squad would then get together and the tree would be riddled with rifle fire and the Germans would be seen tumbling out of it.

The entire company was then ordered down a hill into the valley in broad daylight with the Germans on the other side of another mountain and firing shells directly at Company C. Reber was sent back to get the hash wagon. He had a horse by this time and after he got up on top of the mountain, the animal refused to move.

Shells were dropping all around him and still the animal would not move. Reber said this was because the horse had been in so many gas attacks that he became winded and really couldn't go. Finally he started off at a walk. Nothing was left for Reber to do but put on his gas mask, fold his arms and let the horse take his time of it. He wouldn't go faster than a walk. He finally reached the commissary department and brought up the hash wagon. It was rainy weather and this was the time when Reber was in the saddle 48 hours straight, not even getting out to feed the horse or water him but doing so while in the saddle. He got a new horse and when the hash wagon was finally brought up to where he had left Company C on the other side of the mountain, the Germans were still shelling the place. The 103rd Regiment had by this time put up 40 bridges.

As runner, Reber had to go up to the company to tell them feed was ready and bring the company back. When they got to where the chuck wagon was the captain reported he had forgotten his kit of toilet articles. Reber of course was ordered to go down the mountain and bring them up to the captain. This he had to do under heavy shellfire. The Germans had blocked the road with wooden frames filled with rocks and these had to be torn down by the company. The men had to be afraid that whenever they moved a rock it was liable to set off a shell set by the Germans but this did not happen and they finally moved all the barriers and got through. The Boche had been driven back so far by this time that they could not shell any more.

On September 8th, the French were sent up to relieve them and they were given lots of Bull Durham tobacco by Company C. That night while the company was sleeping a peculiar moaning was heard and some of the fellows were awakened. They knew what it was. It was German bombing planes and a bomb was dropped on either side of the dugout in which John Reber and Lester Reber were. The roof fell in on top of them, sandbags and all, but no one was injured. In this bombing raid 40 men were killed and 52 wounded. In the 112th Infantry, 13 were killed and 40 injured. Many horses were also killed in this raid but Company C did not lose a man.

The company was then ordered back 20 miles and headed for the St.-Mihiel salient. They hiked for three days and two nights. They were then brought back to Les Islette and remained there for four days in some Italian barracks and here caught a fine supply of cooties.

Orders then came to move up to the Argonne Forest. This was on Sept. 25th. The American barrage began at eleven at night and continued till five in the morning. This was prior to the attack. Tanks, artillery, infantry, were all lined up for the attack. The three inch guns or the 75's as they were called, were lined up hub to hub, or just space between them to allow them to pass one another on the rebound after firing. Back of these heavies, the howitzers, the trench mortars and the 11-, 12- and 15-inch cannon were mounted on the railroads. This was the only time the company had so much support of their own guns. The tanks moved forward first and then a wave of doughboys were sent ahead. By the time the first wave of doughboys were half a mile ahead the engineers had built roads for the three inch guns and they were being brought up.

At this place there was a mountain peak something similar to the mountaintop at Cape Horn, above, Schuylkill Haven. This peak was filled with German machine gun nests and they had a clean sweep and killed many before they were routed. Volunteers were called to bring back the wounded who were on this hill. Sergt. Mengle and John Reber were two of them and were given a stretcher between them. There were about 30 volunteers and they had 15 stretchers between them. They had to travel through the Germans' second line trench, up to a ravine through which water was flowing which they had to wade for quite a distance to the base of the mountain, and then climb over rocks and fallen trees and pick up the wounded. Mengle and Reber made two trips up the mountain and brought a wounded man down each time. One of the men was shot through the back and the shell came out his abdomen. He had been hit with an air bomb. With every little jar he would beg them to be more careful in carrying the stretcher, but making their way over rocks, fallen trees, etc. at night was no easy task. The volunteers, between them brought 42 wounded out, some of whom had been lying there from 5 a.m. in the morning.

The infantry had gone ahead and were chasing the Germans but the third line or moppers up were cleaning up what was left. It was a platoon of this third line that went up to the mountainside after the German machine gun nests on top of the mountain. Of the platoon sent up, 42 were brought out wounded. They did not succeed in cleaning the Germans out at that time as they signaled for the German aeroplanes and these then dropped bombs on the platoon.

When they got the wounded to the base of the mountain there were no ambulances to take them back to the rear. The major in charge ordered them to go back and bring any ambulances or trucks in, at the point of a gun if it was necessary. They had to wait from 9 p.m. until 3 a.m. before they could secure ambulances to take them back to the dressing stations. Mengle and Reber remained with the wounded until the ambulances came and tried to make them as comfortable as possible. Several of the wounded begged and pleaded for water which they were compelled to refuse them because of the nature of their wounds. Some of them, of course, they could give water to.

After working the night before, all day and doing the volunteer work at night and until 3 a.m. he was ordered by the captain to go back and bring up the chow wagon, seven miles in the rear, and he had to walk at that, too. The roads were blocked with ammunition trains going to the front and after he reached the chow wagon and got started about noon, they were compelled to get in line and take turns in going along the road. They reached the company at three a.m. the next morning. The company then had been without regular food for three days and were living on rations, of hardtack and corn beef.

Here the Germans were driven that fast that by the time the American artillery would get set and find the range they would receive orders to move up front further, because they were out of range.

The company was given orders to move to Montfaucon and there lay in an apple orchard and with a woods on the left of them. Reber was sent back to direct the wagon train, which he did. He then reported to regimental headquarters, where his physical condition was found to be such that he was ordered to report to the Red Cross station. After an examination here he was found to have been gassed and was sent back to the hospital. This was October 2nd.

Reber had a most thrilling experience and one quite unusual in that he was riding a bicycle on no man's land under the impression that he was riding back to his company. It happened thus. When the company returned from St. Agnan and received orders to go to Dormans from which the French had been forced by the Germans, unknown to Company C, the company was halted at Charleroi, which is on the opposite side of the river from Dormans, by a French sentinel, who had been placed there to them head off. He ordered them to stop. The company got under cover in wine cellars at Charleroi, leaving a sentinel to stop Reber who was bringing up a wagon train. Reber left the wagon train at the top of the hill and went ahead on a bicycle he got from the tool wagon earlier in the day, to locate the company and find what disposition was to be made of the wagon train. Not knowing that the company had been stopped there and the sentinel failing to hold him up, he rode right down to the river Marne. Here he noticed that the American shells were falling on Dormans. Suspecting that something was wrong he started back, when the sentry who had been placed to stop him from going down, held him up and gave him the location of his captain to whom he reported. After the captain inquired as to where he had been he informed him that he had gone over the top on a bicycle and was really cycling on no man's land.

Reber stated that the boys never thought about being shot wounded or gassed. At least the majority did not and when they went up to the front they were always joking, singing or laughing. The entire 28th Division of which the 103rd Engineers was a part were in the hardest battles right along. The division was continually used as shock troops and after they had withheld or driven the Huns back the other troops were brought up and would be placed in position and the 28th would be sent on ahead to do more of the hardest fighting.

I Have About Ten Heinies Working Under Me

January 31, 1919
Private Francis Whalen
Co. A, 1st. Engineers
1st Infantry Division
Army of Occupation
Montabaur, Germany

Dear Brother:

Well, Thomas, I am in fine health and am getting plenty to eat so why worry about the high cost of living when you are seeing the world in the army.

I am on detached service from my outfit and am in Montabaur, Germany in charge of a Dutch sawmill. There are several things to consider when you have taken charge of a concern like that over here. In the first place, you have to speak the lingo a little bit at the least but I am all right here. When I come home don't get excited if I can't talk your language, for a guy over here must have his tongue split to compare all. I have about ten Heinies working under me for the army has taken over all the mills, but the real joy of the thing is being boss over the bunch which caused me to come over [to] this God forsaken place to live on cornmeal and hardtack.

I have seen a lot of things and had a great experiences in the last two years and believe me, I wouldn't miss it for anything. Being in the regular army and also being a volunteer, I hear we have to stay over here till June, while our replacements who are drafted will go home pretty soon, that's handing it to the regulars pretty rotten don't you think.

I sure would like to see some nice girl from the U.S.A. for believe me Tom, I've seen quite a few of them in my travels over here and England, France, Germany, and Luxembourg and none of them come near like those in the States. Well Tom give all the boys my regards.

> Your brother,
> Francis

I Was Wounded and Gassed, and I Got 7 Huns

> February 21, 1919
> Pvt Allen "Dewey" Knarr
> Co. H, 112th Infantry Regiment
> 28th Division
> A.E.F.

We arrived in England on May 15 and arrived in Calais, France, on May 25. On July 29, I was wounded in the neck at Fismes with a rifle grenade. I was sent to a dressing station and then to a Paris hospital. I was discharged and was also fortunate to join my company again at Fismes. On October 31st I received a double dose of mustard and chlorine gas and was unconscious for 48 hours and could not see for eight days. My eyesight is

***Members of the 103rd Engineers, 28th Division, march in a postwar parade in
downtown Pottsville, Pennsylvania, 1919.***

all right now but my lungs are not so good and I get short of breath very
easy. I was sent to hospital no. 55 at Toole [Toul] and then to the University of Pennsylvania at Angreas. I was at this hospital for four weeks and
then sent to a hospital at a seaport. I never experienced such rainy weather
as in France. At the last hospital I was at, it rained for five weeks straight
going and that it had been raining from time to time for three months
before I left. I arrived in the states on the "Manshore" on January 22nd. I
was sent to Camp Meritt and then to Camp Meade where on February 13th
I received an honorable discharge. I expect to remain here for some time
and then to take advantage of the opportunity offered by this government
to go to college. I did not receive any pay for seven months, until I was discharged. I always got good treatment from the Y.M.C.A. and mostly always
able to buy things at less than cost price, when the Y.M.C.A. had it. 15 cent
cigarettes in this country could be bought for 8 cents at the "Y" over there.

When we arrived in France we did a good bit of drilling for a time,
we were required to get up at four a.m. and hike ten miles to a drilling
ground. On July 3, 1918 at two o'clock we hiked until ten the next evening,
July 4th. We were put in reserves at the famous hill no. 204. We then went
down to the Marne River and crossed it on July 15th.

On July 16th I was in Château-Thierry and followed in back of the tanks through the streets of that place driving Germans out. After resting for eight hours, they moved us to Sergy. Here I experienced the hardest fighting. Nine times an attempt was made to dislodge the Germans, who were located in stone quarries. Here I got my first two Germans. I did not know for sure if I killed them but I thought I did, I did not have time to stop and investigate. I knew I got them pretty hard because I bayoneted both of them in through the stomach and each time my bayonet came out on the other side of them. Here my company was with Company C of the 112th and we lost very heavily in this action.

After driving the Germans and fighting all the way, my company finally arrived near Fismes. The first day in Fismes I got three more Huns with my trusty rifle. The second day in Fismes I was wounded with a rifle grenade. It happened during the night. I was taken to the hospital but came back to my company on August 20th. We crossed the Vesle River and was in the Argonne Forest drive. Here I got two more Germans. In the first drive in this forest we were in the reserves. My company was filled up to exceptional strength, there being 270 men in it.

After lying in reserve for a time, I was put in a raiding party and we made seven raids in three days. On one of these raiding parties I saved 58 men of our party from being cut up with machine gun fire. This was on October 28th. A heavy barrage was begun at six p.m. and the raiding party followed the barrage only eighteen feet back of it. The boys went over, singing, "Where do we go from here." My party got far to the front line trenches along the railroad leading into Metz. There we got tangled up into barbwire. The Germans sent up a flare and I found I was alone. I turned to go back to my lieutenant to see what the orders were. And on the road back after I had gone only a few paces, I found my butty who generally traveled with me. I noticed a Hun loading a machine gun nearby and which had been effectively concealed and which up to that time we had not heard from. Me and my butty turned and dashed toward the machine gun and captured a lieutenant, a sergeant and two privates. They were more than surprised at their capture but being down in some kind of a hole quickly consented to surrender at the point of our guns. We took all the souvenirs off them and then marched them back to the company headquarters and then to battalion headquarters. The German Lieutenant could speak English pretty well and considerable valuable information was gotten from him. Had not this machine gun crew been taken it was stated at that time they could have cut the entire raiding party to pieces.

On another raiding party that I was on we got within 75 yards of the German front line when the Germans opened up with the machine gun. I dropped in a shell hole and had to crawl from one shell hole to another in order to get back to the company. This was on October 29th.

On October 30th one hundred of my company was placed in a raiding party that made a day light raid starting at three o'clock in the afternoon. They captured two officers, 3 sergeants and 6 privates. They tried to take a small town nearby but got caught between the lines when the Germans put up a barrage.

On October 31st while up in the front lines I was gassed. I had charge of a platoon. Fourteen hundred one pounders and wizz bang were sent over by the Germans. I was going along to report to my lieutenant, when I narrowly escaped having my head taken off with a wizz bang, having ducked just in time. I was near the upper end of the lines when I was told that two of my men were gassed. I had to ask permission to take them back. I received permission and in dropping down into the shell hole where they were I got some gas but not enough to put me out of commission. I carried the men back to a dressing station and was then sent up to the front lies to bring the men back who had been on duty for 22 hours without any rest. While bringing these men back I got into more gas and this second lot of gas I had already taken into my lungs was too much for me and I collapsed. I was taken to the base hospital where I was for a number of days and then sent to another hospital and finally to the states.

Heroes, Welcome Home

We're filled with a thrill when we see you
For we look at the best in the land,
And to each soldier and sailor
We extend the welcoming hand;
We are proud to honor our heroes,
You men who were willing to give
Your lives on our country's altar,
That freedom and justice shall live.

God bless you, American Warriors,
You inspire our souls at a glance;
The cream of American manhood
That battled in far away France.
You have won a glorious victory,
You have ne'er let defeat in your wake
When you fought for honor and justice
And freedom for humanity's sake

You've let the march of world freedom,
You have silenced the autocrat's brag,
You've succored the poor down trodden,
As you fought for the dear old flag.
When you fought and crossed the Marne river,

Along the Château-Thierry "bend,"
You raised the moral in each sector
From Switzerland up to Ostend.

Our allies morale kept ascending
Till the eighteenth day of July.
And Marshall Foch knew that every Yank
Would fight to the last though he die,
Then came the counter offensive,
Our nation prayed with loud Amen;
Oh, Historic Pennsylvania!
Proud are we of thine Iron Men.

Then the Kaiser learned that you Warriors
Were never to proud to fight,
For liberty, justice and freedom,
The flag, the home and the right.
He learned that American soldiers
Were not made of tin, dough or hay,
For he was forced to abdicate
Through you boys of the U.S.A.

It was not for greed or commerce
Nor for territorial gain,
It was not for filthy lucre
That you sailed across the main,
It was not for insidious "Kultur"
Which teaches that might makes right
And emperors be great as God—
Not for these did you boys fight.

It was for those lofty principles
That are born in a free man's breast,
And for the rule "square deal to all"
That none be dismayed, depressed,
That men shall everywhere be free
With autocracy cast aside,
These are the noble principles
For which your comrades died.

All Honor, Praise and Glory
To those who were slain in the fight,
To those who would give to their country
Their hearing, their limb, or their sight;
To all American Warriors,
The dauntless in battle array,
Who feared nothing but Almighty God
The heroes of the world today.

Ben. W. Thomas, Schuylkill Haven, Penna.

APPENDIX

American Combat Divisions, World War I

Regular Army Divisions

FIRST DIVISION

Was the first division formed, the first in France and the first American division to engage in combat on the Western Front. They fought at Cantigny, Soissons, St.-Mihiel, Argonne and along the Rhine.

Infantry—Regular Regiments, 16th, 18th, 26th, 28th;
Artillery—Regular Regiments, 5th, 6th, 7th;
Machine Gun Btlns.—Regulars, 1st, 2nd, 3rd;
Engineers—1st and Ammunition train.

SECOND DIVISION

Organized in France in the fall of 1917, from miscellaneous units, which included an entire brigade of Marines. They fought at Bouresches, Belleau Wood, Château-Thierry, St.-Mihiel, Argonne, Mont Blanc and the Rhine.

Infantry—Regular Regiments, 9th and 23rd;
Artillery—Regular Regiments 12th, 15th, and 17th;

Machine Gun Btlns.—4th, 5th, and 6th;
Engineers—2nd and Ammunition Train;
Marines—Regulars, 5th and 6th.

THIRD DIVISION

Arrived in France in the spring of 1918. Was known as the "Marne Division." Fought at Château-Thierry, Jaulgonne, Mt. St. Père, Argonne, Meuse and Rhine.

Infantry—Regular Regiments, 4th, 7th, 30th, 38th;
Artillery—Regular Regiments, 10th, 18th, 76th;
Machine Gun Btlns.—Regulars, 7th, 8th and 9th;
Engineers—Regulars, 6th and Ammunition Trains.

FOURTH DIVISION

Arrived in France in the spring of 1918. Fought at Château-Thierry, Ourcq Heights, Vesle, Argonne, Rhine.

Infantry—Regular Regiments, 39th, 47th, 58th, 59th;
Artillery—Regular Regiments 13th, 16th, 77th;
Machine Gun Btlns.—Regulars, 10th, 11th, 12th;
Engineers—Regulars, 6th and Ammunition Train.

FIFTH DIVISION

Arrived in France in the spring of 1918. Fought at St.-Mihiel, Argonne, Meuse, and the Rhine.

Infantry—Regular Regiments, 6th, 11th, and 60th, 61st;
Artillery—Regular Regiments, 19th, 20th, 21st;
Machine Gun Btlns.—Regulars, 16th, 17th, 18th;
Engineers—Regulars, 318th and Ammunition Train.

SIXTH DIVISION

The Sixth Division arrived in France in the summer of 1918. Has the record for marching more than any other division. Known as the "Sight seeing Sixth."

Infantry—Regular Regiments, 51st, 52nd, 53rd, 54th;

Artillery—Regulars, 3rd, 11th, 78th;
Machine Gun Btlns.—16th, 17th, 18th;
Engineers—Regulars, 318th and Ammunition Train.

SEVENTH DIVISION

Arrived in France in the later part of the summer of 1918; occupied a sector in Lorraine from October to November. Was stationed at Didier.

Infantry—Regular Regiments, 34th, 55th, 56th, 64th;
Artillery—Regulars, 8th, 79th, 89th;
Machine Gun Btlns.—Regulars, 22nd, 23rd, 24th;
Engineers—Regulars 319th and Ammunition Trains.

EIGHTH DIVISION

Organized in 1917 but only a third of the division served in France just in time of for the armistice.

Infantry—Regular Regiments, 8th 12th, 13th, and 62;
Artillery—Regulars, 2nd, 81st, 83rd;
Machine Gun Btlns.—Regulars, 22nd, 23rd, 24th;
Engineers—Regulars, 319th and Ammunition Train.

National Guard Divisions

TWENTY-SIXTH DIVISION

Organized in New England arrived in Europe in the fall of 1917. Fought at Seicheprey, Soissons, St.-Mihiel, Rhine.

New England National Guard Infantry Regiments, 101st, 102nd, 103rd;
Artillery—101st, 102nd, 103rd;
Machine Gun Btlns.—101st, 102nd, 103rd;
Engineers—101st and Ammunition Train.

TWENTY-SEVENTH DIVISION

"The New York Division" arrived in France in the spring of 1918; they fought along the Hindenburg Line with the British Army for their entire stay.

New York National Guard, Infantry Regiments 105th, 106th, 107th, 108th;
Artillery—104th, 105th, 106th;
Machine Gun Btlns.—104th, 105th, 106th;
Engineers—102nd and Ammunition Train.

TWENTY-EIGHTH DIVISION

The "Keystone Division" from Pennsylvania fought at Château-Thierry, Aisne, Argonne, and suffered the highest casualties of the National Guard units. Arrived in France in the spring of 1918.

Pennsylvania National Guard Infantry Regiments—109th, 110th, 111th, 112th;
Artillery—107th, 108th, 109th;
Machine Gun Btlns.—107th, 108th, 109th;
Engineers—103rd and Ammunition train.

TWENTY-NINTH DIVISION

The 29th was known as the "Blue and the Gray Division" because of both the northern and southern units assigned to it. It arrived in France in the summer of 1918. They fought in the Argonne campaign.

New Jersey, Delaware and Maryland National Guard Infantry—113th, 114th, 115th, 116th;
Artillery—110th, 111th, 112th;
Machine Gun Btlns.—110th, 111th, 112th;
Engineers—104th and Ammunition Train.

THIRTIETH DIVISION

Arrived in France in the spring of 1918 and fought with the British Army on the Hindenburg Line. They were known as "The Old Hickory Division."

Tennessee and North and South Carolina National Guard Infantry—117th, 118th, 119th, 120th;
Artillery—113th, 114th, 115th;
Machine Gun Btlns.—113th, 114th, 115th;
Engineers—105th, and Ammunition Train.

THIRTY-FIRST DIVISION

Arrived in Brest, France, as the armistice was signed, so no action. They were known as the "Dixie Division."

Alabama, Florida, and Georgia National Guard troops, Infantry—121st, 122nd, 123rd, 124th;
Artillery—116th, 117th, 118th;
Machine Gun Btlns.—116th, 117th, 118th;
Engineers—106th and Ammunition Train.

THIRTY-SECOND DIVISION

Arriving in France in February 1918, the division fought at Gimpette Woods, Bellevue Farm, Fismes, Argonne, and the Rhine. The division was composed of units from Wisconsin and Michigan troops.

Wisconsin and Michigan National Guard Infantry Regiments—125th, 126th, 127th, 128th;
Artillery—119th, 120th, 121st;
Machine Gun Btlns.—119th, 120th, 121st;
Engineers—10th and Ammunition Train.

THIRTY-THIRD DIVISION

Trained By Australian troops, the 33rd Division arrived in France in the spring of 1918, and fought at Hamel, St.-Mihiel, Chipilly, Argonne, and the Meuse.

Illinois National Guard Infantry Regiments—129th, 130th, 131st, 132nd;
Artillery—122nd, 123rd, 124th;
Machine Gun Btlns.—122nd, 123rd, 124th;
Engineers—108th and Ammunition Train.

THIRTY-FOURTH DIVISION

This Division never saw combat after arriving in France too late.

Iowa, Nebraska, Minnesota, S. Dakota Infantry Regiments—133rd, 134th, 135th, 136th;
Artillery—125th, 126th, 127th;
Machine Gun Btlns.—125th, 126th, 127th;
Engineers—110th and Ammunition Train.

THIRTY-FIFTH DIVISION

Arriving in France in the spring of 1918, the "Santa Fe Division" fought at St.-Mihiel, Argonne and the Meuse.

Missouri and Kansas National Guard Infantry Regiments—137th, 138th, 139th, 140th;
Artillery—128th, 129th, 130th;
Machine Gun Btlns.—128th, 129th, 130th;
Engineers—110th and Ammunition Train.

THIRTY-SIXTH DIVISION

Served with the French Army and fought at Argonne and Champagne.

Texas and Oklahoma National Guard Infantry Regiments—141st, 142nd, 143rd, 144th;
Artillery—132nd, 133rd;
Machine Gun Btlns.—132nd, 132nd, 133rd;
Engineers—111th and Ammunition Train.

THIRTY-SEVENTH DIVISION

Arriving in France in the summer of 1918, the 37th fought with the French Army at Flanders, Escault River.

Ohio National Guard Infantry Regiments—145th, 146th, 147th, 148th;
Artillery—134th, 135th, 136th;
Machine Gun Btlns.—134th 135th, 136th;
Engineers—112th and Ammunition Train.

THIRTY-EIGHTH DIVISION

The "Cyclone Division" arrived too late in 1918 to see any action. They were stationed at Le Mans.

Indiana, Kentucky, W. Virginia National Guard Infantry Regiments— 149th, 150th, 151st, 152nd;
Artillery—137th, 138th, 139th;
Machine Gun Btlns.—137th, 138th, 139th;
Engineers—114th and Ammunition Train.

THIRTY-NINTH DIVISION

The division held the depots at St. Florent, providing replacements for the other divisions.

Alabama, Mississippi, Louisiana National Guard Infantry Regiments— 153rd, 154th, 155th, 156th;

Artillery—140th, 141st, 142nd;
Machine Gun Btlns.—140th, 141st, 142nd;
Engineers—114th and Ammunition Train.

FORTIETH DIVISION

The "Sunshine Division" arrived in France in the late summer of 1918, and served as a depot division at Revigny and St. Didier.

Calif., Utah, New Mexico and Arizona National Guard Infantry Regiments—157th, 158th, 159th, 160th;
Artillery—143rd, 144th, 145th;
Machine Gun Btlns.—143rd, 144th, 145th;
Engineers—115th and Ammunition Train.

FORTY-FIRST DIVISION

The 41st was the first of the depot divisions to arrive in France. They served at St. Aignan, and Noyon.

Washington, Oregon, Montana and Idaho National Guard Infantry Regiments—161st, 162nd, 163rd, 164th;
Artillery—146th, 147th, 148th;
Machine Gun Btlns.—146th, 147th, 148th;
Engineers—116th and Ammunition Train.

FORTY-SECOND DIVISION

The "Rainbow Division" was composed of left over state units and had one of the finest fighting records during the war. They fought at Red Cross Farm, St.-Mihiel, Argonne, and the Rhine.

Infantry Regiments—166th, 167th, 168th;
Artillery—149th, 150th, 151st;
Machine Gun Btlns.—149th, 150th, 151st;
Engineers—117th and Ammunition Train.

National Army Divisions

SEVENTY-SIXTH DIVISION

This division was formed from the first draft and arrived in the following summer of 1918. They held the depot at St. Amant and Montrond.

New York and New England Troops Infantry Regts.—305th, 306th, 307th, 308th;
    Artillery—301st, 302nd, 303rd;
    Engineers—301st and Ammunition Train.

SEVENTY-SEVENTH DIVISION

New York City troops. Fought at the Vesle River and Argonne.

Regts. 305th, 306th, 307th 308th;
Artillery—304th, 305th, 306th;
Machine Gun Btlns.—307th, 308th, 309th;
Engineers—302nd and Ammunition Train.

SEVENTY-EIGHTH DIVISION

Fought at St.-Mihiel and Argonne.

New York and New Jersey troops—Regts. 305th, 306th, 307th 308th;
Artillery—304th, 305th, 306th;
Engineers—302nd and Ammunition Train.

SEVENTY-NINTH DIVISION

Fought in the Argonne.

Pennsylvania Maryland, D.C. Troops, Infantry Regts. 313th, 314th, 315th, 316th;
    Artillery 310th, 311th, 312th;
    Machine Gun Btlns.—310th, 311th, 312th;
    Engineers—304th and Ammunition Train.

EIGHTIETH DIVISION

Fought at St.-Mihiel and Argonne.

Virginia, West Virginia, Pennsylvania, Infantry Regts. 317th, 318th, 319th, 320th;
    Artillery—313th, 314th, 315th;
    Machine Gun Battalions—313th, 314th, 315th;
    Engineers—305th and Ammunitions train.

EIGHTY-FIRST DIVISION

On the Somme.

Carolinas, Florida, Porto Rico Infantry Regts. 321st, 322nd, 323rd, 324th;
Artillery—316th, 317th, 318th;
Machine Gun Btlns.—316th, 317th, 318th;
Engineers—306th.

EIGHTY-SECOND DIVISION

Fought at the Argonne.

Georgia, Alabama, Tennessee, Infantry Regts. 325th, 326th, 327th, 328th;
Artillery—319th, 320th, 321st;
Engineers—307th.

EIGHTY-THIRD DIVISION

Held Depot Division at LeMans, and Castres.

Ohio and Pennsylvania Troops, Infantry Regts. 329th, 330th, 331st, 332nd;
Artillery—322nd, 323rd, 324th;
Machine Gun Btlns.—322nd, 323rd, 324th;
Engineers 308th;
Ammunition Train.

EIGHTY-FOURTH DIVISION

Supply at Neuvic.

Illinois, Indiana, Kentucky Troops, Infantry Regts. 333rd, 334th, 335th, 336th;
Artillery—325th, 326th, 327th;
Machine Gun Btlns.—325th, 326th, 327th;
Engineers—309th.

EIGHTY-FIFTH DIVISION

Depot at Pouilly.

Michigan and Wisconsin troops, Infantry Regts. 337th, 338th, 339th, 340th;
Artillery—328th, 329th, 330th;
Machine Gun Btlns.—331st, 332nd, 333rd;
Engineers—311th.

Eighty-Sixth Division

Supply at St. Andre de Cubzac.

Chicago Infantry—341st, 342nd, 343rd, 344th;
Artillery 331st, 332nd, 333rd;
Machine Gun Battalion—331st, 332nd, 333rd;
Engineers—311th.

Eighty-Seventh Division

Supply service at Pons.

Arkansas, Mississippi, and Louisiana Troops, Infantry Regts. 345th, 346th, 347th, 348th;
Artillery—334th, 335th, 336th;
Machine Gun Btlns.—334th, 335th, 336th;
Engineers—312th.

Eighty-Eighth Division

Fought at the Alsace Sector.

Illinois, Iowa, Minnesota, N. Dakota Troops, Infantry Regts. 349th, 350th, 351st, 352nd;
Artillery—337th, 338th, 339th;
Machine gun Battalion—337th,338th, 339th;
Engineers—313th.

Eighty-Ninth Division

Fought at the Argonne and along the Rhine.

Kansas, Nebraska, Colorado, Missouri Troops Infantry Regts. 353rd, 354th, 355th, 356th;
Artillery—340th, 341st, 342nd;

Machine Gun Battalions—340th, 341st, 342nd;.
Engineers—314th and Ammunition train.

NINETIETH DIVISION

Fought at the Argonne and along the Rhine.

Texas and Oklahoma Troops, Infantry Regts. 357th, 358th, 359th, 360th;
Artillery—343rd, 344th, 345th;
Machine Gun Battalions—343rd , 344th, 345th;
Engineers—315th, and Ammunition Train.

NINETY-FIRST DIVISION

Fought at St.-Mihiel, Argonne, Flanders, Spittal Bossichen.

Alaska, Washington, Nevada, Wyoming, Infantry Regts. 361st, 362nd, 363rd, 364th;
Artillery—346th, 347th, 348th;
Machine Gun Battalion—346th, 347th, 348th;
Engineers—316th, and Ammunition Train.

NINETY-SECOND DIVISION

Fought on the Alsace Front.

Negroe Infantry troops—365th, 366th 367th, 368th;
Artillery—349th, 350th 351st;
Machine Gun Battalions—349th 350th 351st;
Engineers—317th, and Ammunition Train.

Bibliography

Newspapers and Journals

Philadelphia Inquirer, 1918.
Pottsville Daily Miners Journal, 1917, 1918, 1919, 1920, 1921, 1922.
Pottsville Daily Republican.
Pottsville Evening Republican, 1917, 1918, 1919, 1920, 1921, 1922.
Schuylkill Haven Call, 1917, 1918, 1919, 1029.
Shenandoah Herald.

Books and Articles

Awards of Foreign Decorations, Manual G.O.1, Headquarters Pennsylvania National Guard, Adjutant Generals Office, Harrisburg, Pennsylvania, 1923.
Ayres, Leonard P. *The War with Germany: A Statistical Summary*. Government Printing office, 1919.
Clifford, E. L. *Schuylkill County Pennsylvania in the World War*. J. H. Zerby Press.
Emprey, Guy Arthur. *First Call*. New York and London: Knickerbocker Press, 1919.
Emprey, Guy Arthur. *Over the Top*. New York and London: Knickerbocker Press, 1917.
The Great War Society. www.worldwar1.com, established 1987.
McDonald, Charles D. *World War I: The U.S. Army Overseas*. Reprinted from American Military History, Office Chief of Military History.
O'Neil. *History and Rhymes of Our Boys in the Great War*. 1926.
The Story of the Sixteenth Infantry in France, American Expeditionary Forces, written by Regimental Chaplain, Frankfurt, Germany, Martin Flouck Montabar Printing, 1919.

Index

www.ingramcontent.com/pod-product-compliance
Ingram Content Group UK Ltd.
Pitfield, Milton Keynes, MK11 3LW, UK
UKHW041354190726
13851UKWH00014B/107